UNITING GERMANY
Documents and Debates, 1944-1993

UNITING GERMANY
Documents and Debates, 1944-1993

Edited by
Konrad H. Jarausch and Volker Gransow

Translated by
Allison Brown and Belinda Cooper

Berghahn Books
Providence • Oxford

Published in 1994 by
Berghahn Books
Editorial offices:
165 Taber Avenue, Providence, RI 02906, U.S.A.
Bush House, Merewood Avenue, Oxford OX3 8EF, UK

Library of Congress Cataloging-in-Publication Data
Deutsch Vereinigung. English.
Uniting Germany: documents and debates, 1944-1993 /edited by Konrad H.
Jarausch and Volker Gransow; translated by Allison Brown and Belinda Cooper.
p.   cm.
Includes bibliographical references.
1. German reunification question (1949-1990) – Sources.
2. Germany – History – Unification, 1990 – Sources. I. Gransow,
Volker. II. Title.
DD290.22.D4813   1994b
943.087 – dc20   94-20694
CIP

British Library Cataloguing in Publication Data
A CIP catalog record for this book is available from
the British Library.

ISBN: 1-57181-010-2 $64.00
1-57181-011-0 pb $18.95

Printed in the United States.

Contents

5.   Economic Union and International Breakthrough   143

Preface

German unification was a "historic" event. After four decades of division, the Germans recovered their unity within one short year in 1989-90. Time and again politicians claimed to be making history. Especially in East Germany, unification fundamentally transformed daily lives. The caesura was so deep that many people started to date events in relationship to this upheaval. The sudden return of German unity ended the post-war era by confirming the territorial changes left by World War II. The unforeseen merger of the two successor states from competing blocs also marked the conclusion of the Cold War. The reemergence of a German national state has altered the power balance within Europe and provided new challenges for American foreign policy.

The documents presented in this volume are intended to help the reader understand these confusing changes. In Germany, myths of heroic liberation or dastardly annexation have clouded the elation. In the United States, a dearth of information has made it difficult to judge the accuracy of journalistic fears. To facilitate an independent judgment, this collection presents a wide range of materials. It offers state treaties and government speeches as well as opposition responses and intellectual criticism of unification. The volume also includes samples of foreign reaction and of international negotiations. Through vivid descriptions it seeks to convey a sense of the hopes and fears of ordinary people. Because any documentation must necessarily be selective, the editors have allowed both proponents and opponents to speak by balancing official statements with personal views.

For ease of use, the material is arranged chronologically. The first chapter presents the background of the German division after 1945. The second section focuses on the democratic awakening in the fall of 1989, while the third deals with the end of the GDR during the subsequent winter. The fourth chapter concentrates on the turn towards unity during the spring of 1990, whereas the fifth analyzes the economic and diplomatic breakthroughs of the summer. The sixth section treats formal unification, and the final chapter concludes with assessments of its consequences. An introductory essay, brief headnotes, and explanatory footnotes on unfamiliar terms make each selection more accessible. A glossary, selected bibliography, and index facilitate comprehension. Though trying to be brief, the excerpts provide substantial passages that reproduce the original intent and tone of a document.

This book is the result of transatlantic cooperation between an American historian and a German social scientist. A Lurcy professor at the University of North Carolina at Chapel Hill, Konrad H. Jarausch has long been interested in questions of German political and social development. Teaching at the Free University of Berlin, Volker Gransow has dealt extensively with GDR issues as well as West German intellectual controversies. The former conceived the bulk of the introduction as well as chapters one through three and coordinated the English production. The latter supervised the German version and compiled chapters four to seven. The editors would like to acknowledge the help of the GDR section of the Institute for Social Research at the Free University of Berlin, members of the civic movement, and government agencies such as the Federal Press Office. They would also like to thank the authors and publications listed as source notes for the reprinting of their texts.

This volume has been translated and revised for its English language edition. It originally appeared in German under the title *Die deutsche Vereinigung: Dokumente zu Bürgerbewegung, Annäherung und Beitritt* (Wissenschaft und Politik, Cologne, 1991). The translators, Belinda Cooper and Allison Brown, strove to reconcile the conflicting imperatives of intelligibility, accuracy and stylistic faithfulness. Whenever possible, they used existing translations. Treaties which have the force of law are cited verbatim, but other documents such as newspaper articles have been retranslated where necessary. Of course, English-language passages are included in their original form. With the benefit of greater perspective, the editors have rewritten the preface, recast the introduction, and added a seventh chapter on post-unification problems. They have also provided explanatory footnotes, expanded the glossary, and updated the bibliography.

The present becomes the past through critical reflection. While some aspects of German unification were overexposed, others remained in the dark. Media images of the fall of the Wall evoked powerful emotions insufficiently counterbalanced by accurate information. Participants and observers were stunned by the collapse of the GDR, and still wonder what it might mean. This volume seeks to provide reliable source materials for analyzing and interpreting the bewildering changes in Central Europe. It is addressed to students of German politics, history, and culture as well as to journalists and general readers interested in European affairs. The editors have consciously refrained from presenting a finished interpretation of German unification. Instead the following materials and commentaries intend to challenge every reader to develop his or her own point of view.

Konrad H. Jarausch and Volker Gransow

Chapel Hill and Berlin, November 1993

The New Germany
Myths and Realities

German unification came as a complete surprise. As late as 1989 politicians and pundits were convinced that the Germans had been divided for good. To be sure, Western speeches on June 17, the holiday commemorating the 1953 uprising, had continued to invoke the goal of eventual reunification. Allied governments had professed to go along, certain that their bluff would never be called. But in practice, almost everyone had accepted the division and tried to manage its consequences. Progressive opinion considered the existence of two German states to be the foundation for peace in Europe. Therefore the sudden East German awakening in the fall of 1989 caught virtually all actors and commentators unprepared.

The speed of the transformation proved shocking. Decades of immobility had created an expectation that the stalemate could be overcome only by incremental changes. But instead of moving like a glacier, events rushed forward like a flood. The overthrow of post-Stalinism did not stop with the democratization of the GDR but created an unstoppable rush to national unity. Despite growing misgivings, one incredible year brought the reunification that had proven so elusive for the preceding decades. From the mass exodus on, time horizons shortened from decades to years, from years to months, from months to days. No wonder that many participants felt giddy, as if they were riding on a runaway train.

The extent of the changes was stunning as well. All elaborate confederation scenarios of gradual reconciliation turned out to be wrong. The two countries did not meet somewhere in the middle through piecemeal reforms; rather, the GDR simply dissolved itself, and its component states joined the FRG. In the clash of ideologies, the "free democratic order" won out over the utopia of "real existing socialism." In the military arena, the hostile blocs did not just disarm, but a key member of the Warsaw Pact actually switched to the NATO side.

In economic competition socialist planning lost out to the superior performance of "the social market economy." As a result even the once superior teams of the East joined less talented athletes of the West to compete together for Olympic medals. When the Iron Curtain lifted at last, a German national state suddenly began to reemerge.

The rapidity and depth of the upheaval have left many people incredulous. Inside and outside the new Germany, a heated debate has arisen about its causes, form, and consequences. With more emotion than information, old fears of German aggression and repression confront new hopes of democracy and prosperity. This cognitive lag has spawned powerful myths. Supporters of unity romanticize the East German rising of 1989 as a heroic struggle and applaud the subsequent turn to the West. Critics deprecate the implosion of the GDR experiment and denounce its annexation as a capitalist plot. The elation of self-liberation has turned into depression over the disastrous results of the merger. A whiff of nostalgia is in the air, making the GDR more alluring after its demise than during its lifetime. Resolving such contradictions requires a closer look at the residual images and chief interpretations of the unforeseen events before turning to the documents themselves.

Pictures of the Upheaval

Since German unification was a media event, it left behind a kaleidoscope of confusing images. Astute commentators called the Eastern rising "a television revolution" in order to emphasize the important role of radio, television, and the press in its course. With their sympathies for dissidents, Western journalists accelerated the pace of change by offering to broadcast their views. Once the GDR media gained some independence, they suddenly blossomed with accurate and biting reports about the deficiencies of their own system. At the same time, Western professionals began to manipulate Eastern opinion by producing slickly packaged promises of a better life. In the babble of sound-bites, former Communists and regime opponents soon found themselves outclassed. The upheaval left a welter of conflicting pictures that continues to evoke some of the drama of the change.

The central symbol of the Cold War had been the Berlin Wall. The GDR had closed off its frontiers in August 1961 to halt the westward emigration of 3.5 million of its citizens. The East German Communist Party (SED) lamely justified the barrier as "anti-fascist protection" against West German revanchism. By stopping the population hemorrhage, East Berlin managed to stabilize its state for almost three decades. The ugly edifice sent a clear message to its citizens and neighbors that the GDR was here to stay. But the Wall also came to symbolize repression, since it penned in an unwilling population and desperate attempts to cross it cost almost 500 lives. For Western observers, the concrete and barbed wire served as visual proof of the inferiority of the barrier's communist regime.

Bonn's red-carpet reception of Erich Honecker in 1987 suggested that both German states tried to improve relations nonetheless. During the state visit, chancellor Helmut Kohl received the East German leader with full honors in the West German capital. The Christian-Democratic host had continued the *Ostpolitik* of his Social-Democratic predecessors Willy Brandt and Helmut Schmidt in order to improve human relations between East and West. By recognizing the GDR de facto and granting crucial economic credits, these FRG leaders had sought "change through closeness." Their conciliatory stance made the border more permeable for East German citizens and allowed greater numbers to travel to the West. But in dealing with the East Berlin government, Bonn had to swallow its ethical objections to Communism. While both sides continued to try to undermine one another, they started to live with each other in a kind of abnormal normality.

In September 1989 news stories of embassy occupations suggested the end of this intra-German stability. One snapshot showed a desperate refugee straddling the fence of the Prague legation: While Czech police pulled on his legs to keep him out, GDR emigrants tugged on his arms to get him into safety. Polish reforms and Soviet perestroika made the Iron Curtain rust through in Hungary, when the improving climate allowed Budapest to remove the barbed-wire fence at the Austrian border. This unexpected chance for vacationers to escape created a mass exodus from the GDR during the summer and fall. SED vacillations between sealing off East German borders and allowing embassy refugees to leave only increased the flow. By voting with their feet, ordinary citizens began to undermine Honecker's post-Stalinist regime. In effect, the flight from the GDR was a kind of individual reunification with the West.

By October 1989 unprecedented images of mass demonstrations dominated the news. The media showed tens of thousands of East Germans marching peacefully with candles in their hands. Instead of shouting "We want to get out," they intoned "We are staying here."

Led by small groups of dissidents advocating human rights, these growing crowds wanted to remain in order to reform the GDR. Since Mikhail Gorbachev refused to authorize the use of Soviet troops, the old men of the politburo did not dare turn to force. When courageous Leipzig citizens and party reformers agreed to avoid bloodshed on October 9, protesters could take to the streets without fear. In order to preserve its power, the SED had no choice but to dismiss the aging Honecker and to appoint a more pragmatic successor, Egon Krenz. The civic courage of the slogan claim "We are the People" had forced the overthrow of the post-Stalinist regime.

During the evening of 9 November, pictures of people dancing on the Wall flashed around the world. On the broad crown of the barrier in front of the Brandenburg gate, hundreds of happy Germans celebrated the opening of the frontier. In a desperate bid for popularity, the Krenz government had promised to ease travel restrictions. Since the SED was fracturing into competing factions of hard-liners, opportunists and reformers, the party sought to regain the initiative by leading the movement toward change. When thousands of impatient East Berliners thronged to the border, the unprepared guards had little choice but to let them through. With the two halves of the divided city coming face to face, a tearful reunion ensued. The opening of more crossing points allowed many GDR citizens to see for themselves the glittering "social market economy" of the West. Ordinary Easterners began to doubt the need for a separate state of their own. Intended to shore up a tottering system, the opening of the Wall hastened its demise.

In early December the wire-services ran photos of earnest discussions at the central Round Table. The new prime-minister Hans Modrow had agreed to meet with the leaders of the opposition to discuss the future of the GDR. Nineteen members of the SED and the nomenklatura, in baggy suits, faced an equal number of men and women of the civic movement, in sweaters and jeans. Mediated by the churches, these debates sought to avoid violence between the embattled authorities and an aroused populace. Both sides were forced to compromise, since the government had power without legitimacy and the opposition popular support without office. Inspired by the Czech dream of a "socialism with a human face," the Round Table members sought to find a Third Way between discredited Stalinism and unrestrained capitalism. By joining forces, the party elite and the dissidents tried to democratize socialism in order to maintain the independence of the GDR.

On 15 January 1990 television showed dramatic footage of the storming of Stasi headquarters in East Berlin. A peaceful demonstration against the East German secret police got out of hand when enraged crowds, led by provocateurs, rampaged through the compound. Prime Minister Hans Modrow and opposition leader Ibrahim Böhme desperately tried to restore order. In effect, the storming of the GDR bastille marked the collapse of socialist renewal. This popular revolt forced the government to broaden its base by including members of the opposition in the cabinet in order to speed up reforms. But a failing economy made popular demands for unification irresistible by early February. In a Moscow visit Modrow obtained Soviet approval for developing a confederation that would eventually lead to national unity. At the same time, the international community surprisingly agreed on a negotiation formula of two-plus-four which combined the World War Two victors with the two German states.

By early March, the screens were filled with shots of Chancellor Kohl campaigning in the GDR. Waving banners and shouting "Helmut, Helmut!" hundreds of thousands enthusiastically welcomed his promises of Western help. During their first free election, Easterners were all too eager to believe that the big brother from Bonn could magically turn their shabby towns into "flourishing landscapes." After scraping by and making do for four decades, they no longer wanted to be second class citizens and demanded prosperity now. Dissident warnings that the Eastern economy would collapse fell upon deaf ears and not even the gradual transition advocated by the SPD seemed to be rapid enough. On 18 March the East German electorate handed the centrist-conservative Alliance for Germany a stunning victory. Despite international fears, the unexpected outcome was a clear mandate for quick unity through accession of the GDR via paragraph 23 of the Basic Law.

At midnight on 1 July, the spotlight shifted to the Deutsche Bank at Berlin Alexanderplatz. Reporters filmed hundreds of people pressing against the plate-glass doors in order to be the first to receive the long-awaited D-mark. The next day banks all over the GDR converted the "aluminum chips" and small bills of the East into the heavier and harder money of the West. With the arrival of monetary, economic and social union, the GDR in effect left the Eastern COMECON and joined the Western Economic Community (EC). Overnight it abandoned the egalitarian and secure poverty of socialist planning for the unequal and risky prosperity of capitalist competition. With salaries exchanged at

1:1 and savings converted at 1:1.5, consumers could finally buy many previously unobtainable goods. Little did they realize that their precipitous merger with a stronger economy would force the closing of inefficient factories and the merciless world market throw many of them out of work!

During the middle of July network news showed Mikhail Gorbachev welcoming Helmut Kohl to his Caucasus retreat. In unaccustomed amity the Soviet President and German Chancellor strolled along scenic mountain streams. At the concluding press conference reporters could hardly believe their ears when the leaders jointly announced a bargain that settled the international issues of unification. With surprising largesse, the Soviet Union offered to withdraw its forces from its World War II conquest in exchange for German disarmament and economic aid. Instead of insisting on neutrality, Moscow accepted the extension of NATO to East Germany as long as no alliance troops were stationed there. In gratitude Bonn promised to recognize its Eastern frontiers and help Russia rejoin Europe. The Caucasus breakthrough on the external terms of unity also hastened agreement in the complicated internal negotiations on an unification treaty that established numerous legal rules for the merger between East and West Germany.

On the evening of 2 October, TV-cameras were trained on the unification ceremony in Berlin. Hundreds of thousands of citizens from East and West crowded in front of the restored Reichstag building to celebrate the merger in quiet dignity. The strains of classical music gave way to cheers from the crowd when athletes unfolded a huge German flag. At the stroke of midnight, fireworks exploded into the sky to mark the reemergence of a united Germany. The holiday was a result of the decision of the first freely elected GDR government to dissolve its separate state. When the economy failed after the currency union, East Germany had to speed up unification in the hope of being rescued by the wealthier West. The haste to join was so great that the Eastern states (*Länder*) could only be constituted two weeks after accession. In early December a hard-fought federal election ratified the decision through a victory of its champions in the CDU and FDP. After forty-one years the GDR dissolved itself and its states rejoined the FRG.

During the summer of 1992, Germany was once again in the news. This time, disturbing pictures showed youthful skinheads throwing rocks at foreigners and setting asylum homes ablaze. In towns like Rostock, Mölln, and Solingen regular citizens cheered them on while the police stood helplessly by. This outbreak of xenophobia showed that unification had not only solved the old problems of division but created new ones in turn. The collapse of the Eastern economy surpassed all predictions and created mass unemployment of around 50 percent. The purge of institutions spawned resentment against Western colonization, and the psychological strain of combining two such contradictory cultures was immense. While Easterners complained of insufficient help, Westerners got tired of having to foot the bill. But in the fall hundreds of thousands of citizens took to the streets for a different purpose, marching with candles in their hands to urge tolerance towards foreigners. At present it remains to be seen which spirit will ultimately dominate the new German State.

This glance at the picture album suggests that German unification was a contradictory process. Time and again, surprises confounded the experts. The development was so rapid that people felt they were losing control. One can hardly imagine a more drastic change than having one's country disappear under one's feet. Hence both the celebratory and the catastrophic narratives contain some kernels of truth. Compared to Bismarck's wars of unification, the restoration of German unity was remarkably peaceful and democratic. This time self-determination had the approval of the neighbors and the support of the majority of the electorate. But the merger was also more bureaucratic and destructive than campaign promises suggested. The priority of privatizing state property destroyed Eastern industry, while the dictates of Bonn officials forced an alien system upon the new citizens. Hence the sudden and massive changes unleashed by unification brought both euphoria and despair.

Explaining the Inexplicable

Understanding this upheaval is a daunting intellectual challenge. The chief difficulty in explaining the events is the unanticipated transformation of the democratic awakening into a push for national unification. While the former is clearly part of the general East European repudiation of communism, the latter again constitutes a special German case. Instead of leading to unity, the revival of ethnic passions in other countries broke up larger states. Moreover, the renewal of socialism was propelled by protagonists and programs that differed from the reunification of the German successor regimes. And yet both processes were fundamentally linked, since the communist collapse was an essential precondition for the recovery of national unity. How can one make sense of this unexpected and ambiguous relationship?

A further complication is the varying speed of the process. First, there was the very slow development of division and détente, which took more than forty years. In the post-war era, the hostile blocs seemed frozen and changes appeared virtually impossible. Second, there was the headlong rush from democratic awakening in the GDR in 1989 to the political unification of Germany in 1990. During this astounding year, events accelerated with breathtaking speed. Third, after unification the process once again slowed down markedly. The internal integration on the political, social, economic, and cultural level is taking much longer than expected. Predictions about the time-span for this task have changed from a few years to whole decades that reach well into the next century.

It should not be surprising that this precipitous process was accompanied by ever-changing explanations. Because they often turned out to be partisan myths rather than dispassionate analyses, unresolved questions abound: What were the special characteristics of the German upheaval in comparison to the general features of the transition from post-Stalinist socialism? While many aspects of the civic revolution seem similar, in other important respects East Berlin differed markedly from Warsaw or Prague. What shape is the newly emerging order taking? The notion of "post-Communism" seems to imply everything from "democracy" and "capitalism" to "civil war," "ethnic strife," "nationalism," and even "fascism." Even less clear are the consequences for the future. What implications will the return of German unity have for that country's domestic stability and for European integration?

In German public discourse, two polarized legends compete as stylized accounts of the surprising events. In a celebratory narrative of the right, enshrined in the new national holiday, the East German people heroically overthrew an alien dictatorship. As a kind of founding myth for the reunited state, this government-sponsored version emphasizes that for the first time Germans proved capable of achieving a revolution of their own. Because it fears that the new country might misbehave like the old, the left is instead inclined to take a catastrophic view. Intellectual members of the civic movement denounce the "unity wave" among the East German population and most West German politicians as a form of "annexation," thus recalling the blackmailing of Austria by the Nazis. Another myth that fits Marxist anti-capitalist sentiment is the charge that East German "social achievements" were "sold out" to greedy Western industrialists.

Much of the scholarly discussion focuses on the problem of revolution. Participants talk simply about a "turn" (*Wende*) to demarcate the change in their lives without actually assigning responsibility. People close to the "civic movement" tend to stress the notion of "civil society." From their own opposition experience, they argue that the East German upheaval was based on the demand of active citizens for the recovery of individual and collective rights against the control of a repressive state. Many social scientists who are uncomfortable with the notion that Germans could actually revolt prefer to speak of an "implosion" of the GDR. But this mechanistic metaphor begs the important question of agency. More analytical observers emphasize post-totalitarian transition from dictatorship to democracy, resembling the transformation of southern Europe or Latin America. While illuminating some common features of collapsing authority, this approach fails to explain the national turn of the East European transformations.

Other explanations fasten upon the national dimension of the events. Especially conservative commentators like Thomas Nipperdey argue that unification was a quasi-natural event that was bound to happen, once the obstacles against it were removed. In their understanding any nation strives to be unified, because ethnic groups want to obtain self-determination through a state of their own. Regarding the nation not as a political, social or cultural construct but as an intrinsic entity, this approach views unification as a self-evident result of the overthrow of Communism. In contrast, liberal historians suggest that it might be more useful to refer to the turbulent events of 1848 as an example of the complicated connections between "revolution" and "nation." Only if such concepts are clearly defined and treated as historical creations can they offer any interpretation of the confusing events. The interpretative challenge is to explain the actual linkage between the civic rising of 1989 and the national turn of 1990.

As they do not fit one overarching concept, German developments should be analyzed in four different, but related, arenas. First, the basic precondition was the general *collapse of Communism* in Europe and Central Asia. The implosion of "actually existing socialism" linked several different dynamics. Economic production failed to master the transition to new technologies (with the exception of armaments). The widening gap between socialist rhetoric and reality made the population disillusioned in the system. The aspiration of internationalism came increasingly into conflict with Russian dominance and military occupation. Democratic centralism reached a legitimacy crisis as the goal of a communist future became ever more opaque. Such accumulated problems inspired Gorbachev's perestroika and the lifting of the "Brezhnev doctrine" that justified intervention. These Soviet changes opened Poland's and Hungary's way towards democracy, and de-legitimized Honecker's style of post-Stalinist rule.

Secondly, the speed of the communist collapse led to a *civic revolution* in East Germany. This neologism seeks to mark the special quality of the civic movement's peaceful revolt that overthrew the post-Stalinist regime. The disparate developments of the mass exodus, the protest demonstrations for human rights, and the reform debates within the communist elite combined in an unstoppable dynamic. On the one hand this revolt aimed at restoring those civil rights granted in the GDR constitution that were never actually practiced. Dismantling repression and establishing freedom of opinion, association, and travel began to democratize the GDR in the fall of 1989. On the other hand instituting a "council democracy" in the Round Tables also tried to develop new forms of social participation, ecological reform and gender relations appropriate for the 21st century. Though it remained nonviolent, the speed and extent of the East German transformation was, indeed, revolutionary.

Thirdly, in Germany the post-Communist transition took a peculiar *national turn*. In the spring of 1990, the GDR population abandoned the Third Way and embraced the slogan "we are *one* people" as quickest path toward a better life. The provisions of the FRG constitution that maintained citizenship for all Germans and allowed for the accession of other parts of Germany created the legal preconditions for a merger. Instead of supporting the continued existence of an Austrian-style GDR, the Bonn cabinet offered economic help only if it led to the restoration of a national state. Invoking the experience of 19th century unification, it argued that the mass exodus and economic collapse could be stopped only by a union of currencies. As a result, the majority of East Germans decided to have a reforming GDR join the FRG during the first free elections in March 1990. Although West Germans were loath to pay the costs, the public ratified this decision in the national ballot in December 1990 out of a lingering sense of national solidarity.

Ultimately, the unification of the German states was made possible by the *détente of the superpowers*. At the height of the Cold War, the

Soviet Union would never have relinquished its prize of World War II. The lessening of East-West tensions, demonstrated by disarmament, changed Central Europe from a potential battle-ground to a pillar for peace. Moscow reformers could argue that Russian security would be enhanced by the creation of a united but friendly Germany that extended economic aid. Steadfast American support helped persuade France and Britain, the other victor powers, to settle the German question in order to speed up European integration. At first, some neighbors were reluctant to permit unification because they feared the reemergence of German dominance over the continent. But eventually they accepted the result of the "Two - Plus - Four-" negotiations, since it guaranteed European frontiers in exchange for granting full sovereignty to the united Germany.

German unification was, therefore, the product of a unique combination of internal and external developments. The failure of forty years of attempts to achieve reunification indicates that progress was impossible with even one of the four major factors missing. In the international realm, Gorbachev's departure from the Brezhnev doctrine and the growing détente between the superpowers made reuniting the Germans less problematic than before. Domestically, the overthrow of the post-Stalinist regime in the East and the continuation of national solidarity in the West allowed the post-Communist transition in Germany to take the form of unification. Instead of being determined by a single overriding cause, the upheaval of 1989-90 was the result of a constellation of forces that seemed highly unlikely before it actually occurred. This example suggests that just when everything looks immutable, history can sometimes take a surprising turn.

Consequences of Unity

German unification has transformed the face of Central Europe. Most importantly, the fall of the Wall cleaned up the territorial debris of World War II and ended the Cold War on the continent. After four decades of division, a national state that existed for only three-quarters of a century has returned to Germany. Compared to previous incarnations, this latest version is a smaller and more homogeneous country. Hitler's and Stalin's ethnic cleansing have reduced German minorities so drastically that they no longer pose any irredentist threat in the East. Geographically, the new Germany is only the third largest state in Europe after France and Spain. Nonetheless, its population of about 80 million and potent economy restore it to a position of latent hegemony. Too large to fit in easily, the FRG is nonetheless too small to dominate the continent outright. Perhaps European integration and NATO membership will finally resolve this structural incompatibility.

The recovery of unity has also profoundly reoriented German politics. In the fall of 1989 the CDU was unpopular and the SPD seemed on the verge of taking power in the upcoming election. But by gambling on unification with a Protestant and socialist state, Chancellor Kohl trounced his populist rival Oskar Lafontaine. His success derailed the post-national and post-materialist agenda of 1968 advanced by leftist intellectuals. Instead of saving rain forests and helping the Third World, priorities have shifted to rebuilding the devastated Eastern states. Though given grudgingly, the annual transfer of 150 billion DM from West to East is the largest peacetime redistribution of funds in German history. Now parties, interest groups, and organizations face the challenge of integrating the new citizens psychologically and politically. Older class divisions and religious animosities have been superseded by the new cleavages between East and West.

In the short run, incorporating the East has proven more of a fiscal strain than an economic benefit. The GDR legacy of outdated equipment, polluted soil and casual work habits was far worse than anyone had expected. In structural terms, Eastern industry faced an impossible double transition from smokestack to high-tech production and from a planned economy to market competition. But the neo-liberal illusions of the CDU/FDP coalition also complicated the transition unnecessarily. To spare Westerners from sacrifice, the government followed the myth that the market would unleash another economic miracle. The decision to return nationalized property to its erstwhile owners tied up many properties needed for rebuilding in endless litigation. Though improving consumption and services, the hasty privatization policy of the Trusteeship Agency produced massive deindustrialization and unemployment. After the unification boom fizzled in the West, the unparalleled social experiment of integrating the East has turned out to be an enormous liability.

By destroying old certainties, unification also triggered a deep identity crisis among the citizens of the new states. The national turn of the Eastern electorate disappointed critical intellectuals who were hoping to find their own Third Way between the camps. Revelations of widespread complicity with the Stasi added another painful layer to the confrontation with the already troubled Nazi past. To a shocking extent politicians like Lothar de Maizière and Manfred Stolpe or writers like Christa Wolf and Sascha Anderson had collaborated with the secret police. The sudden juxtaposition of once separate populations revealed deep differences between a cosmopolitan but consumer-oriented West and a provincial but egalitarian East. The influx of half a million asylum seekers and a quarter-million ethnic refugees into the united country posed new questions about what was German and what was foreign. By especially undercutting leftist intellectual positions, unification forced many Germans to redefine themselves.

The return of unity called Bonn's international role into question as well. The increase in size and the lifting of restrictions rendered the FRG's posture of being an economic giant and a political dwarf obsolete. The clash between new expectations of responsibility and old fears of hegemony placed the German government in a no-win situation. If it took the lead as in the recognition of Croatia, it was criticized as overbearing. If it held back as in the Persian Gulf war, it was attacked for shirking its duties. In spite of strained resources, East European neighbors expected economic help without accompanying control. Western friends looked for greater leadership without having their own importance diminished. The UN hoped to use German troops for peacekeeping missions in exchange for the prospect of a permanent Security Council seat. While the right was only too willing to assume a larger role, the left clung to a moralism that eschewed force. No wonder that a new consensus on transcending D-mark diplomacy without excessive assertiveness has yet to emerge.

Finally, the German merger also complicated the process of European integration. Paris agreed to unification only if Bonn would be anchored more firmly in a united Europe. But an enlarged Germany, though preoccupied with absorbing its new states, deserved a greater voice in European institutions and needed subsidies for the underdeveloped East. The collapse of communism made the choice of "deepening" or "widening" the European Community harder, since poor Eastern cousins like Czechia and Poland now joined attractive Western suitors like Austria and Sweden. As a solution, the Maastricht agreement committed the members to a currency union by the end of the century and authorized the inclusion of new countries. However, high Bundesbank interest rates, designed to fight inflation, forced Britain and Italy to abandon the European Monetary System and compelled a broadening of the exchange range. Though the treaty weathered several plebiscites, popular resentment against Brussels bureaucrats grew so strong that the goal of a European superstate seemed to recede into an indeterminate future.

Will the new Germany become a "normal" state like other West European countries? The evidence presented below shows that unification was not a revanchist effort to undo the defeat of World War II. While historic fears centering on renewed aggression or another holocaust are likely to be misplaced, new problems created by unity arouse concern instead: The addition of seventeen million who lived for fifty-six years under dictatorship is testing democratic stability. A prolonged economic recession is trying the assumption of continuing material prosperity. Bouts of xenophobia are straining the civility of a Westernized society. But there are also hopeful signs that the Germans have learned from their problematic history: The hundreds of thousands who demonstrated for tolerance during the winter of 1992 showed a deep commitment to human rights. The debate about an out-of-area deployment of troops reveals an ingrained pacifist timidity. No doubt, the process of internal unification will be contested and painful. But the return of unity also offers the Germans another chance to combine nationality with liberty.

1

Division, Cold Civil War, and Détente

The division of the German nation-state at the end of World War II prompted continual efforts at reunification. The victorious Allied powers demanded the destruction of the Third Reich as punishment for Hitler's brutal expansionism, which had inflicted unspeakable suffering upon the European continent. Lasting protection of neighboring countries against a repetition of German aggression was imperative in light of the 35 million war casualties and victims of persecution. Pragmatic preparations for military occupation (Document 1) merged with plans for effective denazification in the resolutions at the Potsdam Conference (Document 2), which, despite continued reference to Germany as a whole, divided the territory of the German Reich de facto. In the face of total collapse, the German people accepted this division as a necessary condition for their survival in those central and western regions that were neither returned to eastern neighbors like the Sudetenland nor given over to Polish or Russian administration like East Prussia and Upper Silesia. Contrary to reactionary myths, partition was not only a retribution for Nazism, but it was also supported by the Germans themselves, who accepted the system set up by the occupation powers.

The Cold War between East and West hastened the founding of two separate successor states, the GDR and FRG. The claims of both constitutions to speak for all Germans (Documents 3 and 4) existed merely on paper, as any concrete efforts to regain unity such as the 17 June 1953 revolt (Document 5) were repressed by force. Instead, the GDR and the Federal Republic became integrated into their respective ideological blocs (Documents 6 and 7), tearing apart the social and cultural fabric of unity. The division culminated in the summer of 1961

Uniting Germany

with the building of the Berlin Wall and the fortification of the East German border, which provided a powerful symbol of the separation (Documents 9, 10 and 13). In spite of unification dreams (Document 11), the ideological clash between communism and the "free world" lent the partition the character of a "cold civil war" (Document 12).

In the late 1960s, the policy of détente lessened the severity of the confrontation. Reducing tension to the level of competition between two systems opened up possibilities for pragmatic cooperation. The social-liberal cabinet's abandonment of the claim to sole representation as stated in the Hallstein Doctrine (Document 8) made a new FRG policy towards the East possible. The Berlin Agreement (Document 14) and the Basic Treaty (Document 15) between the two Germanys decreased border conflicts and gradually improved the general atmosphere. Whereas East Germany insisted upon defining its own national identity (Document 16), the conservative West German government of the 1980s continued to strive for "change through rapprochement" (Document 17). Across the ideological divide, inter-German relations developed an ambivalent, "love-hate" character, resulting in close economic cooperation, a sense of mutual responsibility for peace, and finally, efforts to ease the conditions of the citizens (Documents 18 and 19). Despite rhetorical reunification pledges on national holidays, until 1989 German development from division to confrontation was limited to an ambiguous rapprochement between the two successor states.

Document 1:

The London Protocol of the European Advisory Commission delineated three Allied occupation zones for conquered Germany and thereby created the pragmatic basis for the later division of the country.

London Protocol, 12 September 1944

(Source: J. Nawrocki, *Relations Between the Two States in Germany*, Bonn, 1985, 84ff.)

The Governments of the United States of America, the United Kingdom of Great Britain and Northern Ireland, and the Union of Soviet Socialist Republics have reached the following agreement with regard to the execution of Article 11 of the Instrument of Unconditional Surrender of Germany:

1. Germany, within her frontiers as they were on December 31, 1937, will, for the purposes of occupation, be divided into three zones, one of which will be allotted to each of the Three Powers, and a special Berlin Area which will be under joint occupation by the Three Powers.

2. The boundaries of the three zones and of the Berlin area, and the allocation of the three zones as between the U.S.A., the U.K., and the U.S.S.R. will be as follows:

Eastern Zone

The territory of Germany (including the province of East Prussia) situated to the east of a line . . . will be occupied by armed forces of the U.S.S.R., with the exception of the Berlin Area, for which a special system of occupation is provided below.

Northwestern Zone

The territory of Germany situated to the west of the line defined in the description of the Eastern Zone, and bounded on the south by a line . . . will be occupied by armed forces of the United Kingdom.

Southwestern Zone

The territory of Germany situated to the south of a line . . . will be occupied by armed forces of the United States of America.

Berlin Area

The Berlin area (by which expression is understood the territory of "Greater Berlin" as defined by the Law of the 27th April, 1920) will be jointly occupied by armed forces of the U.S.A., U.K., and U.S.S.R., assigned by the respective Commanders-in-Chief. For this purpose the territory of "Greater Berlin" will be divided into the following three parts . . .

Document 2:

After the defeat of the Third Reich, the Potsdam Agreement between Great Britain, the Soviet Union, and the United States determined the principles of occupation policy and established provisional frontiers in the East. Though promising to treat Germany as an economic unit, the treaty ratified its partition de facto.

Potsdam Agreement, 2 August 1945

(Source: Nawrocki, *Relations*, 88ff.)

III. The Allied armies are in occupation of the whole of Germany, and the German people have begun to atone for the terrible crimes committed under the leadership of those whom, in the hour of their success, they openly approved and blindly obeyed.

Agreement has been reached at this Conference on the political and economic principles of a coordinated Allied policy towards defeated Germany during the period of Allied control.

The purpose of this agreement is to carry out the Crimea Declaration on Germany. German militarism and Nazism will be extirpated, and the Allies will take in agreement together, now and in the future, the other measures necessary to assure that Germany never again will threaten her neighbors or the peace of the world.

It is not the intention of the Allies to destroy or enslave the German people. It is the intention of the Allies that the German people be given the opportunity to prepare for the eventual reconstruction of their life on a democratic and peaceful basis. If their own efforts are steadily directed to this end, it will be possible for them in due course to take their place among the free and peaceful peoples of the world. . . .

A. Political Principles

1. In accordance with the Agreement on Control Machinery in Germany, supreme authority in Germany is exercised, on instructions from their respective Governments, by the Commanders-in-Chief of the armed forces of the United States of America, the United Kingdom, the Union of Soviet Socialist Republics, and the French Republic, each in his own zone of occupation, and also jointly, in matters affecting Germany as a whole, in their capacity as members of the Control Council.

2. So far as is practicable, there shall be uniformity of treatment of the German population throughout Germany.

3. The purposes of the occupation of Germany by which the Control Council shall be guided are:

I. The complete disarmament and demilitarization of Germany and the elimination or control of all German industry that could be used for military production. . . .

II. To convince the German people that they have suffered a total military defeat and that they cannot escape responsibility for what they have brought upon themselves, since their own ruthless warfare and the fanatical Nazi resistance have destroyed the German economy and made chaos and suffering inevitable.

III. To destroy the National Socialist Party and its affiliated and supervised organizations, to dissolve all Nazi institutions, to ensure that they are not revived in any form, and to prevent all Nazi and militarist activity or propaganda.

IV. To prepare for the eventual reconstruction of German political life on a democratic basis and for eventual peaceful cooperation in international life by Germany. . . .

9. The administration of affairs in Germany should be directed towards the decentralization of the political structure and the development of local responsibility. To this end...:

IV. For the time being no central German government shall be established. Notwithstanding this, however, certain essential central German administrative departments headed by State Secretaries, shall be established, particularly in the fields of finance, transport, communications, foreign trade, and industry. Such departments will act under the direction of the Control Council. . . .

14. During the period of occupation Germany shall be treated as a single economic unit. To this end common policies shall be established in regard to:

a) mining and industrial production and allocation;

b) agriculture, forestry, and fishing;

c) wages, prices, and rationing;

d) import and export programs for Germany as a whole;

e) currency and banking, central taxation and customs;

f) reparations and removal of industrial war potential;

g) transportation and communications.

In applying these policies account shall be taken, where appropriate, of varying local conditions.

VI. City of Königsberg and the Adjacent Area

The Conference examined a proposal by the Soviet Government that pending the final determination of territorial questions at the peace settlement, the section of the western frontier of the Union of Soviet Socialist Republics which is adjacent to the Baltic Sea should pass from a point on the eastern shore of the Bay of Danzig to the east, north of Braunsberg-Goldap, to the meeting point of the frontiers of Lithuania, the Polish Republic, and East Prussia.

IX. Poland

The Conference considered questions relating to the Polish Provisional Government and the western boundary of Poland . . .

b) The following agreement was reached on the western frontier of Poland.

In conformity with the agreement on Poland reached at the Crimea Conference, the three Heads of Government have sought the opinion of the Polish Provisional Government of National Unity in regard to the accession of territory in the north and west which Poland should receive. The President of the National Council of Poland and members of the Polish Provisional

Government of National Unity have been received at the Conference and have fully presented their views. The three Heads of Government reaffirmed their opinion that the final delimination of the western frontier of Poland should await the peace settlement.

The three Heads of Government agreed that, pending the final determination of Poland's western frontier, the former German territories east of a line running from the Baltic Sea immediately west of Swinemünde, and thence along the Oder River to the confluence of the western Neisse River and along the western Neisse to the Czechoslovak frontier, including that portion of East Prussia not placed under the administration of the Union of Soviet Socialist Republics in accordance with the understanding reached at this Conference and including the area of the former free city of Danzig, shall be under the administration of the Polish state and for such purposes should not be considered as part of the Soviet Zone of occupation in Germany . . . .

XIII. Orderly Transfers of German Populations

The Conference reached the following agreement on the removal of Germans from Poland, Czechoslovakia, and Hungary:

The three Governments, having considered the question in all its aspects, recognize that the transfer to Germany of German populations, or elements thereof, remaining in Poland, Czechoslovakia, and Hungary, will have to be undertaken. They agree that any transfers that take place should be effected in an orderly and humane manner.

Document 3:

The constitution of the West German successor state of the Deutsches Reich attempted to cure the causes of the collapse of the Weimar Republic and sought to achieve a lasting democratization. In the hope of overcoming division, the authors incorporated a reunification mandate in the preamble and articles 23 as well as 146.

(Source: R. Merker, ed., *Grundgesetz für die Bundesrepublik Deutschland vom 23. Mai 1963*, Stuttgart, 1963, 16 ff.)

Basic Law of the Federal Republic of Germany, 23 May 1949

Preamble:

The German people in the Länder of Baden, Bavaria, Bremen, Hamburg, Hesse, Lower Saxony, North-Rhine Westfalia, Rhineland-Palatinate, Schleswig-Holstein, Württemberg-Baden, and Württemberg-Hohenzollern, conscious of its responsibility before God and man, animated by the resolve to preserve its national and political unity, and to serve the peace of the world as an equal partner in a united Europe, desiring to give a new order to political life for a transitional period, has enacted, by virtue of its constituent power, this basic law of the FRG. It has also acted on behalf of those Germans to whom participation was denied.

The entire German people is called on to achieve by free self-determination the unity and freedom of Germany. . . .

Article 20: (1) The FRG is a democratic and social federal state.

(2) All state authority emanates from the people. It is exercised by the people by means of elections and voting and by separate legislative, executive, and judicial organs.

(3) Legislation shall be subject to the constitutional order; the executive and the judiciary shall be bound by the law. . . .

Article 21: (1) The parties participate in the shaping of the political will of the people. Their foundation is free, their inner structure must correspond to democratic principles, they have to account for the source of their funds in public.

(2) Parties which are inclined to harm or to overthrow the free democratic order or to endanger the existence of the FRG according to their goals or to the behavior of their supporters are unconstitutional. The Federal Constitutional Court decides on the question of constitutionality.

(3) Further details are regulated by federal law.

Article 22: The federal flag is black-red-gold.

Article 23: For the time being, this basic law applies in the territory of the Länder of Baden, Bavaria, Bremen, Greater Berlin, Hamburg, Hesse, Lower Saxony, North-Rhine Westfalia, Rhineland-Palatinate, Schleswig-Holstein, Württemberg-Baden, and Württemberg-Hohenzollern. In other parts of Germany, it shall be put into force on their accession. . . .

Article 116: (1) This Basic Law understands as German, except for other legal stipulations, whoever has German citizenship or whoever lived as a refugee or expellee of German ethnic origin or as his spouse or descendant on the territory of the German Empire on 31 December 1937.

(2) Former German citizens who lost their citizenship between 30 January 1933 and 8 May 1945 for political, racial or religious reasons, and their descendants are to be repatriated on appeal. They are regarded as not expatriated, if they were residing in Germany after 8 May 1945 and have not expressed a contrary desire. . . .

Article 146: This Basic Law becomes invalid on the day on which a constitution comes into being which has been created by the German people in a free decision. . . .

Document 4:

Conceived as a progressive alternative to the restoration of capitalism in the West, the East German constitution did not mention the communist character of the GDR. Like its Western counterpart, it did claim to speak for all of Germany.

Constitution of the German Democratic Republic, 7 October 1949

(Source: L. Holborn, *German Constitutional Documents Since 1871*, New York, 1970, 186ff.)

In the desire to guarantee freedom and human rights, to shape communal and economic life in social justice, to serve social progress, to support friendship with all nations, and to secure peace, the German people have given themselves this constitution.

Article 1: Germany is an indivisible democratic republic; it is composed of the German states.

The republic decides in all matters which are essential to the existence and the development of the German people as a whole; all other matters are decided by the states themselves. As a matter of principle, the decisions of the republic are carried out by the states. There is only one German citizenship.

Article 2: The colors of the GDR are black-red-gold. The capital of the republic is Berlin. . . .

Document 5:

The revolt of 17 June 1953, which was suppressed by Soviet tanks, grew out of a demonstration by East Berlin construction workers against an increase in production quotas. Public protests developed into a general call for the resignation of the SED government, and finally a demand for reunification. Beginning in 1955, June 17 was celebrated in the West as the Day of German Unity.

Central Committee Resolution, 24-26 July 1953

(Source: I. Spittmann, ed., *Der 17. Juni 1953: Arbeiteraufstand der DDR*, 2d ed., Cologne 1988, 21ff.)

7. As tools of American imperialism, West German monopoly capitalist and Junker circles played an important role in preparing the fascist putsch attempt

on June 17. Ever since the power of the workers was established in the GDR, ever since the capitalist monopolies and Junkers were expropriated and banned, these circles, which hold power in West Germany, have been waging a bitter battle for restoration of the old capitalist order in the GDR. They shrink from no crime in order to subvert popular control and the peaceful construction of the GDR, and to take back the factories from the workers and the land from the peasants. Their political representatives, Adenauer and Kaiser, openly announced the fascist Day "X" in advance. The particular focus of the hatred of these reactionary circles is the SED, the leading force in creating the foundations of the popular democratic order.[*]

The intentions of West German monopoly capitalists and Junkers were reflected on June 17 in the hostile demands of fascist provocateurs for the overthrow of the government of the GDR and restoration of the power of big capitalists and Junkers.

8. The fascist putsch attempt on June 17 was unsuccessful. The majority of the population of the GDR, especially the working class, did not support the provocateurs; instead, it firmly rejected them. The general strike planned and proclaimed by the putschists did not take place because the overwhelming majority of workers did not participate. Only some five percent of the workers of the Republic took part in strikes. Many of the Republic's leading factories — such as the Unterwellenborn mill, the Lauchhammer coking plant, the Döhlen steel mill, the "Wilhelm Pieck" synthetic fiber plant, the "Otto Grotewohl" combine in Böhlen, Secura in Berlin, Klingenberg power plant in Berlin, Plamag in Plauen, and many others — rebuffed the provocateurs with disciplined work and increased production. The great majority of the working intelligentsia also stood firmly behind the GDR government. The provocateurs faced the disapproval of the majority of the farming community as well. In most cities and enterprises, the party organizations of the SED, at the head of the working class, actively confronted the provocateurs, thus frustrating the putsch attempt. This rejection of the provocateurs by the majority of the population was the main reason for the defeat of the fascist putschists on June 17.

The official organs of the Republic, and especially the Soviet occupation troops, contributed decisively to thwarting the fascist war provocation.

The unsuccessful putsch attempt on June 17 proved that the democratic order in the GDR is firm and unshakable, because it is supported by the majority of workers. . . .

29. Despite this correct general line, the party recently committed a number of errors. These errors were as follows:

---

[*] Konrad Adenauer and Jacob Kaiser were the leaders of the conservative CDU. Day "X" was a communist construct marking the day when reactionary forces would invade the GDR.

a) The party, which had taken the correct course to construct the foundations of socialism in the GDR, took the incorrect course in accelerating completion of this task without considering the actual internal and external conditions. This exaggerated the pace of development in the economy, especially in heavy industry, and led to improper attempts to suppress and liquidate the urban middle class and petite bourgeoisie as well as the wealthier peasantry in the countryside; this had a negative effect on supplies for the population, and to a certain extent led to a disturbance of the proper relationship between the party and the working masses, as well as to an application of administrative methods rather than broad-based, patient informational work among the masses.

b) The party organizations were right to support the movement to create agricultural collectives in the GDR, which was initiated by the working peasants. However, in some areas party organizations tolerated violations of the principle of strict voluntarism in creation of such collectives; they attempted to force quantitative growth without devoting enough attention to firmly establishing the organizational and economic basis of existing collectives — which is the main task for the party in creating collectives in rural villages. . . .

30. Because of the division of Germany, a great misfortune for the German people and a threat to peace in Europe, the main task of the party has become the struggle for German reunification on a peaceful democratic basis. Therefore, it is necessary that all activity in the GDR be carried out in such a way that it both contributes to German unification and is understood by West German workers. We must remember that the majority of the West German population, as a result of the constant influence of the bourgeois press and radio, is under heavy reactionary influence, which hinders actions to increase democratic awareness.

The policy of the party in the GDR must therefore be simple and clear, open and determined, so that it can be understood by simple people. This policy is the party's new line. . . .

Document 6:

As the basis for the integration of the Federal Republic with the West, this general treaty ended the occupation regime of the Western powers and at the same time pledged their support for German reunification.

General Treaty on Germany, 23 October 1954

(Source: P. Longerich, *"Was ist des Deutschen Vaterland?" Dokumente zur Frage der deutschen Einheit 1800 bis 1990*, Munich, 1990, 196f.)

Article 1. (1) When this treaty goes into effect, the United States of America, the United Kingdom of Great Britain and Northern Ireland, and the French Republic (in this treaty and supplementary treaties thereafter also referred to as the "Three Powers") will end the occupation regime in the Federal Republic, repeal the occupation statute and dissolve the Allied High Commission and the offices of the State Commissioners in the Federal Republic.

(2) The Federal Republic will thereby have the full powers of a sovereign state over its internal and external affairs.

Article 2. In view of the international situation, which until now prevented German reunification and the conclusion of a peace treaty, the Three Powers retain the rights and duties exercised or held by them with regard to Berlin and Germany as a whole, including German reunification and a peace settlement. The rights and duties retained by the Three Powers in regard to stationing armed forces in Germany and protecting the security of these forces are determined by Articles 4 and 5 of this Treaty. . . .

Article 7. (1) The signatory states agree that a significant goal of their joint policies is a settlement for all of Germany through a peace treaty freely agreed to by Germany and its former opponents, which will form the basis for a lasting peace. They further agree that a final determination of Germany's borders must be postponed until such a settlement is reached.

(2) Until conclusion of a peace treaty settlement, the signatory states will cooperate by peaceful means to implement their common goal: a reunited Germany possessing a free, democratic constitution similar to the Federal Republic and integrated into the European Community. . . .

(4) The Three Powers will consult the Federal Republic in all matters affecting the exercise of their rights with regard to Germany as a whole. . . .

Document 7:

As a counterpoint to the Paris treaties, the Soviet Union offered the GDR autonomy and promised support for reunification under socialist auspices.

Treaty Between the GDR and the USSR, 20 September 1955

(Source: Holborn, *German Constitutional Documents*, 14)

The President of the GDR and the Presidium of the Supreme Soviet of the Soviet Union . . . in view of the new situation which has arisen owing to the coming into force of the Paris Agreements of 1954; convinced that the concerted efforts of the GDR and the Soviet Union to cooperate in the preservation and consolidation of peace and of security in Europe, to restore the unity of

Germany as a peace-loving and democratic state, and to bring about a peace settlement with Germany in the form of a treaty are in accordance with the interest of the German people and the Soviet people and alike with the interests of the other European peoples; taking into consideration the obligations of the GDR and the Soviet Union under the international agreements that concern Germany as a whole, have decided to conclude this treaty. . . .

The contracting parties solemnly confirm that the relations between them are based on complete equality of rights, mutual respect of sovereignty, and noninterference in domestic affairs.

In accordance with this, the GDR is free to decide on questions of its internal and foreign politics, including those pertaining to its relations with the FRG, as well as those pertaining to the development of relations with other states. . . .

The Soviet troops at present stationed on the territory of the GDR in accordance with the existing international agreements, remain temporarily in the GDR with the approval of the government of the GDR on conditions to be settled by an additional agreement between the government of the GDR and of the Soviet Union.

The Soviet troops temporarily stationed on the territory of the GDR will not interfere with the internal affairs of the GDR and with the social and political life of the country.

There is accord between the contracting parties that it is their main aim to bring about a peaceful settlement for the whole of Germany by means of appropriate negotiations. In accordance with this, they will make the necessary efforts toward a settlement by a peace treaty and toward the restoration of the unity of Germany on a peaceful and democratic basis.

Document 8:

In the 1950s, the West German government pursued what is often referred to as the Hallstein Doctrine, under which it claimed sole representation of all of Germany, attempting to encourage non-recognition of the GDR by third nations.

Konrad Adenauer on the Moscow Treaties, 20 September 1955

(Source: Bundesministerium für gesamtdeutsche Fragen, ed., *Die Bemühungen der Bundesrepublik um Wiederherstellung der Einheit Deutschlands durch gesamtdeutsche Wahlen*, vol. 2, Bonn, 1958, 246f.)

On the occasion of establishing diplomatic relations between the government of the FRG and the government of the USSR, I declare:

1. The establishment of diplomatic relations between the government of the

FRG and the government of the USSR does not represent any recognition of present territorial possessions on both sides. Final determination of the German boundaries remains reserved for a peace treaty.

2. The establishment of diplomatic relations with the government of the Soviet Union does not signify any change in the legal standing of the FRG regarding its authority to represent the German people in international affairs and the political relationship in those German areas which presently lie outside of its effective jurisdiction. . . .

These reservations eliminate the possibility that third nations misinterpret our decision to establish diplomatic relations with the Soviet Union. All states having diplomatic relations with us can clearly see that the standpoint of the FRG toward the so-called "GDR" and to boundary issues has not changed in the least. . . .

A settlement of Germany's territorial situation that is binding under international law does not yet exist. Such a settlement can be made only within the scope of a peace treaty to be concluded with a freely elected all-German government. The position of the government of the Federal Republic toward the government of the Soviet zone — as follows from the first reservation — will not be affected by the establishment of diplomatic relations between the Soviet Union and the FRG. The government of the so-called "GDR" was not formed on the basis of truly free elections and therefore has not received any real authorization by the people. In fact, it is rejected by the overwhelming majority of the population; there is neither legal protection nor freedom in the Soviet occupied zone, and the constitution exists only on paper.

The FRG therefore remains the only free and legal German government, with sole authorization to speak for all of Germany. . . . We have notified the Soviet government of our viewpoint in order to remove any doubts whatsoever as to the firmness of our position. If the Soviet government nevertheless establishes diplomatic relations with us, it is doing so, though without granting approval, with full knowledge of our stand toward the so-called "GDR" and our claim to speak for all of Germany. Where third nations are concerned, we also maintain our standpoint regarding the so-called "GDR." I must clearly and in no uncertain terms declare that the government of the FRG will interpret as an unfriendly act the establishment of diplomatic relations with the "GDR" by third nations with which it has official relations, as this act would serve to deepen the division of Germany.

Document 9:

In response to a never-ending flood of defections, the GDR erected a wall in Berlin and fortified the entire border. This drastic measure stabilized East Germany's population, economy, and politics; but it also created more than a "certain discomfort" for the people and deepened the division of Germany.

Resolution of the GDR Council of Ministers, 12 August 1961

(Source: J. Rühle, ed., *13. August 1961: Die Mauer von Berlin*, Cologne, 1981, 93ff.)

On the basis of the declaration of the Warsaw Pact member states and the Volkskammer resolution, the Council of Ministers of the GDR has resolved:

In the interest of peace, the actions of West German revanchists and militarists need to be stopped and, by means of a German peace treaty, the way must be paved for peace and the rebirth of Germany as a peace-loving, anti-imperialist, neutral state. The standpoint of the government in Bonn — that World War II has not yet ended — is tantamount to a call for a license for militaristic provocation and civil war measures. Such imperialistic policy disguised as anti-communism represents a continuation of the aggressive goals of fascist German imperialism at the time of the Third Reich. The defeat of Hitlerian Germany in World War II has led the Bonn government to give the criminal politics of German monopoly capitalism and its Hitler generals another try by renouncing the policy of a German nation-state and transforming West Germany into a NATO state, a satellite of the United States.

This new threat to the German and European peoples through German militarism could become an acute danger, since the West German Federal Republic and the front city of West Berlin have continually violated the basic stipulations of the Potsdam Agreement that call for eradication of militarism and Nazism.

Revanchism has intensified in West Germany, with increasing territorial claims against the GDR and neighboring states. This sentiment is closely tied to accelerated rearmament and acquisition of nuclear weaponry by the West German army. The Adenauer administration is making systematic preparations for civil war against the GDR. Citizens of the GDR who visit West Germany are increasingly subject to terrorist persecution. West German and West Berlin espionage headquarters are systematically soliciting citizens of the GDR and organizing the smuggling of human beings.

As formulated in official government documents and the declaration of principles of the CDU/CSU party leadership, the goal of this aggressive policy and these disruptive activities is to incorporate all of Germany into NATO, the western military bloc, and extend the militaristic rule of the Federal Republic onto the territory of the GDR. West German militarists wish to use all kinds of deceptive maneuvers, such as "free elections," in order to expand their military basis first as far as the Oder River and then begin the great war.

West German revanchists and militarists are abusing the peaceful policies of the USSR and Warsaw Pact states in regard to the German question. Their intentions are to use hostile agitation, solicitation, and diversionary maneuvers to harm not only the GDR but other socialist states as well.

For all these reasons, the Council of Ministers of the GDR, in accordance with the resolution by the Political Advisory Committee of the states of the Warsaw Pact, is instituting the following measures to secure peace in Europe and protect the GDR, and in the interest of ensuring the security of states in the socialist camp:

To stop hostile activities by revanchist and militaristic forces in West Germany and West Berlin, a border control will be introduced at the borders to the GDR, including the border with western sectors of Greater Berlin, as is common on the borders of sovereign states. Borders to West Berlin will be sufficiently guarded and effectively controlled in order to prevent subversive activities from the West. Citizens of the GDR will require a special permit to cross these borders. Until West Berlin is transformed into a demilitarized, neutral free city, residents of the capital of the GDR will require a special certificate to cross the border into West Berlin. Peaceful citizens of West Berlin are permitted to visit the capital of the GDR (democratic Berlin) upon presentation of a West Berlin identity card. Revanchist politicians and agents of West German militarism are not permitted to enter the Capital of the GDR (democratic Berlin). For citizens of the West German Federal Republic wishing to visit democratic Berlin, previous control regulations remain in effect. Entry by citizens of other states to the capital of the GDR will not be affected by these regulations.

For travel by citizens of West Berlin via routes through the GDR to other states, previous regulations remain in effect.

Transit traffic between West Germany and West Berlin through the GDR will not be affected by this resolution.

The Minister of the Interior, the Minister for Transport, and the Mayor of Greater Berlin are called upon to enact any measures necessary for the implementation of this resolution.

This resolution on measures to secure peace, protect the GDR, in particular the capital city of Berlin, and assure the security of other socialist states will remain in effect until conclusion of a German peace treaty.

Document 10:

Because the Western allies did not want to risk the outbreak of World War III with a military response, West Germany had no alternative but to condemn the building of the Wall and reaffirm its desire for self-determination.

Adenauer on the Building of the Wall, 13 August 1961

(Source: Rühle, *13. August 1961*, 96)

This evening, those in power in the Soviet zone began to cut West Berlin off from its surroundings, in open violation of the Four-Power Agreement. This measure is being taken because the regime forced upon the people of central Germany by a foreign power can no longer overcome the internal problems in its sphere of power. The other East bloc states demanded from the Zone government that it eliminate this condition of weakness and insecurity. Every day, mass flight from the Zone showed the world the pressure under which its citizens lived, as well as the fact that they were denied the right of self-determination recognized throughout the world.

Through the despotism of the Pankow regime, a serious situation has developed. Necessary countermeasures will be taken along with our allies. The federal government asks all Germans to have confidence in these measures. We are called upon now to meet the challenge from the East firmly but calmly, and not to do anything which could only worsen the situation rather than improve it.

We continue to feel close ties to Germans in the Soviet zone and East Berlin; they are, and remain, our German brothers and sisters. The federal government holds unswervingly to the goal of German unity in freedom. Given the significance of the action, I have asked the Foreign Minister to inform foreign governments through the German embassies.

Document 11:

At the end of the Adenauer era, comedian Wolfgang Neuss used satire to attack bourgeois hopes for a restoration of "Greater Germany."

Wolfgang Neuss on Reunification (ca. 1963)

(Source: *Ästhetik und Kommunikation*, 1990, Nos. 73-4, 41)

Why I am looking forward to reunification

Because then we will be one power. A million soldiers. Twice as many police officers. A car for every German. Hundreds of thousands of jails. An incalculable number of tax officials. Barges on the Oder. Danzig brandy. Königsberg meatballs. The Baltic Sounds. Downhill skiing on the Schneekoppe. Rübezahl, the spirit of the Sudeten Mountains, in Kattowitz. Schweidnitz restaurant. Zeiss-Ikon for Münnemann.[*] The descendants of Pferdmenges[**] as the lessors of the fishing sites in Brandenburg and all the beautiful lakes which would be ours again. The Century Hall in Breslau. The boys' choir in Stettin. The Dresden Zwinger Castle. The Auerbach cellar in Leipzig, and the Thomas Church boys' choir. The Wittenberg Church. Goethe's city of Weimar. The West Berlin Theater, which could move back to Cottbus. Swimming in the Baltic Sea.

---

[*] West German industrialist.

[**] Adenauer's banker.

Smoked sausage spread from the Rügenwald. Chalk cliffs. A national population of 70 million. And a high wall along the German-Polish border of 1937. And the border police would have orders to shoot. So that no Poles can come over, because we want to keep to ourselves. Because we don't want to be separated from our family.

And because then we wouldn't have any trouble any more with foreign police who search our cars in our own country. Because then we wouldn't need to give development aid to foreign countries. Because no one will need to recognize anything anymore. Or they won't be able to, whatever. Because then we couldn't be blackmailed. Because then we wouldn't have any fateful questions regarding the nation anymore. Just answers. Based on democracy. And anybody who isn't a democrat gets a punch in the nose. Because we have learned. Because we'll do it better this time. Because we don't need the French anymore. Because the Russians will have to pay. The warships from Rostock and Swinemünde and Danzig will be in Wilhelmshaven and Kiel. And because the National Soccer League will get new blood and because the 1. FC Köln will have to play against Beuthen 09.[***]

Because we won't need any concentration camps anymore. Because the Jews from Berlin, Hamburg, and Munich will have to move to Israel. And Ulbricht's thugs will get put in the camp. Because that's part of self-determination. And international law has done enough. And the cherry blossoms in Werder. Finally, potteries in Bunzlau again. And Peenemünde[****] will be expanded.

Then the Chinese will get nervous.

That's why I'm looking forward to reunification. Because in the end, the Chinese are responsible for the division of Germany. To think of all that they want to do to us in the future, just because we're letting them starve to death today. That's why we have to become one nation again, with several leaders (that's what we need in a democracy!). And we also have to stay rich, because of our force of attraction reaching as far as the Ural Mountains.

I am also looking forward to it because the intellectuals won't be able to say "I told you so!" They want to do without. But our claim is undeniable. Because we belong together. That's why I'm looking forward to reunification. Because then things will be even better for us. From the Saar Region all the way to Allenstein.

Document 12:

Dissatisfied with the "policy of strength" towards the East, West German intellectuals criticized the West German government's reuni-

---

[***] Professional soccer teams from Cologne and Upper Silesia.

[****] Nazi rocket center.

fication rhetoric in a "Catechism on the German Question," compiled by Hans-Magnus Enzensberger.

Hans-Magnus Enzensberger on the Cold Civil War, February 1966
(Source: "Katechismus zur deutschen Frage," *Kursbuch* 4, February 1966, 1ff.)

1. What is the German question?

The German question is often referred to, but rarely formulated. There are those who talk about it but do not know how to put it into words. Depending on who asks it and whom it is asked of, it can express all sorts of things: self-pity, resentment, narrow-mindedness, chauvinism, reason, realism, vision, solidarity. It can be asked belligerently and peacefully, from within and from without. In practice, it permeates a whole host of political, social, economic, strategic, and legal questions whose common source is World War II. The war, begun and lost by the Third Reich, destroyed that Reich and replaced it with two German states and the city of Berlin, a zone protected by the victorious powers. This legacy has not been settled to this day.

2. Is such a settlement possible?

Yes.

3. Are the Germans, and are German governments, prepared to make such a settlement?

That is the German question. . . .

22. What are the legal doctrines upon which the government's policies are based?

Reunification, right of self-determination, claim to sole representation, four-power responsibility: these four concepts can be considered the legal correlates to official political and military doctrines. They deserve more careful analysis simply because legal illusions are more difficult to penetrate than the policies based upon them.

23. What does the federal government mean by "reunification"?

Those who talk of reunification have essentially surrendered to the legal standpoint of the federal government. For in its view, that which is popularly termed reunification is the creation, in reality, of a situation which is supposed to have existed legally all along. That is, the Federal Republic is none other than the German state founded in 1867 as the North German Union and expanded into the German Reich in 1871, which survived all changes in its state form and was not even destroyed by the total collapse in 1945. The Federal Republic is a continuation of the German Reich as a subject of international law, with its legal identity preserved; it is the only sovereign state. The area of the GDR and the areas under Polish and Soviet administration on the other side of the Oder and Neisse are, in this view, part of its territory; the Federal Republic cannot exercise its power there only because it is prevented from doing so by foreign despotism.

Reunification thus means the elimination of Soviet control and that of its German governors; it is not reunification at all, in the sense of a union of separate but equal parts, but "reconnection" or "liberation of occupied territory."

There are good reasons why the view held by the federal government that the Federal Republic is identical with the German Reich (the identity theory) is also called the "civil war theory." According to this theory, a rebellious government has been established on the territory of the Federal Republic with the help of a foreign power; the Federal Republic is involved in a "cold civil war" with it. Reunification — that is, repossession of the territory illegally held by the rebels — thus requires the opponent's capitulation. Reunification, in the sense used by the federal government, means a victory in the cold war; its necessary correlate is a policy of strength. . . .

Document 13:

As sign of the consolidation of the GDR, 94.49 percent of the East German population approved a new constitution in a plebiscite in April 1968. It emphasized the socialist character of the workers' state and the leading role of the SED but continued to refer to the concept of a German nation.

GDR Constitution, 6 April 1968

(Source: Holborn, *German Constitutional Documents*, 186ff.)

The people of the GDR — imbued with the responsibility of guiding the entire German nation on its path toward future peace and socialism, fully cognizant of the historical fact that imperialism has divided Germany and that West Germany has become the base for imperialism and for the fight against socialism under the leadership of the United States and with the consent of the West German circles of capitalist monopoly, aware that this division is against the vital interests of the nation, firmly founded on the achievements of the antifascist and democratic-socialist transformation of the social order, united in the goal of its working classes and people to continue in the spirit of the Constitution of 7 October 1949, and imbued with the will to pursue peace, social justice, democracy, socialism, and friendship with all peoples freely and resolutely — have given themselves this socialist constitution.

Article 1: The GDR is a socialist state of German nationality. The GDR is the political organization of the urban and rural working people. Under the leadership of the working class and its Marxist-Leninist party, it is making socialism a reality. Berlin is the capital of the GDR. The flag of the GDR is black, red, and gold with the state emblem of the GDR in the center on both sides. The state emblem of the GDR is the hammer and compass in a wreath of ears of grain entwined at the base with a black, red, and gold ribbon. . . .

Article 8. 1. The generally recognized provisions of international law that encourage peaceful cooperation among people are also binding for all state authorities and citizens. The GDR will never start a war of aggression or use its armed forces against the freedom of another people.

2. The establishment of normal relations between the two German states and their cooperation on the basis of equality is the national concern of the GDR. Moreover, the GDR and its citizens seek to overcome the division of Germany that was forced upon the German nation by imperialism and, step by step, to bring about the rapprochement of the two German states on the basis of democracy and socialism.

Document 14:

One of the first results of the détente between East and West was the 1971 Berlin Agreement among the World War II victors. It improved the practical situation of West Berlin through a renewed guarantee of unhindered transit and better travel to the GDR.

Berlin Agreement, 3 September 1971

(Source: Nawrocki, *Relations*, 98ff.)

The Governments of the French Republic, the Union of Soviet Socialist Republics, the United Kingdom of Great Britain and Northern Ireland, and the United States of America, represented by their Ambassadors, who held a series of meetings in the building formerly occupied by the Allied Control Council in the American Sector of Berlin,

Acting on the basis of their quadripartite rights and responsibilities, and of the corresponding wartime and postwar agreements and decisions of the Four Powers, which are not affected,

Taking into account the existing situation in the relevant area,

Guided by the desire to contribute to practical improvements of the situation,

Without prejudice to their legal positions,

Have agreed on the following:

Part I

1. The four Governments will strive to promote the elimination of tension and the prevention of complications in the relevant area.

2. The four Governments, taking into account their obligations under the Charter of the United Nations, agree that there shall be no use or threat of force in the area and that disputes shall be settled solely by peaceful means.

3. The four Governments will mutually respect their individual and joint rights and responsibilities, which remain unchanged.

4. The four Governments agree that, irrespective of the differences in legal views, the situation which has developed in the area, and as it is defined in this Agreement as well as in the other agreements referred to in this Agreement, shall not be changed unilaterally.

Part II

A. The Government of the Union of Soviet Socialist Republics declares that transit traffic by road, rail and waterways through the territory of the GDR of civilian persons and goods between the Western Sectors of Berlin and the FRG will be unimpeded; that such traffic will be facilitated so as to take place in the most simple and expeditious manner; and that it will receive preferential treatment.

Detailed arrangements concerning this civilian traffic, as set forth in Annex I, will be agreed by the competent German authorities.

B. The Governments of the French Republic, the United Kingdom, and the United States of America declare that the ties between the Western Sectors of Berlin and the FRG will be maintained and developed, taking into account that these Sectors continue not to be a constituent part of the FRG and not to be governed by it. . . .

C. The Government of the Union of Soviet Socialist Republics declares that communications between the Western Sectors of Berlin and areas bordering on these Sectors and those areas of the GDR which do not border on these Sectors will be improved. Permanent residents of the Western Sectors of Berlin will be able to travel to and visit such areas for compassionate, family, religious, cultural or commercial reasons, or as tourists, under conditions comparable to those applying to other persons entering these areas.

The problems of the small enclaves, including Steinstücken, and of other small areas may be solved by exchange of territory.

Document 15:

The Basic Treaty between the two Germanys was an achievement of the *Ostpolitik* of the social-liberal coalition under Willy Brandt. It improved relations between the German states by de facto recognition of the GDR, although Egon Bahr maintained the FRG claim to reunification in a separate letter.

Basic Treaty between the FRG and the GDR ,21 December 1972

(Source: Nawrocki, *Relations*, 112ff.)

The High Contracting Parties,

Conscious of their responsibility for the preservation of peace,

Anxious to render a contribution to détente and security in Europe,

Aware that the inviolability of frontiers and respect for the territorial integrity and sovereignty of all states in Europe within their present frontiers are a basic condition for peace,

Recognizing that therefore the two German states have to refrain from the threat or use of force in their relations,

Proceeding from the historical facts and without prejudice to the different views of the FRG and the GDR on fundamental questions, including the national questions,

Desirous to create the conditions for cooperation between the FRG and the GDR for the benefit of the people in the two German states,

Have agreed as follows:

Article 1: The FRG and the GDR shall develop normal, good neighborly relations with each other on the basis of equal rights.

Article 2: The FRG and the GDR will be guided by the aims and principles laid down in the United Nations Charter, especially those of the sovereign equality of all States, respect for their independence, autonomy, and territorial integrity, the right of self-determination, the protection of human rights, and non-discrimination.

Article 3: In conformity with the United Nations Charter, the FRG and the GDR shall settle any disputes between them exclusively by peaceful means and refrain from the threat or use of force.

They reaffirm the inviolability now and in the future of the frontier existing between them and undertake fully to respect each other's territorial integrity.

Article 4: The FRG and the GDR proceed on the assumption that neither of the two states can represent the other in the international sphere or act on its behalf.

Article 5: The FRG and the GDR shall promote peaceful relations between the European states and contribute to security and cooperation in Europe.

They shall support efforts to reduce forces and arms in Europe without allowing disadvantages to arise for the security of those concerned.

The FRG and the GDR shall support, with the aim of general and complete disarmament under effective international control, efforts serving international security to achieve armaments limitation and disarmament, especially with regard to nuclear weapons and other weapons of mass destruction.

Article 6: The FRG and the GDR proceed on the principle that the sovereign jurisdiction of each of the two states is confined to its own territory. They respect each other's independence and autonomy in their internal and external affairs.

Article 7: The FRG and the GDR declare their readiness to regulate practical and humanitarian questions in the process of normalization of their relations. They shall conclude agreements with a view to developing and promoting, on the basis of the present treaty and for their mutual benefit, cooperation in the fields of economics, science and technology, transport, judicial relations, postal and telecommunications, health, culture, sport, environmental protection, and other fields. The details have been agreed upon in the Supplementary Protocol.

Article 8: The FRG and the GDR shall exchange Permanent Missions. They shall be established at the respective government's seat.

Practical questions relating to the establishment of the Missions shall be dealt with separately.

Article 9: The FRG and the GDR agree that the present treaty shall not affect the bilateral and multilateral international treaties and agreements already concluded by them or relating to them.

Letter from the Government of the FRG to the Government of the GDR on German Unity, 21 December 1972

In connection with the signing today of the Treaty on the Basis of Relations between the FRG and the GDR, the Government of the FRG has the honor to state that this treaty does not conflict with the political aim of the FRG to work for a state of peace in Europe in which the German nation will regain its unity through free self-determination.

Document 16:

In order to escape the Western policy of "change through closeness," the GDR tried to distance itself from the FRG. The constitution of 1974 defined East Germany only as a socialist state of workers and peasants and omitted any reference to reunification.

GDR Constitution, 7 October 1974

(Source: D. Müller-Römer, ed., *Die neue Verfassung der DDR*, Cologne, 1974, 78ff.)

The people of the GDR, carrying on the revolutionary tradition of the German working class, and aided by the liberation from fascism, in accordance with the processes of the historical development of our epoch, have realized thier right to social, economic, state and national self-determination and created a developed socialist society.

Intent on freely determining their fate and proceeding undeterred on the road of socialism and communism, of peace, democracy, and international friendship, the people of the GDR have given themselves this socialist constitution.

Article 1: The GDR is a socialist state of workers and peasants. It is the political organization of the workers in town and country under the leadership of the working class and its Marxist-Leninist party.

The capital of the GDR is Berlin.

The state flag of the GDR consists of the colors black-red-gold with the state emblem of the GDR in the center on both sides. The state emblem of the GDR is hammer and compass in a wreath of ears of grain entwined at the base with a black, red and gold ribbon. . . .

Article 8: The generally recognized provisions of international law that encourage peaceful cooperation among nations are also binding for our state authorities and citizens. The GDR will never start a war of aggression or use its armed forces against the freedom of another people.

Document 17:

Despite anti-Communist rhetoric and an emphasis on reunification, Helmut Kohl's conservative coalition government held to the policy of German cooperation, attempting to coax further humanitarian concessions from the GDR through economic incentives.

Helmut Kohl on the State of the Nation, March 1984

(Source: J. Nawrocki, *Die Beziehungen zwischen den beiden Staaten in Deutschland*, Berlin, 1986, 64ff.)

We stand behind the agreements we have signed. We hope to further tighten the network of relationships. . . . We hope to preserve and increase what we have achieved; we want to utilize the opportunities created by the Basic Treaty and other inter-German treaties and agreements. We are prepared to develop further our relations with the GDR on the basis of balance, fulfillment of treaties, and predictability, with the goal of attaining practical results of immediate value to the people. The FRG and the GDR form a community of responsibility for peace and security in Europe; both must make efforts to reduce international tension. . . .

By agreeing to more than a billion marks in loans from West German banks, the Federal Republic sent a clear signal to the GDR leadership last summer. At the same time, this decision was a message to the Germans in the GDR, which they interpreted correctly: We will protect our security and alliance interests but are of course prepared to cooperate in inter-German relations.

Document 18:

Despite Honecker's prediction "that socialism and capitalism can combine as little as fire and water," bilateral relations between West and East Germany improved considerably in the late 1980s, relieving some of the negative effects of the division.

Joint Communique by Erich Honecker and Kohl, 8 September 1987

(Source: *Ein Erfolg der Politik der Vernunft und des Realismus,* Berlin, 1987, 39ff.)

General Secretary Erich Honecker and Chancellor Helmut Kohl agreed that the GDR and the FRG, in view of the mutual responsibility to deal with their common history, must take special action to secure peaceful coexistence in Europe. Never again shall war emanate from German soil; Germany shall unleash peace.

Heads of State Honecker and Kohl emphasized that the relationship between the two states must remain a stabilizing factor for constructive East-West relations. It must provide a positive impetus for peaceful cooperation and dialogue in Europe and beyond. . . .

In consideration of existing circumstances, and despite differences of opinion regarding basic issues, including the national question, it is the intention of both states, in the spirit of the Basic Treaty [of 21 December 1972], to develop normal, neighborly relations on an equal basis and to continue to take advantage of all opportunities for cooperation provided by the treaty.

The two heads of state agreed to preserve and expand prior achievements, keeping in mind the basic principle that the states respect one another's independence and sovereignty regarding their domestic and foreign affairs. Willingness to negotiate and realism should be the guidelines for constructive, practical cooperation between the two states. . . .

General Secretary Honecker and Chancellor Kohl dealt with travel and visit issues, including trips in the event of urgent family matters. They acknowledged progress up to now, and reaffirmed their intention to continue improving and simplifying procedures in the interests of the people. . . . They welcomed the establishment of partnerships between cities in the GDR and the FRG as important in facilitating meetings among the citizens of the two states, including cultural events, and developing peaceful neighborly relations. They will continue to support such efforts in the future. . . .

The heads of state discussed humanitarian issues, including uniting families and dealing with hardship cases. They acknowledged positive results so far and agreed to continue relevant, constructive efforts. . . .

General Secretary Honecker and Chancellor Kohl stated that they attach great significance to protecting the natural foundation of human existence. They assessed the agreement which further structures relations in the area of environmental protection as an expression of the desire to intensify cooperation in this area. . . .

They both welcomed the agreement on cooperation in the fields of science and technology and concur in their intention to intensify relations, including contacts among scientists and research facilities within the scope of particular, mutually beneficial projects.

The two heads of state emphasized the great significance of comprehensive, objective reporting by the press, radio, and television for the further development of good neighborly relations. Accordingly, both sides assure journalists of the greatest possible support in doing their jobs. . . .

They were pleased to announce that, all in all, economic relations between the two states have developed positively in the last few years. They consider trade to be an important stabilizing factor in the overall relationship and declared their interest in steadily expanding economic cooperation on the basis of equality and reciprocal benefit, which will also include smaller and mid-sized enterprises. They confirmed their intention to improve trade structures and to put more effort into the exchange of capital goods, particularly products in the areas of mechanical and electrical engineering, and energy and environmental technology. Both sides stressed the significance of cooperation with outside markets. . . .

The heads of state further discussed international development. In the awareness that different social systems exist in the two states and that they belong to different alliances, the heads of state expressed their opinions on the status and prospects of East-West relations.

They announced their wish to contribute, within the scope of their respective alliances, to a policy of détente and peace, while continuing dialogue and long-range cooperation.

In a joint effort to develop to the fullest all opportunities for a broader and more constructive dialogue on the needs of people in East and West, and in the firm conviction that a long-term, stable and lasting state of peace in Europe cannot be achieved solely by military means, both states attach particular significance to the CSCE process. Balanced, tangible progress in all areas relating to the Helsinki Accords is an important measure of openness to détente and of readiness to solve security problems by building confidence. Both sides are committed to seeing all principles and stipulations of the Helsinki Accords and the concluding document of Madrid achieve their maximum effectiveness, for the good of the people and in the interest of cooperation between the states.

In this context, General Secretary Honecker and Chancellor Kohl exchanged opinions on the protection of human rights. . . .

They emphasized results of negotiations within the framework of the East-West dialogue on effective measures for arms control and disarmament in all areas. Based on the principles of equality and parity, a stable, truly verifiable balance of power at the lowest possible level must be achieved, and any imbalance dismantled. This must be able to be verified effectively. . . .

General Secretary Honecker and Chancellor Kohl regarded their exchange of opinions as necessary and beneficial for the further development of relations. They declared their support for the continuation and intensification of such contacts at high political and other levels.

Document 19:

As a reaction to the growing desire of East German citizens to travel, this ordinance made private trips and emigration somewhat easier; however, the government, fearing unlimited contacts, insisted on including countless reasons to deny permission.

GDR Travel Ordinance, 30 November 1988

(Source: U.-E. Böttger, ed., "DDR-Verordnung über Reisen und Ausreisen," *Deutschland Archiv*, 22, 1989, 108ff.)

Article 6: Private trips to the People's Republic of Bulgaria, the Korean Democratic People's Republic, the Mongolian People's Republic, the People's Republic of Poland, the Socialist Republic of Romania, the Czechoslovakian Socialist Republic, the Union of Soviet Socialist Republics, and the Hungarian People's Republic may be undertaken without presenting particular reasons unless otherwise stipulated.

Article 7: (1) Applications for private trips to foreign countries other than those listed in Article 6 can be made by grandparents, parents (including stepparents), children (including stepchildren), and siblings (including half-siblings) on the occasion of births , baptisms, name days, school entry,

"Jugendweihen,"* confirmations and first communions, civil and church marriages, 25th, 50th, 60th, 65th, and 70th anniversaries of civil and church marriages, 50th, 55th, and all birthdays thereafter and including the 60th, for installation in church offices, ordinations and anniversaries in office, for necessary care in the case of life-threatening illnesses, for deaths and funerals.

(2) Applications for private travel to countries other than those listed in Article 6 can be made by grandchildren, parents-in-law, daughters-in-law, sons-in-law, aunts, uncles, nieces, nephews, cousins, brothers- and sisters-in-law . . . .

(3) Applications for private trips by citizens who have reached legal retirement age or invalids can be made without presentation of particular reasons. . . .

Article 10: (1) Permanent emigration can be permitted where humanitarian reasons exist.

(2) Humanitarian reasons exist if:

a) parents are to be reunited with minor children of whom they have custody;

b) minors whose parents are deceased are to be cared for by their siblings, or, if they have no siblings, by relatives living abroad, where permission is given by the responsible organs of the Youth Relief Organization of the GDR. . . ;

d) permission is to be granted to spouses, where marriage occurs with permission of the responsible organs under Article 18 of the Implementing Law of 5 December 1975, or if a spouse has taken up residence abroad with permission of the responsible organs of the state;

e) single non-minors are to be reunited with their relatives who live exclusively abroad;

f) because of their physical or psychological condition, single non-minors are to be cared for by parents or siblings, or, if parents or siblings are no longer living, by relatives living abroad;

g) citizens who have reached legal retirement age or are invalids wish to join relatives or friends in order to spend their old age with or be cared for by them. . . .

Article 13: (1) Permission is to be denied if necessary to protect national security or national defense.

(2) Permission can be denied if the applicant has not yet actively served in the military or other equivalent service, or served in the military reserve, and has not reached his 26th birthday, or if he is presently serving in defense or

---

*Secular youth rite of passage in the GDR.

security organs, or if the period following release from service set by the responsible state organs has not yet elapsed.

Article 14: (1) Permission can also be denied if necessary to protect public order or other state interests of the German Democratic Republic. This is in particular the case if:

a) because of present or former employment, the applicant possesses knowledge that must be kept confidential in order to prevent danger, damage, disruption, or other harm;

b) investigation of legal complaints against the applicant has not yet been completed, there is an official investigation against him, he is involved in a criminal procedure, or a sentence is being served;

c) in connection with the application, actions were committed in violation of the GDR legal order, or the exclusive responsibility of the state organs of the GDR was disregarded;

d) there is reason to suspect that the foreign trip will be used for activities that would be crimes under the laws of the GDR;

e) during previous trips abroad, the laws of the GDR were violated or the reputation of the GDR harmed;

f) the private trip or permanent emigration is to be made to citizens of the GDR living abroad in violation of the laws of the GDR;

g) the applicant provided false information during the application process.

(2) Permission for permanent emigration can also be denied in order to protect the rights of citizens, the principles of socialist morality or social necessities. This is in particular the case if:

a) the applicant has purposely withdrawn from his social obligations in order to achieve permanent emigration, in particular by giving up his employment, with the result that an impairment of the citizens' quality of life has occurred or can be expected;

b) the applicant has not settled his financial obligations to the GDR;

c) a relationship with a minor would be affected;

d) husbands and wives or guardians would be separated from minor children;

e) proper administration of the applicant's real estate, houses, or other property could not be guaranteed. . . .

2

Emigration, Opposition, and
Inability to Reform

Imprisonment behind the Wall made travel an obsession for East German citizens. Some 3.5 million had "voted with their feet" and left the country between the late 40s and 1961. Following the fortification of the border, another 616,066 had resettled in West Germany by 1988 (62.1 percent legally, 26.6 percent through other countries, 6.5 percent by crossing the border illegally; the remaining 4.3 percent were ransomed by the FRG). The SED's consistent policy of separation (Document 2) did not succeed in eliminating the deep dissatisfaction with "real existing socialism" felt by an increasing number of East Germans (Document 4). Thus in the first half of 1989, 36,484 East Germans emigrated legally and 4,849 illegally, while another 2,070 were caught in the attempt. The erosion of communism in neighboring states led, in the autumn of 1989, to distressing scenes during embassy occupations in Budapest, Prague and Warsaw. When Hungary opened its border (Document 7), the SED defiantly rejected the emigrants as victims of revanchist media propaganda (Document 10). Thousands of refugees hoped to improve their lives through a personal reunification with the West.

Attempts to create an opposition in the GDR were particularly difficult because of the cold civil war against West Germany and repeated deportation of dissidents. The expulsion of Wolf Biermann in 1976 was one of the first incidents to spark internal protests; this critical potential was strengthened by impulses from the peace movement, beginning in the early eighties ("swords into ploughshares") (Document 1). Stimulated by concerns about environmental degradation, opposition networks formed within the Protestant Church; despite persecution by the secret police, the *Stasi*, they protested human rights violations and election fraud. In order to initiate a public dialogue on the country's problems, dissidents founded the "New Forum" (Document 5), while critics within the governing "bloc parties," such as the East German Christian Democratic Union, also spoke up (Document 6). Impressed by the wave of emigration, democrats sought to free the Social Democratic Party from its coerced unification with the SED (Document 8); "Democracy Now" (Document 9) and other groups, such as "Democratic Awakening," demanded greater freedom (Document 11). These rapidly-growing, wide-ranging grass roots citizens' movements aimed less at national unity than at renewal of the GDR.

The SED leadership's inability to reform turned the wave of emigration and opposition protest into a crisis of the system. To the old men surrounding Erich Honecker, only a socialist GDR had any right to exist (Document 3); thus they clung proudly to their achievements in building up the country under difficult conditions and stuck to their repressive doctrines (Document 12). Not even Mikhail Gorbachev's warning during the celebration of the fortieth anniversary of the GDR (Document 13) succeeded in swaying their determination to put down the swelling demonstrations by force (Documents 14 and 15). Only local cooperation between secretaries of the Leipzig district party leadership and prominent citizens such as the conductor Kurt Masur succeeded in preventing a bloodbath on 9 October like the Chinese massacre in Tiananmen square (Documents 16 and 17). When the younger party leaders finally rebelled, they used the exodus and demonstrations to force the resignation of SED chief Honecker (Document 18) and the appointment of Egon Krenz, former secretary of the party youth (FDJ). US President George Bush then responded publicly by discussing the possibility of reunification at some future time (Document 20).

Document 1:

Despite intensive Stasi spying and numerous repressive measures, a multilayered network of opposition groups began to form in the mid-1980s under the umbrella of the Protestant church. These dissidents attempted to create a socialist democracy on East German soil.

Stasi Analysis of the East German Opposition, 1 June 1989

(Source: A. Mitter and S. Wolle, eds., *Ich liebe euch doch alle! Befehle und Lageberichte des MfS*, Berlin, 1990, 46 ff.)

A main thrust of the opponents' subversive activities against socialism is the attempt to create and legalize a so-called internal opposition, as well as to inspire and organize underground political activity in the socialist states, creating "internal pressure" to soften, subvert, politically destabilize, and ultimately eliminate socialism. To carry out the anti-socialist "program for democracy" of imperialist circles in the USA, leading political forces in the NATO states, under the banner of "democratization, liberalization, and advocacy of political pluralism along Western lines in communist countries," are developing and promoting opposition parties and movements in these states, while actively supporting legalization of existing so-called independent groups. This behavior is reflected both in the policies of the major imperialist powers and in manifold subversive activities by hostile centers and organizations, as well as by other anti-socialist forces operating against the socialist states. (By misusing the CSCE process and referring to certain developments in some socialist countries, these activities increasingly aim to support hostile opposition forces and groups politically, materially, and morally and to inspire and provoke behavior aimed against the socialist political and social order.)

It must be assumed that opposing political, ideological, and subversive developments, as well as the impact of current developments in some socialist countries, exercise a certain influence on sectors of the GDR population. This can be seen in particular in the existence of groups (still controllable and under state and social supervision) that attempt to act in the spirit of this opposing strategy, in accordance, or cooperation with reactionary members of the clergy and external enemies.

Since the early 1980s, continuing attempts at gathering and organizing by persons aiming to soften, subvert, politically destabilize, and even change the social system in the GDR have led to the creation of such groups. They are integrated almost without exception into the Protestant Church in the GDR, or use its material and technical facilities for their activities. Correspondents accredited in the GDR and employees of diplomatic corps from non-socialist countries (including secret service members camouflaged as diplomats), especially from West Germany, the USA, and Great Britain, play a decisive role in this process. They inspire hostile opposition forces and groups of individuals to anti-socialist activities, provide them with continued support and popularize such activity, with the goal of placing such persons and associations under the protection of international publicity. . . .

There are presently some 160 such associations in the GDR. Among them, a large number is responsible for hostile-negative or other activities aimed against the socialist state and social order, continually or on particular occasions. They are subdivided into some 150 so-called grassroots church groups that, depending on the demagogic "goal" and "content" of their activities or their personal composition, call themselves "peace groups" (35), "environmental groups" (39), mixed "peace and environmental groups" (23), "women's groups" (7), "doctors' groups" (3), "human rights groups" (10), or "third world groups" (39), and so-called regional groups of draft resistors. . . .

As derived from so-called founding declarations and strategy papers . . . as well as views and demands announced in other ways, the following anti-socialist contents and thrusts form the main focus of the hostile opposition forces:

1. Attacks aimed at the foundations and laws of socialism find concentrated expression in demands for change in the socialist state and social order and the "renewal of socialism." These forces refer increasingly to the process of transformation and related developments in the USSR and other socialist countries. Concepts such as glasnost, democratization, dialogue, civil rights, freedom for "those who think differently," or pluralism are misused demagogically in order to cover up their own political conceptions and goals. . . .

2. Attacks on security and defense policies appear primarily in the guise of "demilitarization" of society, demands for the elimination of para-military education and training of young people (including the school subject "military training"), elimination of military service, creation of a social or civil "peace service" as a substitute for military service, and the right to refuse military service for reasons of conscience.

3. Attacks on communist education of youth include, for example, demands for abandonment of the "claim to totality" of the Marxist-Leninist world view as a valid doctrine and practice in all educational facilities, as well as dismantling the "claim to totality" of social institutions of political education. . . .

4. Environmental problems form a broad field with which to discredit the party's policies on environmental issues; content and methods are aimed mainly at state institutions and, despite their scientific appearance, often do not correspond with reality. . . .

Considering the development and activities of the groups of persons existing in the GDR, we suggest:

1. Under the leadership of the party, further activity by existing groups and the creation of new groups of persons should be consistently opposed through uniform, conceptually founded political-ideological and operative cooperation and action by all responsible state organs and social organizations and forces; measures by the security organs to subvert and dissolve the same and to paralyze anti-socialist activities by these groups should be supported in an effective and sophisticated manner.

2. It is considered advisable to present evidence, using the media and other public means, that these groups of individuals and their ideas, so-called open letters, petitions, demands, and similarly propagated hostile oppositional

views correspond to similar ideological attacks by the enemy, and to carry on an offensive political-ideological discussion on this basis.

3. To preserve and implement socialist legality, various consistent, suitable sanctions should be employed against persons and groups that particularly threaten security through public action against the socialist state and social order, thereby significantly violating legal norms.

4. In the future, differentiated travel restrictions should be employed against persons from the non-socialist world who act as advocates or organizers of underground political work in the GDR and as contact persons to hostile, opposition persons and the aforementioned groups. . . .

Document 2:

Joachim Herrmann's statements in the summer of 1989 were typical of the SED's rigidity which made it insensitive to the people's wishes and hopes. The "old guard" could see popular aspirations only through the lens of anti-Communist propaganda.

Joachim Herrmann on the Need to Stand Firm, 22-23 June1989

(Source: J. Herrmann, *Aus dem Bericht des Politbüros an die 8. Tagung des ZK der SED*, Berlin, 1989, 5ff.)

The great demonstration by the working class on May 1, the mandate for our policies in the local elections, the younger generation's pledge to socialism in the GDR during the FDJ meeting at Pentecost, the farsighted discussions at the Ninth Educational Conference – all these events which took place during the period of this report express the firmness with which the values of socialism are rooted among the people. The unity of economic and social policy is being consistently achieved, in turn sparking new activity by the working people. In a cosmopolitan climate, we continue the construction of socialism as a historic process of far-reaching political, economic, social, intellectual and cultural transformation.

We are currently being subjected to very intensive efforts by certain politicians in capitalist countries to apply political, economic, and ideological pressure upon socialist countries, to encourage them to adopt capitalist structures and concepts of society, bourgeois pluralism, and bourgeois ideology. Under the banner of "renewing socialism," forces seeking to eliminate socialism are at work. In this context, developments in Hungary cause us great concern. Attacks on socialism are accompanied by demands that the present realities in Europe be called into question. However, anyone who attempts to change these realities, in particular the European borders; anyone who proclaims the revanchist slogan of restoration of the German Reich within its 1937 borders; anyone who attempts to interfere with the internal affairs of the socialist states or censor their sovereignty undermines the foundations of the postwar European order, and in the end endangers the transformation of international relations from confrontation to détente. Those politicians in the West who, in recent days, do not let a public appearance go by without attacking the "Wall," the state border between the GDR and West Berlin, should be aware of this. They want the GDR to give up its security against economic plundering, against infiltration by criminal elements of psychological warfare, even including drug traffic. Of course, this will not happen. Our experience in the period before August 1961 was bitter enough, and everyone knows that peace in Europe was endangered more than once. That is why the GDR has stated repeatedly that the "Wall" will continue to exist until the conditions leading to its construction are eliminated. . . .

Regarding recent events in the People's Republic of China, the GDR has published all relevant statements and declarations from the party and state leadership of the People's Republic of China, in order to make objective information available and counter Western horror stories. The peaceful demonstrations by students in Peking were to be exploited for a counterrevolutionary revolt against the people's government in China. In a declaration introduced by the SED delegates, the Volkskammer of the GDR emphasized the fact that the Chinese party and state leadership's efforts to find a political solution to domestic problems were hindered by violent, bloody incidents by anti-constitutional elements, and that the popular government was therefore forced to restore order and security through the use of armed force. The Volkskammer emphasized the fact that it considers the events in Peking exclusively the internal affairs of the People's Republic of China, and opposes any foreign interference. The deputies of the highest popular representative body expressed their firm conviction that the party and state leadership of the People's Republic of China, closely linked with its people, will take steps to clarify the problems and serve the continued progress on the road to socialism that the Chinese people freely chose forty years ago. . . .

Document 3

This widely quoted statement by the rector of the Academy of Social Sciences of the Central Committee presented the official SED viewpoint on the German Question, which blocked any internal reform of the GDR by equating the current party line with the existence of the state.

Otto Reinhold on East German Identity, 19 August 1989

(Source: *Blätter für deutsche und internationale Politik*, 1989, 1175)

Today the relationship between the GDR and the FRG has changed significantly. Even the Springer press[*] has had to take note of the new reality in some way, leaving off the quotation marks around our country's name. But the contradiction between the two social systems remains, even if it appears in another form. The claims that the German question must be kept open, that the German Reich in its 1937 borders still exists, and many others indicate that those who promote such theses continue hoping they will be able to liquidate the GDR and reconquer the old spheres of power.

At the same time, it is necessary, in the interests of both German states, to work together closely in political, economic, cultural, humanitarian, and other areas. Thus, unlike any other socialist country in Europe, the dialectical link between cooperation and conflict is an indispensable characteristic of our concept of society. The central question involved is, to a particularly great extent, what one might call the socialist identity of the GDR. In this question, there is very clearly a basic difference between the GDR and other socialist countries. Those countries all existed, before undergoing socialist restructuring, as states with capitalist or semi-feudal orders. Thus their state identity did not rest primarily upon a social order.

The GDR is different. It can be conceived only as an anti-fascist, socialist state, a socialist alternative to the FRG. What right would a capitalist GDR have to exist alongside a capitalist Federal Republic? None, of course. Only if we are constantly aware of this fact is it clear how important a social strategy is which aims without compromise to consolidate the socialist order. There is no room to play thoughtless games with socialism or the socialist government. . . .

Document 4:

This blunt analysis by the Ministry for State Security reveals the background of the mass exodus and the full extent of the failure of "real existing socialism."

Stasi Report on Motives for Emigration, 9 September 1989

(Source: Mitter and Wolle, *Ich liebe euch doch alle*, 141ff.)

The overwhelming majority of these people has an essentially negative view of problems and failures in the development of society, especially in their private lives, personal living standards, and so-called everyday shortcomings; based on this attitude and on comparisons with conditions in the FRG and West Berlin, they assess developments in the GDR negatively.

The advantages of socialism, such as social security and protection, are acknowledged; however, they are no longer seen as decisive factors in

---

[*]Conservative West German newspapers like the *BILD-Zeitung*.

comparison with the problems and failures that have emerged. To some extent, they are taken for granted; thus they are no longer included in these assessments at all, or are completely negated. Doubt and disbelief exist as to the achievability of goals and the correctness of party and government policies, especially in regard to domestic developments, guarantee of appropriate living standards, and satisfaction of personal needs. This is accompanied by the view that developments have not brought any perceptible improvements for the people and that, in many areas, things in the GDR had once been better. Such viewpoints are observed in particular in people who were once socially active, but who, for the aforementioned reasons, became "tired," resigned themselves, and in the end capitulated.

There is insufficient understanding of the complexity and objective contradictions involved in building socialism; from their point of view, goals and results that have not been attained, as well as existing problems, shortcomings, and defects, are interpreted and judged as mistakes in policy.

As the result of a long-term process, these people come to the conclusion that a perceptible, rapid, and permanent change in their living standards, especially pertaining to satisfaction of personal desires, is only attainable in the FRG or West Berlin.

Although in each individual case, a complex of concrete, individual facts, manifestations, events, etc. helps create the motive for leaving the GDR, a summary of the essential factors leading to such motives is attempted in the following:

The essential reasons for, and causes of, efforts to leave the GDR, either illegally or through emigration – which are echoed in numerous petitions to central and local organs or institutions – are:

- dissatisfaction with the supply of consumer goods;

- annoyance at inadequate services;

- impatience with problems of medical care and treatment;

- limited opportunities for travel within and outside the GDR;

- unsatisfactory working conditions and discontinuity in the production process;

- inadequacy and inconsistency in applying or carrying out the principle of merit pay, as well as dissatisfaction with the development of wages and salaries;

- annoyance at bureaucratic behavior by the heads and employees of state organs, industries, and institutions, and at unfeeling treatment of citizens;

- lack of understanding of the GDR's media policy.

In greater detail:

Dissatisfaction with the supply of consumer goods

Criticism of distribution of goods to the population is the most significant factor in the motivational structure. In particular, there is little understanding of continuing problems with consistent supply of quality consumer goods (cars, furniture, textiles, shoes, home electronics, etc.), as well as spare parts, construction materials, and certain everyday goods (for example, quality groceries, fresh fruit, vegetables, and items on the continually changing list of "1,000 little things"). This includes distribution of goods, freshness of groceries, gaps in supply, a lack of constant availability until store closing time, and the related transport problems.

The persons concerned point in particular to the "standing in line" caused by this, the need to run around and search for particular items, the "procuring and organizing" that goes on even during working hours, and the possibility of obtaining certain goods only through "connections"; they conclude that they can no longer bear all this.

The chief complaint revolves around the fact that those who possess foreign currency can obtain almost anything (not only in Intershop[*] stores).

There is criticism of the so-called double currency system, of Intershops, luxury hotels and "privileges" for those with foreign currency.

The aforementioned persons – often pointing to the continuation or increase in such phenomena – doubt the possibility of a solution to these problems of concern to citizens.

Annoyance at inadequate services

Closely related to the views regarding the supply situation are various problems in the service sector. In particular, reference is made to a lack of, or limits on, available facilities for repairs and services. Shortages of spare parts, long waiting periods and unfriendly treatment of citizens in the service sector, in restaurants and in stores are the main focus of criticism. . . .

In summary, it must be pointed out that the motivational factors mentioned are in part linked with:

- illusions about "Western" lifestyle, especially expectations of a life with "better" material security and "better" earnings, more "freedom," enabling one to attain a lifestyle based on selfish striving for consumption and ownership;

- attitudes, viewpoints and characteristics such as selfishness, greed, careerism, immorality, overestimation of self, etc.

---

[*] Special hard currency stores for Western goods.

These factors are inseparably linked to current developments in other socialist states, in particular the Hungarian People's Republic, the People's Republic of Poland, and the Soviet Union; through these, significant doubts have arisen as to the unity, and thus the strength, of the community of socialist states, which lead increasingly to doubts about the prospects and chances of victory of socialism itself.

Additional motives for leaving the GDR are based to a small extent on truly humanitarian reasons (for example, marriage, reuniting families), "solutions" to family or personal conflicts, a yearning for adventure, and efforts to escape legal punishment.

In making an overall assessment, it must be taken into account that those applying for emigration or persons who leave the GDR illegally are, as a rule, no longer politically bound to the GDR in any way. However, the majority does not act out of a basically hostile attitude.

Manifestation of hostile attitudes can in many cases be explained by the fact that the citizens involved believe this improves their chances of having permanent emigration authorized. As a rule, they use the arguments of opponents without being able to explain them convincingly, for example, to the responsible organs of state.

Document 5:

The appeal for an "Awakening 1989," signed by intellectuals such as B. Bohley, K. Havemann, R. Henrich, R. Meinel, C. and S. Pflugbeil, E. and J. Reich, and H. J. Tschiche, called for the initiation of a non-partisan dialogue in order to democratize the GDR.

Founding Appeal of the New Forum, 9 September 1989

(Source: *Die ersten Texte des Neuen Forums*, Berlin, 1990, 11)

Communication between the state and society is obviously disrupted in our country. Evidence of this is widespread disillusionment, to the point of withdrawal into private niches or mass emigration. Elsewhere, refugee movements of this size are the result of poverty, hunger, and violence. None of that exists here.

This disturbed relationship between state and society is paralyzing our creative potential and preventing the solution of existing local and global problems. We are wasting our time in sullen passivity, while there are more important things we could be doing for our lives, for our country, and for humanity.

The interests of groups and classes in the state and the economy are poorly balanced. Communication on the situation and these interests is also hampered. All of us offer our private diagnoses and suggest measures we consider most important. But such wishes and desires vary greatly; they are never weighed rationally against each other and examined for feasibility. On the one hand, we want an increase in available consumer products and improved supply; on the other, we are aware of the social and ecological costs, and advocate a renunciation of unlimited growth. We want leeway for economic initiative but not degeneration into a dog-eat-dog society. We want to preserve that which is proven, while creating room for something new, in order to live more frugally and less at odds with nature. We want order, but do not want to be told what to do. We want free, self-confident citizens who nevertheless behave responsibly. We want protection from violence without having to put up with a state full of henchmen and spies. Those who are lazy and do nothing but talk are to be driven from their comfortable jobs; yet we do not want to disadvantage the socially weak and defenseless. We want effective health care for everyone but do not want people taking sick leave at others' expense. We want to participate in export and world trade without becoming either debtors and servants to the leading industrial states, or exploiters and creditors of economically weaker nations.

In order to recognize all these contradictions, hear and evaluate opinions and arguments, and distinguish between special and general interests, we need a democratic dialogue on the responsibilities of the state, the economy, and culture. We must think about these issues and talk to one another about them, publicly, together, throughout the country. Whether we can find a way out of the present crisis in the foreseeable future will depend on our readiness and willingness to do so. Given current social developments, it is necessary for a large number of people to participate in the process of social reform [and] for the many individual and group activities to unite in joint action.

Therefore, together we are creating a political platform for all of the GDR that allows people from all professions, parties, and groups to take part in the discussion and resolution of crucial social problems in this country. We have chosen the name

NEW FORUM

for this comprehensive initiative.

We wish to place the New Forum's activities on a legal footing. We refer to the basic right, governed by Article 29 of the Constitution of the GDR, to achieve our political goals through common activity in an association. We will register the founding of the association with the responsible organs of the GDR, in accordance with the decree of 6 November 1975 on "Founding and Activities of Associations" (*Gbl.* I, No. 44, 723).

The desires that the New Forum hopes to express and give voice to are based on a wish for justice, democracy, peace, and protection of nature. It is this impulse that we would like to see brought to life in the coming reorganization of all areas of society.

We call on all citizens of the GDR who would like to participate in the reorganization of our society to become members of the New Forum. The time is now.

Document 6:

Encouraged by the wave of emigration, this open letter by synod member M. Huhn, Senior Church Secretary M. Kirchner, Pastor C. Lieberknecht, and Church Secretary G. Müller was a first attempt to introduce a discussion on reform within one of the "bloc parties."

Weimar Letter to the East German CDU, 10 September 1989

(Source: *Deutschland Archiv*, 22, 1989, 1185ff.)

1. As employees or members of the Church who belong to the CDU, we address ourselves to the party's members and its executive body. We ask them to consider with us the contribution the CDU can make to the solution of acute social and political problems. We are convinced that the party can do more than it has, as yet, believed possible.

2. Above all, we are concerned that the problem of legal and illegal emigration from the GDR has escalated this year, rather than gradually losing significance. When we look at the ages, educational levels, and vocations of the emigrants, it becomes apparent that [their loss] affects not the margins, but the heart, of our society. Our country is suffering – and the longer it continues, the worse the damage becomes.

3. Our churches are also suffering from the wave of emigration. No one is interested in their appeal to citizens to remain in the country and be patient. The ability to resist the temptation to emigrate is weakening not only among parishioners, but even among employees of the diaconate and the clergy. Often those wishing to emigrate attempt to use the Church to achieve their ends.

4. In addition, the attempt to trace the causes of the emigration movement and contribute to eliminating or reducing them burdens the churches with the role of substitute for the responsible social authorities. To some extent, the churches are forced into this role against their will; to some extent they succumb to the temptation to gain the attention often denied them in fulfilling their actual tasks in our secularized society. In any event, the churches largely lack the competence and strength to play this role of substitute.

5. In this situation, we advocate preservation of the principle of separation of church and state as a basic element of the conception of the "church in

socialism." This includes the right of the churches to take a position, from their own point of view, on fundamental issues concerning the people and questions of the survival of humanity.

6. The principle of separation can, however, be upheld only if all forces responsible for shaping the state carry out their tasks decisively and actively. For this reason, we must guard against any tendency to play down or deny social problems, or to make them taboo, in order to justify inaction.

7. We believe the CDU in the GDR is being challenged to measure its social responsibility by the higher standards appropriate to the state of development forty years after the GDR's creation. We consider ourselves, along with all members and the executive board of the party, obligated to take notice of our country's present problems, realistically and honestly; to discuss them openly and make suggestions on how to solve them.

8. Regarding the current, particularly distressing emigration problem, it is necessary to recognize the causes and help to eliminate them – causes that lead people who have grown up in our country, who were raised and trained by the GDR, and who were active in the labor process, to emigrate in disproportionately high numbers.

9. Political responsibility, involvement, and participation by the party and its members must attain a new quality in three main areas: 1. within the party, 2. within the community of the Democratic Bloc, 3. within the broader society.

10. 1. Further Development of Democracy Within the Party:

Party work is to be shaped so that the will of the members enjoys absolute priority. . . .

11. 2. Defining the Party's Contribution Within the Community of the Democratic Bloc:

A small party like the CDU, subordinate to the leading forces in the Democratic Bloc, gains stature primarily through the proposals it can introduce in the social process of opinion formation and decision making. . . .

15. 3. Decisive Approach to Social Problems:

The CDU is obligated to the broader society to face the current situation of our country. In the following, we list some of the problems in need of urgent solutions. They are a representative sample; others are no less important.

16. Encouragement of public opinion formation. . . .

21. Respect for the people's ability to take responsibility for themselves. . . .

23. Giving travel issues the importance they deserve. . . .

28. Revealing economic problems. . . .

Document 7:

The gripping emotions of liberation, as well as their exploitation by the anti-Communist media, are apparent in the reports of the mass circulation tabloid *BILD* celebrating the opening of the Hungarian border in anticipation of German unity.

The *BILD-Zeitung* on the Opening of the Hungarian Border, 12 September 1989

(Source: BILD, *Guten Morgen, Deutschland: Das Tagebuch der Freiheit*, Hamburg, 1989, 68ff.)

It began with a hole in the fence

Budapest – It began with a hole in the Iron Curtain:

2 May: Hungarian border guards cut holes in the border fence with wire cutters.

20 June: The first reports arrive of "three or four" East German citizens refusing to leave Bonn's embassy in Budapest until they are permitted to emigrate to the Federal Republic.

21 July: Hungary no longer returns refugees to the GDR.

8 August: 130 GDR citizens refuse to leave [West Germany's] permanent mission in East Berlin. The mission is closed.

13 August: Bonn closes its embassy in Budapest. 180 GDR citizens are waiting there.

19 August: Mass flight by 660 GDR citizens during an event sponsored by the "Pan-Europa Union."

22 August: Bonn closes its embassy in Prague. 140 refugees still wait there.

8 September: 116 GDR citizens leave the permanent mission in East Berlin and voluntarily return to their homes.

10 September: The Hungarian government allows all refugees to travel to the West.

11 September: At exactly midnight, Hungary opens its border.

Germany, 12 September 1989:

They Kiss Freedom

Hamburg – They danced, they fell into one another's arms, they cried for joy, they kissed the ground and symbolically meant freedom. Yesterday, nearly

10,000 GDR citizens stormed across the Hungarian border to Austria. They came in buses and in their own cars; most continued on to the Federal Republic immediately. It was the largest refugee trek since the end of the war. "I'm shaking all over," said 24-year-old Jens Lorenz as he stepped on Bavarian soil after an eight-hour ride. They celebrated with mineral water, champagne, and beer. A toast made the rounds: "We drink a drop to German unity."

They Danced Through the Barrier

At three minutes past midnight, a rust-brown Lada is the first to cross the border. In the car are two families, one child.

The strapping driver: "I still can't believe it worked." A group of young people with knapsacks dances, singing and cheering, under the barrier. They are welcomed on the other side of the border by locals with champagne and applause. A young man holds up a poster: "Erich Honecker, give up, aren't 100,000 refugees enough?" The wife of an East Berlin truck driver: "It's like a rubber band bursting. Like when the props fall away from a rocket."

Dagmar Schwochow beams; she holds her poodle tightly. "On August 14, my boyfriend and I applied for a visa to Hungary, and now we're here. We had more luck than brains."

Shortly after five thirty, Frank and Heike Streit of Erfurt (both 26) arrive at the border near Salzburg. "We have quite a trip behind us," says Frank. "Yesterday morning at 10 we left Erfurt, we were in Hungary at seven in the evening, and we went right on to the Federal Republic." In the first five hours after midnight, more than 2,000 GDR citizens had already passed through the border crossing in Burgenland in private cars. By noon it becomes clear there are more than 7,000.

Brunhilde Kiebert (56) got a taxi in Budapest with her last 100 Marks, and took it to the border. "The driver gave me a jacket so I wouldn't freeze." A father from Thuringia tells how happy GDR citizens in Hungary had been about getting permission to leave: "My wife and I sobbed, the little one laughed," says the man, pointing to his young son. A young man in his mid-twenties says in a hoarse voice: "I was in Hungary with my wife, but she went back alone." Their one-and-a-half year old child was still in the GDR. . . .

At the Hungarian Border

"This is incredible. Go on, drive! We're on our way to Germany!"

Nickelsdorf – an hour before midnight, under clear skies, a four-kilometer-long line of Trabis, Wartburgs and Ladas is already backed up at the Hungarian border station near Hegyeshalom. TV teams from as far away as the USA and Japan push their way between the cars.

Many refugees wait near their packed cars, greeting each other with the "V" sign for victory. Some are shivering – a cool easterly wind is blowing through Burgenland tonight.

The Barrier Rises

A friendly Hungarian border guard says: "I'd like to open the border earlier. But my boss said not until midnight."

But he doesn't hold out quite that long. At 11:59 PM, the red, white, and green Hungarian barrier rises – the gate to the West.

Under a blue cloud of exhaust from the spluttering, stinking Trabis, the refugees kiss the ground. Laughing border guards wave their caps and throw them into the cars. The horns toot a concert; people cry for joy, cheer, sob. Then the motors roar. In another two kilometers – covered in three minutes – there's another stop, this time in front of Austria's red and white barrier.

Freedom at Last

Management expert Frank Schneider and his wife Petra stop here in their Lada at 12:03 A.M. Their small daughter Jasmin (3) is asleep on the back seat; the child blissfully hugs her doll. The family from Leipzig waited five weeks in Budapest – now freedom is in sight. Petra is shaken by sobs. She cries over and over, as if possessed, "My goodness! Oh, Frank! This is incredible! Go on, drive! On to Germany!"

In a few minutes, the border crossing is jammed. Red Cross workers pass out hot tea, lemonade, and crackers. Four young men wave black, red and gold flags, singing as if they are at a soccer game: "Ale, Ale, Alemania!"

Lars (22) excitedly throws his last East German coins into the air, rips up his blue East German passport, and cries: "I'm a Trabi mechanic. That was my last trip in my good old Zwickau refugee's suitcase." That's what they call Trabis in the East.

All refugees are supposed to get visas upon entering Austria. But the Austrian officers, overwhelmed by the avalanche of Zwickau-made cars, open all five barriers. Isolde (23), from Werra, springs from her Trabi and kisses a border guard. He turns away, furtively wiping a tear from his eye. Brunhilde Kiebert (56) from Friesach arrives in Austria in a taxi from Budapest: "I paid for it with my last 100 Marks. My brother is waiting in Austria."

Seven Hundred Schillings for Gas

Just beyond the border, Austrians give each driver seven hundred schillings (100 marks) for gasoline, as well as road maps with the fastest route to Passau marked out. In the parking lots along National Highway 10, drivers scrape off their GDR stickers. They paste D stickers[*] to their rear windows. Handmade.

---

[*]International automobile identification for (West) Germany.

Document 8:

The illegal appeal, signed by M. Gutzeit, M. Meckel, A. Noack, and I. Böhme, was an attempt to revive the tradition of democratic socialism by establishing an independent SPD, thus offering a political alternative to the SED.

Founding Appeal for a Social Democratic Party in the GDR, 12 September 1989

(Source: Mitter and Wolle, *Ich liebe euch doch alle*, 161ff.)

It can't go on like this!

Many people are waiting for something to change. But that is not enough! We want to do our part.

The necessary democratization of the GDR demands a fundamental denial of the governing party's claim to absolute truth and power. We need an open, intellectual discussion on the state of our country and its future. This requires a program, as well as people who have, or can attain, the necessary abilities.

We, the undersigned, believe it is important to the future of our society to found a Social Democratic Party. Our goals are:

Ecologically oriented social democracy

This requires a clear separation of state and society,

- making possible, strengthening, and protecting the social, cultural, and political rights of citizens, and the accompanying acceptance of responsibility;

- guaranteeing protection of the natural environment, and securing resources and the possibility of life for coming generations.

We call on those who agree with the following indispensable programmatic orientation to unite locally:

- the rule of law and separation of powers;

- democracy and party pluralism;

- relative independence (financial, economic, cultural) of regions (Länder), districts, cities, and local governments;

- social market economy with strict prohibition of monopolies to prevent undemocratic concentrations of economic power;

- democratization of economic structures;

- free trade unions and the right to strike.

We seek binding organizational ties in solidarity with all those who unite around these basic principles. Those who do not agree with us should describe and define their own democratic perspectives.

We seek alliances with all those who would like to cooperate in fundamental democratization of our country.

We appeal to those who are affected by our country's need. We invite all initiatives with similar aims to join us. We particularly hope for alliances with Christians and critical Marxists. Let us reflect together on our future, on a society in solidarity, in which

- social justice, freedom, and dignity are guaranteed for all,
- social consensus is sought in public dialogue, and implemented through a just balancing of various interests,
- the responsible, creative work of its citizens creates lively pluralism in our community,
- the rule of law and legal security ensure domestic peace,
- economics and ecology are brought into accord,
- prosperity is no longer increased at the expense of poor countries,
- satisfaction can be sought and found, more than in the past, in community life and creative work for the public good.

We invite all those wishing to participate in a dialogue on the principles and concepts of democratic reorganization of our country . . . .

We hope to be able to present a list of candidates for the upcoming elections to the Volkskammer . . . .

Let us stand together, and together restore hope in our country!

Document 9:

Critical intellectuals such as H.-J. Fischbeck, L. Mehlhorn, U. Poppe, W. Ullmann, and K. Weiss launched "A Public Call to Get Involved in Our Own Cause." The citizens' movement "Democracy Now" developed a clear program and supported the creation of "a new unity of the German people within the European community."

Founding Appeal for 'Democracy Now', 12 September 1989

(Source: Flier, Berlin, Fall 1989)

Dear friends, fellow citizens, and all concerned!

Our country is living in a state of internal strife. Some have rubbed themselves sore under the current conditions, and others have simply resigned themselves. A great loss of approval of what has historically developed in the GDR is sweeping the country. Many can hardly justify living here any longer. And many are leaving the country because there are limits to how much conformity one can stand.

Until a few years ago, "real existing socialism" was considered the only option available. It was characterized by a centrist state party enjoying a power monopoly, state control of the means of production, state-organized infiltration and uniformity of society, and the inability of citizens to participate in their affairs. Despite its unquestionable accomplishments in terms of public welfare and social justice, it is now obvious that the era of state socialism is coming to an end. A peaceful, democratic renewal is necessary.

Introduced and emphasized by Gorbachev, democratic reconstruction of society is underway in the Soviet Union, Hungary, and Poland. Enormous economic, social, ecological, and ethnic problems present major obstacles to these changes, threatening them with failure, which would be accompanied by disastrous consequences for the entire world. The social justice and solidarity for which the socialist workers' movement has struggled are at stake. Socialism must rediscover its intended, democratic form if it is not to be lost to history. It cannot be allowed to fail; this endangered species, called humanity, needs other options to save human coexistence than the example set by Western consumer societies, the prosperity of which must be paid for by the rest of the world.

Government whitewashing cannot hide the political, economic, and ecological signs of the crisis of state socialism "GDR style". The SED leadership has not shown any willingness to change. It seems to be speculating on the failure of reform in the Soviet Union. The important thing now is to participate in this process of democratization.

The political crisis of GDR state socialism became particularly apparent in the local elections of 7 May 1989. The doctrine of the "moral-political unity of party, state, and people," which was used to justify a power monopoly independent of elections, could be confirmed only as a result of election fraud. Between 10 percent and 20 percent of the population in major cities openly refused to vote for National Front candidates. This figure would certainly have been considerably higher had balloting been secret.

So many people are no longer represented by the National Front; they lack any political representation at all in society. The wish of many citizens for a more democratic relationship between state and society still cannot be discussed publicly. For this reason, we appeal to all people to join the

CITIZENS' MOVEMENT 'DEMOCRACY NOW.'

Document 10:

Instead of dealing with the fears and hopes of the aroused GDR population, the Communist Party newspaper inveighed against the West German media. In true Cold War style the SED leadership stigmatized those wishing to leave the country as traitors to socialism.

Neues Deutschland on the Exodus, 2 October 1989

(Source: *Neues Deutschland*, 2 October, 1989)

Spokespersons for the Ministry of Foreign Affairs announced that former GDR citizens illegally occupying the West German embassies in Prague and Warsaw had been deported to the FRG via the GDR, on Deutsche Reichsbahn[*] trains. The GDR felt obliged to do so on humanitarian grounds due to the intolerable conditions which had developed at the FRG embassies; the local populations in the countries concerned could have been endangered should epidemics have broken out. It would not have mattered that the situation was not caused by us, but rather by the FRG, due to its violation of the norms granted embassies by international law. In Europe, embassies cannot grant asylum. . . .

Many citizens of the GDR will now rightly ask why we are letting these people travel through the GDR into the FRG, even though they are grossly violating the laws of the GDR. The government of the GDR has been guided by the consideration that these persons would not have found a place within normal society upon return to the GDR, even if such a return had been possible. They have alienated themselves from their workplaces and from the people with whom they have been living and working up to now. Parents have neglected all responsibility for their actions, even regarding their children, who grew up well cared for in the socialist German state, with all children's facilities and education and developmental opportunities available to them. These people would have had difficulty obtaining new apartments, since, of course, their old ones have been assigned to other citizens. They could not expect preferential treatment in the GDR. In addition, according to observations, many of these people represent anti-social elements who have neither employment nor normal living conditions.

Through their actions, they all have trampled upon moral values and cut themselves off from our society. Thus, no tears need be shed for them. There have already been some reports from the FRG as to how they are faring on the other side. Some have been fired from jobs for wanting to take care of errands during working hours. In an automobile factory, a woman was laughed at because she applied for day-care for her children. Workers yelled at her that she was confusing the FRG with the GDR. If she had stayed here, she would not have had to worry about day-care services. How many lives remain in the

---

[*]East German state railroad.

dark after the TV spotlights are turned off! The hypocritical declarations by politicians in Bonn, the blatant attempts to interfere with the internal affairs of the GDR, the Pan-German, nationalistic propaganda which they mount – all this leads only to confrontation, damaging the possibility for reasonable co-operation between the two German states, which is counterproductive to the interests of the people and the interests of Europe in general.

Document 11:

As a result of the civic awakening, I. Böhme, R. Eppelmann, S. Pflugbeil, G. Poppe, and a dozen other representative of various groups met at the beginning of October to demand democratization of the GDR through free elections.

Joint Declaration of the Civic Movement, 4 October 1989

(Source: Mitter and Wolle, *Ich liebe euch doch alle*, 212f.)

On the 4th of October 1989, the representatives of these grass roots citizens' movements

Democracy Now, Democratic Awakening, the Group of Democratic Socialists, the Initiative for Peace and Human Rights, the Initiative Group for a Social Democratic Party in the GDR, the New Forum, as well as representatives of peace groups met to discuss possibilities for joint political activities. We welcome the variety of initiatives which are developing as a sign of emerging, growing courage to express personal political opinions publicly. We are joined by our desire to restructure the state and society in a democratic way. Our goal is to end the situation in which citizens of this society lack the opportunity to enjoy political rights, as guaranteed in human rights conventions of the United Nations and CSCE documents. We declare our solidarity with all those being persecuted for their activities toward this end. We support the release of prisoners, the rescinding of past convictions, and the abandonment of current proceedings. We consider it of prime importance to open a discussion in our country regarding the minimum conditions needed for democratic elections.

A choice among various political positions must be made possible. A secret ballot must be guaranteed, that is, the voters are obliged to use a voting booth. Elections must be free, that is, no one may be coerced to vote in a particular way.

The next elections should take place under UN observation. We wish to work together and determine the degree to which we can create an election coalition with our own, joint candidates. Changing our country politically requires everyone's participation and criticism. We appeal to all citizens of the GDR to participate in the process of democratic change.

Document 12:

Ignoring the seething crisis, the SED leader celebrated the victory of socialism in his speech on the 40th anniversary of the founding of the GDR. He dismissed the mass exodus and the growing opposition as capitalist slander and announced his resolve to hold to his hardline course.

Honecker on the 40th Anniversary of the GDR, 6 October 1989

(Source: *Blätter für deutsche und internationale Politik*, 1989, 1401f.)

Today, the GDR is an outpost of peace and socialism in Europe. We will never forget this fact; this keeps us, and should also keep our enemies, from misjudgment.

Just as the Soviet Union, which liberated us, and the People's Republic of China, which is also celebrating the 40th anniversary of its founding, the People's Republic of Poland, the Czechoslovakian Socialist Republic, and other socialist countries, the GDR will also cross the threshold into the year 2000 with the certainty that socialism is the future. Socialism is a young society, and yet it exerts a great influence on international developments. It has brought about significant social change and will continue to do so. Its existence gives hope, not only to our people, but to all of humankind. . . .

Just when the influential powers in the FRG sense the chance to annul the outcome of World War II and post-war developments through a coup, they have again had to realize that reality cannot be changed, that the GDR, on the western boundary of the socialist countries in Europe, remains firm as a dam against neo-Nazism and chauvinism. The GDR's solid position in the Warsaw Pact cannot be shaken.

It is no coincidence that our opponent is directing its slander against the GDR to a greater extent than ever before. Forty years of the GDR also means forty years since the defeat of German imperialism and militarism. Socialism on German soil is so intolerable to our opponent because it represents proof that the previously exploited masses can determine their fortune without capitalism. . . .

Life in our country and international events presently pose questions which demand clear answers from a firm position. Our position does not come from one of the scandal sheets of the FRG, nor from the radio or television there; it has not evolved out of dated doctrine, but rather from the creative application of Marxism-Leninism, from the interests of the working class and all factory workers. In a word, our position is a policy based on the highest principle, namely, to do everything possible for the well-being of the people and a future in peace. Accordingly, we do not stop at the achievements we have made.

Upon attaining something dependable, we leave behind that which is outdated and restrictive; we are progressing on our course of unified economic and social policy. In this spirit, we will also continue to develop socialist democracy in its many forms. Our aim is for citizens to participate more and more actively and concretely in the activities of the state. . . .

Forty years of the GDR mark a totally new chapter in the history of our people. At the same time, these forty years have impressed upon our consciousness the absolute necessity and also the preciousness of long-lasting peace. Never again shall war emanate from German soil; this declaration arises from a decisive lesson of the past. It has become our state policy. It has been the top priority behind all we have done up to now and all we will do in the future, so that the socialist GDR continues to thrive and the family of European peoples can live in safety and harmony. Our nation is reliably satisfying its responsibility at the center of the continent, at the division between the two major allied blocs. . . .

In sharp contrast to our politics stand the revanchist demands of FRG politicians, spurring concern and protest throughout the world. There is talk of the "reestablishment of the German Reich within the 1937 borders." The post-war settlements are being questioned, the theory of the supposedly open German question is stated more loudly than it has been previously. The revival of the claim of sole representation, from the 1950s and 1960s, has culminated in a claim to so-called responsibility for all Germans. In this regard, there is obviously a considerable amount of common ground between revanchist politicians in Bonn and the increasingly strong neo-Nazis.

The emergence of neo-Nazis on the political stage in the FRG is food for thought. In light of the fact that attempts are being made to deny or downplay the existence of neo-Nazism, I would like to remind you that during the Nazi regime, two other comrades and I were turned over to the prison of Hitler's personal guards for "treatment," at the same time as the present head of the Republikaner was active there as SS leader. There is no doubt that such elements of FRG politics which cause concern among the peoples of the world are in urgent need of reform.

The relentless, internationally coordinated slander campaign currently being led against the GDR aims to confuse the people and sow doubt regarding the strength and advantages of socialism. This can only serve to strengthen our resolve to continue in the future to do everything possible for a peaceful European house. The ability for states with different social orders to live and work together in such a house should be allowed to develop to the fullest. A solid foundation for this is provided in the final act of the Helsinki Conference as well as other CSCE documents. But we will not allow anyone to abuse these agreements for the purpose of destabilizing socialism. Strict respect for sovereignty, territorial integrity, independence, and non-intervention in internal affairs are indispensable.

The GDR has paved its way with achievements serving to strengthen our people in the knowledge of their power and of the worth of all efforts to establish a new, humane, complete life. Socialism and peace are, and remain, key words for that which we have achieved up to now, as well as that which we will continue to accomplish. We tackle the task with vigor and confidence. In its fifth decade, the socialist workers' and peasants' state on German soil will continue to prove – through its actions for the good of its people and through its efforts for peace, security and international cooperation – that its founding in October of 1949 was a turning point in the history of the German people and of Europe. . . .

Document 13:

In contrast to Honecker's emphasis on the achievements of the GDR, Soviet Communist Party Chairman Mikhail Gorbachev displayed a spirit more open to international cooperation and domestic reform, in keeping with his motto, "Life punishes those who come too late."

Mikhail Gorbachev on the 40th Anniversary of the GDR, 6 October 1989

(Source: *Blätter für deutsche und internationale Politik*, 1989, 1402ff.)

Like every other country, the GDR, of course, has its own problems of development which must be considered and for which solutions must be found. These emerge both from society's internal needs for continued development, and from the general process of modernization and renewal underway throughout the socialist world. All countries are affected by processes of integration and by changes within the international economic and political order. No one can remain indifferent in face of global problems and the demands of the scientific-technical revolution. . . .

We do not doubt the capability of the Socialist Unity Party of Germany, with all its intellectual potential, its rich experience, and its political authority, in cooperation with all social forces, to find answers to the questions which the development of the republic has placed on the agenda and which are mobilizing its citizens. It is actually a question of developing possibilities inherent to our socialist order – the order of the working class and popular rule. . . .

The socialist world, as today's civilization in general, is characterized by a growing variety of forms of organization of production, social structures, and political institutions. This is in keeping with the thesis of Vladimir Ilyich Lenin, that each nation will put its own stamp on one form of democracy or another, on one pace of socialist transformation or another. Attempts at uniformity or standardization in questions of social development, either by imitation, or by imposing binding patterns, are a thing of the past. The palette of creative possibilities is growing; the concept of socialism itself is gaining incomparable richness.

The choice among forms of development remains a sovereign decision of each people. As the variety and quality of these forms grow, however, the need for an exchange of experience as well as a discussion of theoretical and practical problems grows as well. And of course, there is a need for joint action. In other words, diversity is not only an obstacle; on the contrary, it is a further important argument for the development of cooperation. This is the standpoint of our party, and this is the basis on which we strive to build our relations with the socialist countries. Equality, autonomy, solidarity – this is what determines our relationship today. . . .

We all know how tedious and complex the struggle was for the international recognition of the GDR. We all remember the dramatic events aimed at destabilizing the republic, which resulted in crisis situations, not only in Europe but internationally.

On the other hand, it is clear to all of us that the positive development now referred to as the CSCE process was possible thanks to the realism demonstrated by participants on both sides. The path to Helsinki opened only after the signing of treaties with the USSR, and then between the GDR and other socialist countries with the FRG, and after conclusion of the quadripartite agreement for West Berlin.

The 50th anniversary of the beginning of World War II spurred intensive debates and discussion in search of historical answers to questions posed by the present.

Unfortunately, it is often the case that only those answers are sought in history which one wants to find. By that I mean the attempts to blame the Soviet Union and its allies for the division of Europe into two opposing military blocs. We are constantly being called upon to take measures to eliminate this division. We have indeed heard such demands as the following: The USSR should take down the Berlin Wall, for only then will their peaceful intentions be taken seriously. And in the FRG, voices have recently been heard demanding the reestablishment of Germany within the boundaries of 1937. Even Polish Silesia has come under discussion. It seems as though the reforms in the Soviet Union and other socialist countries have tempted some politicians to reassert old claims. They have gone so far as to interpret the Soviet-West German declaration signed in Bonn this past June in a dubious manner. These questions have extraordinary significance for the fate of the European peoples and for world peace. This is why absolute clarity is necessary.

Above all, our western partners need to assume that the issues which concern the GDR are decided in Berlin and not in Moscow. The GDR is a sovereign state, undertaking autonomous measures regarding the various tasks to protect its interests and determine domestic and foreign policies.

The Soviet Union, of course, does not mean to shirk its responsibility for solving European problems. And here I mean the responsibility of the Soviet Union concerning international agreements and its role as one of the victorious powers of World War II.

Now, regarding the order which has developed in Europe. We do not idealize it. Yet in essence, recognition of the post-war reality has secured peace in Europe. More than that – the Helsinki process has developed out of this order, and its continuation promises further positive changes in the European situation as a whole and the construction of a common European house. In a word, the realities that exist on the continent, including the key elements of the borders of the sovereign states, do not block the way for progress in international relations. . . .

If it is possible to accomplish everything we have taken on, this will mean the final end of the Cold War era and the start of a period of real peace in the history of Europe. The Soviet Union is genuinely concerned that this unique chance for the European peoples and all of humankind not be lost. I believe that we have proven our sincerity in deed, i. e., through domestic reorganization and a new foreign policy.

I would like to emphasize the important role played by the GDR in securing a stable and peaceful development on this continent. In addition to active participation in collective actions by the states of the Warsaw Pact, the German comrades have introduced a series of independent concepts regarding foreign policy, the realization of which, in our opinion, will contribute to strengthening security in the center of the continent.

Comrades! We all know the great interest with which the people of the GDR follow our affairs, the radical reorganization in the Soviet Union. This restructuring is extremely difficult, requiring the greatest exertion of physical, intellectual, and moral strength by the party and the people. But this is an absolutely necessary process for us, and we firmly believe it will lead our country to successful development of the rich potential of socialism much further than ever before.

Democratization, openness, socialism, free development of all peoples and their equal participation in the country's affairs, dignified living conditions for the entire population and guaranteed rights for all, extensive opportunities for creative expression by each individual – this is what we are striving for, and we will not be diverted from these goals . . . .

Document 14:

One indication of the SED's preparations to quell the growing mass demonstrations by force was the threat to use weapons against provocations to the state. In a "Letter to the Editor" in the *Leipziger*

Volkszeitung, the commander of a workers' militia unit, Günter Lutz, warned that communist patience was running out.

Leipzig Militia on the Monday Demonstrations, 6 October 1989

(Source: Neues Forum Leipzig, *Jetzt oder nie - Demokratie: Leipziger Herbst '89*, Munich, 1990, 63.)

Workers of the District Demand:

Cease Tolerating Activities Hostile to the State

The members of the "Hans Geiffert" Militia Unit condemn the actions which have been organized for some time by unscrupulous elements in the city of Leipzig. We are in favor of Christian citizens gathering in the Nikolai Church to show their reverence in prayer. This is guaranteed by our constitution and the authority of our socialist GDR. However, we are opposed to having the church misused to hold events hostile to the state of the GDR. We feel harassed when confronted with such things after a hard day's work. Thus, we expect that everything possible will be done to secure public order and safety, in order to protect the values and achievements of socialism in the GDR which have been attained after forty years of hard work, so that we can continue to work, determined and according to plan, for the well-being of all citizens. We are willing and able to protect effectively that which we have created through the work of our own hands, in order to stop these counterrevolutionary actions once and for all.

If necessary, with weapons in hand!

We deny these elements the right to use the songs and slogans of the working class. In doing this, they are only trying to conceal their true goals.

Document 15:

A large number of recorded experiences plainly illustrate the SED's attempt to intimidate demonstrators by means of a massive police presence. They also show, however, the growing solidarity and anger of the population about the brutality of law enforcement officers.

A Leipzig Shift-Worker on her Arrest, 7 October 1989

(Source: Neues Forum, *Jetzt oder nie*, 66ff.)

I planned to go with two women I work with to the farmers' market on October 7th, and afterwards to stroll through the city. . . .

About 1:00 P.M., we met a co-worker on the square in front of the Nikolai Church. We stopped and chatted for a little while. Aside from us other people were also there, all engaged in conversation. A few security officers were walking back and forth on the square, which wasn't unusual. Everything was calm and peaceful; nothing gave the impression of unrest. The policemen got together and walked to the edge of the square. All of a sudden, one of them yelled: "Move!" Panic broke out. Within seconds the square was full of police with billy clubs. Military trucks drove up (police vans). Then the officers started bashing people wildly and aimlessly with their clubs. They pulled them by the hair to the trucks. As we were getting in, a civilian on the truck pulled us up onto the back. They screamed at us. We were pulled by our clothes onto the bench in the truck. They called us "pig" and "swine." At exactly 1:33 P.M., the truck drove away with eight citizens and three of the security officers. The truck didn't stop again until we were in a courtyard surrounded by buildings. Who knows where we were. As we were getting out, they pulled us by our clothes again, and sometimes used their clubs. Not until after the clubbing did they ask us if we were male or female. Then we had to go into a building, upstairs. We were ordered to stand there, hands at our sides, and not to lean on the wall – that would be punished. Then we were brought one by one into the hall, and they took our ID. Then we were escorted to a room at the end of the hall. There were a number of police officers guarding the door, outside and inside. Inside, we had to sit down. Hours went by until a non-uniformed policeman called out my name. I had to go with him, had to go upstairs again and then stop. He unlocked a door, and when we were both seated, the questioning began; it's also called the interrogation. Afterwards I had to sign a protocol. We went out and back downstairs. . . .

A policewoman led me through a terrible, barely lit basement hallway. Thousands of things went through my head in that moment; uncertainty overcame me – who knows what would happen now. Then I felt a cold, fresh breeze. We came to the courtyard. Another building; had to go upstairs again. I'm not sure what floor we were on when I was ordered to stay there. There were seven police officers in the hall, and I had to go into a room again. There were three officers on guard inside, and several other people who had suffered the same fate as I were already sitting there. Hours went by again. We had to ask permission to go to the bathroom. Then we had to wait for them to decide, and if they said "yes," then only with an escort. One of us asked about food or something to drink. For such a question, he was taken out to the hall and had to stand with his hands on the wall and his legs spread apart away from the wall.

It was 9:30 P.M. when we were called again. We had to go downstairs again, and were led back to the courtyard. The same police vehicles that we had come in were waiting for us. In that courtyard, a whole lot of police officers were waiting for us too; they had helmets with visors covering their faces, billy clubs, and a few of them had machine guns like I've seen in war movies, and they pushed us all onto the trucks. In school I learned what the Nazis were like. And in peacetime I saw it in practice, because these police officers treated us the same way. On the trucks we sat crowded together, shoulder to shoulder. Then the policemen kicked some of the people away so they could attach the wire screen onto the truck. Shielded from us, four policemen were sitting on guard with machine guns. Then the truck took off. It was raining as if the sky was crying along with the rest of us, and understood as little as us what was going on the whole time. End of the line were the agricultural fairgrounds. The trucks stopped, and the separation screen was taken off. . . .

Then we women had to get off. Just like the men, we had to take off our jackets and stand against the wall. A policewoman did the examination. I told her that I had my period, and then a policeman said: "So what, you pig!" Then a policeman grabbed me by my sweater and dragged me into a horse stall, along with the other women. He was really excited, getting to bring all of us into the horse stall. You could see it in his face. There was an older woman (long since retired) locked in the stall with me, that is, with us. She was crying and shivering all over. You could see fear in her face and her nerves were about to go. We women called a policeman and asked him to let the old woman go. He laughed at us and then rushed away as if he hadn't heard a word. No respect for our senior citizens. . . .

Sunday at 1:00 in the morning, we each got a hotdog, a hard roll and a sip of tea. Our legs were as heavy as lead from standing for hours on end. We were exhausted and frozen, almost indescribable. . . .

Approximately at 12:00 noon we were called again and we got our property back. Then we had to get back on the truck. And then the truck drove away again. Randomly, we were let out in groups of three, and then the truck would drive on. I found my way to the streetcar and went home. About 1:00 P.M. I arrived home, totally worn out.

Document 16:

A Chinese-style bloodbath was avoided because the Soviet forces did not intervene and there were no clear instructions from Berlin due to the crisis in the SED leadership. The courageous Leipzig citizens Kurt Masur, Peter Zimmermann, and Bernd L. Lange, along with three SED district secretaries, appealed for nonviolence shortly before the Monday Demonstration on 9 October.

Leipzig Appeal for a Dialogue, 9 October 1989

(Source: *taz*, 11 October 1989)

Our common concern and responsibility have brought us together today. We are distressed by the developments in our city and are seeking a solution.

We all need to be allowed to enjoy the free exchange of opinions about how to develop socialism in our country. The persons named, therefore, promise all citizens to use their whole strength and authority to ensure that this dialogue takes place, not only in the district of Leipzig, but with our government as well. We urgently appeal to you to remain calm so that a peaceful dialogue will be possible.

Document 17:

This Leipzig newspaper reported on the prevention of violence by the cooperation between demonstrators and SED moderates. The acceptance of a public dialogue on the citizen movement's reform demands shifted the focus from police control to political debate.

Sächsisches Tageblatt on the Monday Demonstration, 11 October 1989

(Source: "Von Besonnenheit geprägt," *Sächsisches Tageblatt*, 11 October 1989)

Characterized by Nonviolence

Tens of thousands of Leipzig residents came out Monday evening for an unauthorized demonstration in the city center following the weekly prayer for peace in the Nikolai Church. The demonstration remained peaceful, on the one hand, due to the calm response of the police force and members of the militia units, who did not intervene in the events, and the absolute lack of provocation on the part of the demonstrators on the other. . . .

This was in keeping with the appeal proclaiming that "violence does not solve any problems" which was read to those attending the services in the churches by the church working groups on justice, human rights, and environmental protection. Other prayers for peace took place on that evening in the St. Thomas Church, the Reformed Church, and in St. Michaelis Church, in which Bishop Johannes Hempel participated.

During the march, which went along Grimmaische Street, Karl Marx Square, Georgi Ring, Republic Square, Tröndlin Ring, and Dittrich Ring to Ross Square, the demonstrators several times called for nonviolence.

Friedrich Magirius, superintendent of the Leipzig-East church district, said in a telephone interview with the *Sächsisches Tageblatt* that he considered the appeal by leading political and cultural personalities read during the demonstration, which asked the demonstrators to act calmly and nonviolently, to be an encouraging initial signal paving the way for a dialogue, which should be followed by concrete offers. The writers of the appeal committed themselves to ensure that such a dialogue would take place. Magirius made reference to the introduction of the peace vigils seven years ago following the announcement of the NATO intermediate missile decision. At that time many considered disarmament utopian, but it has indeed become reality, he said. The same is true for the dialogue to be held in the heart of the country. The signal sent this Monday, said Magirius in closing, must be preserved. . . .

Document 18:

Mounting problems led to a power struggle between the old guard around Honecker, favoring continued repression, and a more flexible younger generation, supporting a political solution. Since the outcome was not yet decided, this declaration contained both Stalinist and reformist messages.

Politburo Declaration, 11 October 1989

(Source: *Deutschland Archiv*, 22, 1989, 1435ff.)

Having just celebrated the 40th anniversary of the GDR, we now turn to the working class, to the cooperative farmers, to the scientists, the artists, and all the intellectuals, to the youth, to members of the protective and security organs, to all citizens of the GDR. The Politburo of the Central Committee of the Socialist Unity Party of Germany thanks all of you who have created socialism on German soil and prepared for the 40th anniversary of the GDR through impressive achievements and deeds. . . .

Socialism needs all of us. It has a place and a future for everyone. It is the future of the coming generation. For that reason, we cannot remain indifferent when people who lived and worked here now disassociate themselves from our GDR. Many of them have given up the security of a socialist homeland and a secure future for themselves and their children. They grew up in our country, attained their professional qualifications here, and built up a good livelihood for themselves. they had friends, colleagues, and neighbors. They had a homeland which needed them and which they needed as well. There may well be many reasons for the step they have taken. We must, and will, seek them in us, each in his place, all of us together.

Many of those who have turned their backs on our republic in recent months were victims of large-scale provocation. Once again, the imperialists of the FRG have confirmed that they will never come to terms with a socialist state on German soil; agreements have been broken and human rights violated. The imperialist powers believe that the 40th anniversary of the founding of the GDR is the right moment to spread doubt regarding socialism and its philosophy through a hateful media campaign. They are trying to distract us all from the most important issue of our time, securing peace. Their interest is to weaken the joint struggle of different peoples in solving global problems. And last but not least, they want to divert attention from their own inability to make necessary reforms. Dreams of a greater Germany, fostered by old revanchist and neo-fascist sources, do not have a chance. Demagogy, deception, blackmail – these methods are not new, as the history of the relationship between the two German states shows. And neither is it a new goal to change the peaceful order in Europe by eliminating socialism on German soil. In violation of international law, the FRG has intervened in the internal affairs of the GDR, arrogating for itself the duty to take care of the citizens of the GDR. By questioning the post-war order, the FRG has absolved itself of joint German responsibility to do everything possible to see that war will never again emanate from German soil. Today, such an action threatens peace to the highest degree. . . .

Therefore, the needs of the moment demand that all those whose actions are determined by political reason and a sense of humanitarian responsibility toward the people of our country clearly disassociate themselves from those trying to misuse our citizens for counterrevolutionary attacks. We will solve the problems of the further development of socialism in the GDR ourselves – through an objective dialogue and political cooperation. . . .

Together we will consult on all the fundamental issues of our society which need to be solved, today and in the future. Together we hope to find answers on how we can meet the difficult challenges of the coming decade, in accordance with the humanitarian ideals of socialism. Together we hope to structure our fatherland in such a way that the growing material and cultural needs of each individual can be better satisfied according to their achievements. This means the continuation of the unity of economic and social policy. And this also means economic productivity and its usefulness for everyone, democratic cooperation and committed work together, a wide range of available consumer goods and achievement-oriented pay, media which are in touch with life, travel opportunities and a healthy environment. It also means our republic's contribution to securing world peace. And literally everything which serves the welfare of the people. Together we hope to cross the threshold into the next millennium in a strong socialist GDR. . . .

At the next meeting of the Central Committee, we will announce to our Party and to the people our suggestions to this end as regards our strategic conception for continuity and renewal. These are based on the thousands of discussions which have taken place within the SED party organization and the suggestions and considerations which we have received from workers throughout the republic. To this end, all opinions and suggestions for an attractive form of socialism in the GDR are important. We are open to discussion.

We have all the necessary forms and forums of socialist democracy. We call upon everyone to use these available methods more fully. We do, however, openly declare our opposition to suggestions and demonstrations which conceal their actual intention to mislead the people and change the constitutional foundation of our state. The GDR is made up of the citizens who created this state for their welfare, in democratic cooperation under the leadership of the SED. The GDR, socialism and peace, democracy and freedom belong together forever. Nothing and no one can stand in our way.

Trusting cooperation is needed now more than ever, in order to find common answers to the questions which occupy many of us and concern all of us – answers which serve us all. They cannot be found in the capitalist past.

Socialism on German soil is not up for grabs. The people of the GDR have chosen socialism, once and for all. With this in mind, let us work together and be guided by the experience that socialism can only be a product of all of us. Our workplace remains our place of struggle for socialism and peace.

Document 19:

Since his unwillingness to reform cost him the support of the Soviet leadership as well as the trust of the GDR population, Erich Honecker and his faithful allies Günter Mittag (Economy) and Joachim Herrmann (Propaganda) felt compelled to resign, transferring power in the party and government to Egon Krenz.

Honecker's Resignation, 18 October 1989

(Source: *Neues Deutschland*, 19 October 1989)

Dear Comrades!

After deep reflection, following yesterday's consultation in the Politburo, I have come to the following decision: As a result of my illness and the surgery I have had, I am no longer able to expend the strength and energy required by our Party and the people, today and in the future. Therefore, I request that the Central Committee release me from my function as Secretary General of the Central Committee of the SED, from my office as chairman of the Council of State of the GDR, and from the function as chairman of the National Defense Council of the GDR. As my successor, I recommend Comrade Egon Krenz to the Central Committee and the Volkskammer, as he is able and committed to accept the responsibilities and the amount of work demanded by the situation, the interests of the Party and the people, and the preparations for the 12th Party Conference, encompassing all aspects of the society.

Dear Comrades!

My entire adult life has been spent in unswerving loyalty to the revolutionary cause of the working class, dedicated to our Marxist-Leninist world view and the establishment of socialism on German soil. The founding and successful development of the socialist GDR, which we celebrated together on the 40th anniversary, is in my opinion the epitome of the struggle of our Party and my own efforts as a Communist.

I give my thanks to the Politburo, the Central Committee, my comrades in struggle during the difficult time of anti-fascist resistance, the members of the Party, and all citizens of this country, for decades of common, fruitful action for the good of the people.

I will also make myself available to my Party in the future to offer my advice and experience.

I wish our Party and its leadership a further strengthening of unity and commitment, and the Central Committee continued success in the future.

Document 20:

In contrast to widespread European fears of a "fourth Reich," U.S. President George Bush, in a perceptive interview, welcomed the prospect of German unification and thereby helped make it possible.

George Bush Interview, 24 October 1989

(Source, *New York Times*, 25 October 1989)

Q. Let me give you two things that are being discussed within your Administration, among the Europeans, among professors. Can you see, presuming that you're here for eight years, any beginning of American troop withdrawal from Europe, or troop reduction?

A. We've already seen that in our proposal. . . . So my answer would be definitely yes.

Q. Can you see any changes in the status of Germany?

A. Yes. . . . I don't share the concern that some European countries have about a reunified Germany, because I think Germany's commitment to and recognition of the importance of the alliance is unshakable. And I don't see Germany, in order to get reunification, going off onto what some are concerned about, and that is a neutralist path that puts them at odds, or potentially at odds, with their NATO partners. . . .

And yet, I don't think we ought to be out pushing the concept of unification, or setting timetables, or coming from across the Atlantic over here making a lot of new pronouncements on this subject. It takes time. It takes a prudent evolution. It takes work between them . . . and understanding between the French and the Germans and the Brits and the Germans on all of this.

But the subject is so much more front and center because of the . . . rapid changes that are taking place in East Germany. . . .

And who knows how Mr. Krenz is going to turn out to be? Is he going to be just a perpetuation of the Honecker view, or is he going to be something different? I don't think he can resist total change.

Q. What's our early appraisal of that?

A. It's too early. I can't get a fix on it. . . . I think you're going to see some accommodation at change. . . . He can't turn the clock back. . . . The change is too inexorable.

3

Awakening, Fall of the Wall, and Bankruptcy

Both the reformers within the SED and the grass-roots citizens' movements strove for a renewal of the GDR. The speeches and press conferences (Documents 1 and 3) by the new head of the SED, Egon Krenz, proclaimed a fundamental change of direction [*Wende*] in communist politics, though this met with skepticism. Opposition protests resulted in a popular democratic awakening (Document 2), in which feminists (Document 4) and the Greens (Document 6) clamored to improve the situation of women and the environment. The dramatic climax of public unrest was a mass demonstration in Berlin on 4 November, 1989. Organized by progressive intellectuals, more than half a million people took to the streets with humorous banners and frank speeches, calling for the establishment of democratic socialism (Document 5). The question of unification, raised by FRG chancellor Kohl (Document 7) played hardly any role at all during this phase of socialist renewal.

The unexpected opening of the Berlin Wall was not so much a result of foreign demands as of domestic pressure. When SED District Secretary Günter Schabowski announced the liberalization of travel rules on 9 November (Document 8), thousands of East Germans immediately rushed to the border. After the guards let them cross, spontaneous celebrations erupted at the former symbol of separation (Document 9). Broadcast on television throughout the world, the heart-rending sight of thousands of people coming together was a peaceful reunion which ex-chancellor Willy Brandt welcomed as a chance for future German unification (Document 10). The new head of the East German government, Hans Modrow, responded to these heightened emotions with a reform program, emphasizing cooperation between the two German states by means of a contractual union (Document 11). Although this signal aroused international concern about the rebirth of a nationalistic Germany (Document 12), West German Chancellor Helmut Kohl went even further by proposing in his "Ten-Point Plan" the creation of "confederative structures" leading up to a federal state (Document 14). East German intellectuals and West German leftists opposed a FRG takeover, preferring instead an independent GDR (Document 13).

While reformers still searched for a "third way" between Stalinism and capitalism, the GDR collapsed as an independent state. In early December the establishment of the "Round Table," bringing together government and opposition, was an attempt to come to grips with the deepening crisis (Document 15). At the same time, the SED hoped to win back its ability to govern through consistent de-Stalinization under its new head, Gregor Gysi (Document 16). But "Democracy Now" sought to channel popular hopes by submitting a three-step plan for unification (Document 17). Moreover, on 19 December Modrow and Kohl met in Dresden to discuss the practical steps for developing the proposed contractual union (Document 18). In early January, the SED used vandalism of the Soviet War Memorial in Treptow to organize an anti-fascist mass demonstration against a "sell-out" to the West (Document 19). Ultimately, the accelerating collapse of the planned economy made any form of renewal in the GDR impossible (Document 20). News of the continued activity of the notorious Stasi enraged the long-oppressed population to such an extent that crowds stormed the secret service headquarters in mid-January, bringing its extralegal power to an end (Document 21).

Document 1:

As the new head of the government, Egon Krenz promised an open dialogue, warned against confrontation, and stressed the independence of the socialist GDR. But the citizens' movement held him co-responsible for the political crisis because of his previous hardline policy.

Egon Krenz's Government Program, 24 October 1989

(Source: Z. and S. Zimmerling, eds., *Neue Chronik DDR*, 2, Berlin 1990, 16ff.)

The task given us by the people, honorable representatives, imposes upon us, today more urgently than ever, the obligation to react to the demands of the times competently, consistently, and with the courage to be truthful, and to find better solutions to the difficult problems in our country. Everything we do is always measured primarily by its effects on the people. . . .

The renewal of our society which we are attempting needs the firm socialist foundation we have laid together. We all agree on this point – all of us in the democratic alliance; renewal requires solidarity and identity rooted in history, without denying the mistakes and distorting biases which also accompanied the establishment of our new order in the past decades. . . .

Diversity of opinion prepares the ground for sound and open dialogue. The chance to find the most effective, and, therefore, the best, solution for our citizens is to listen to the pros and cons in the debate on the best form for the development of our society. The basis for this lies in Article 1 of our country's constitution: "The GDR is a socialist state of the workers and peasants. It is the political organization of the workers in town and country, under the leadership of the working class and its Marxist-Leninist party." All the reforms, honorable representatives, which we must bring about – and we want to bring them about – are dedicated to this task demanded by the people. . . .

The cooperation of all political parties, the democratic alliance of all popular forces in the *National Front*, is taking on a new importance. This requires an objective dialogue that makes it possible to consider questions and suggestions on participation in communal and societal decision making processes, by all those obliged by the constitution to act in the national and international interest. . . .

We should do everything in our power to avoid aggravating the situation or even provoking any confrontation at all. This would threaten much of what has already been set in motion. Regarding demonstrations, no matter how peaceful their planners and organizers intend them to be, in these complex times the danger always exists that they might not end as they began. Many of our citizens have good reason to be concerned when this places our society, already challenged by so many new things, under additional pressure. As important as dialogue and discussion are – and I am strongly committed to these processes – the people's livelihood is earned only through conscientious, collective work, conditioned on the individual responsibility for the whole. . . .

The demonstrations may have served a purpose, but our society – and by this I mean all our citizens – needs more than ever before an objective dialogue on conflicting ideas and opinions. It does not need confrontation among its citizens, as recent events have shown. We all share this responsibility, and I would like to emphasize once more that we are dedicated to finding political solutions to political problems. . . .

No one should draw false conclusions from the political developments in the GDR. The German Democratic Republic is a sovereign socialist state, and everything that happens here is the result of the sovereign decision of our country and its citizens. NATO proposals and "suggestions" aiming to abolish socialism through reform continue to have no chance!

Document 2:

Volker Braun's poems, read to a gathering of writers in the Church of the Savior in Berlin, reflect the stirring of an intellectual opposition. The opening appeal "Against the Sleep of Reason," calls for the awakening of public consciousness.

Volker Braun "Against the Sleep of Reason," 28 October 1989

(Source: U. Bresch et al., eds., *October 1989: Wider den Schlaf der Vernunft*, Berlin, 1989, 154)

Against the sleep of reason. . . .

Awakened from dogmatic slumber

you used the night

I practiced the expectation of it

do you also know the sweet pain, the strange love,

the unknown deed, how, what are you talking about

the veins almost burst in my flesh

how tired I am of it, crossing St. Mark's Square

you are dreaming, aren't you, dreaming determinedly

and on the streets, openness thrives.

I wrote the following texts in commemoration of the Prague Spring and in expectation of a political turn around:

Yesterday, spring was a disgrace. Today, the summer is going well. Once the river disappeared into the sand; today we notice the flow of the tide. The "turn" – this surprising offshore wind in the corridors of smashed desks, the blood which is vomited by newspapers and glory and hunger, history turns itself on its heels, determined for a moment.

Changing the Wallpaper

The management tells me they quietly completed the reconstruction long ago, but the house doesn't have any more space, the stairway is uncomfortable. And do the small rooms have more light? And why are people moving out instead of in?

Eurasian lecture

When the big wall stood, the nations of the world began to migrate.

The farmer to his ox, seventy after October: Oh eminent one, you have shit all over the stall. Your strength is no longer profitable for me, so now I will slaughter you for a tractor.

The Clay Warrior

The tanks drive from the bunkers under the Square of Heavenly Peace into the crowd. Age-old practice of an age-old party.

Document 3:

After being assured of backing by Mikhail Gorbachev, Egon Krenz explained his reform course – called the "turn" [*Wende*] – to the press. During his Moscow visit, he nonetheless defended SED leadership claims and rejected any thought of reunification.

Krenz on his New Course, 1 November 1989

(Source: *Neue Chronik DDR*, 2, Berlin 1990, 48f).

At the subsequent press conference, Krenz judged the conversation to have been "excellent." In answer to questions from journalists, Krenz said that his recent telephone conversation with West German Chancellor Helmut Kohl gave him the impression that they agreed that the existence of two German states should be utilized to improve relations with each other. When asked whether the Wall should be taken down now that freedom of movement had been promised to GDR citizens, Krenz said the reasons leading to the building of the Wall still existed. Real steps needed to be taken, according to Krenz, rather than hanging on to dreams. Neither did he consider the issue of the reunification of Germany to be on the agenda. Regarding the invasion of Czechoslovakia by Warsaw Pact troops in 1968, Krenz said he had nothing to correct, nor did he regret this resolution. On the SED claims to leadership, Krenz declared he would do everything in his power to see that this principle, which was anchored in the constitution, would be realized. In answer to questions on the political changes in East Germany, he said the decision to steer a reform course was not made overnight but was the result of a collective discussion within the Party, which also had the power to implement it. A party with over two million members is capable of surviving difficult times, according to Krenz. The current changes in the GDR are the result of the work of the Politburo and the Central Committee of the SED. Krenz considers the fact that many GDR citizens are attending rallies and meetings as an expression of the irreversibility of the reform program started by the SED.

Document 4:

As a result of a Round Table discussion with the women's magazine *Für Dich*, feminist scholars criticized the discrepancy between the positive-sounding rhetoric regarding women's rights and practical discrimination against women in the SED state.

Open Letter from Feminists to the SED, 1 November 1989

(Source: *Blätter für deutsche und internationale Politik*, 1989, 1453)

Is the renewal of society passing us women by?

The interests of women have not played any significant role in the recent dialogue up to now. No public consciousness exists in our society regarding the actual situation of women and their widespread exclusion from the most important decision making spheres of governmental and political power. Reform will be successful only if the interests of the female half of our society are perceived and taken into account. It is primarily the task of women to introduce this process and carry it through together with others. This requires concrete interest groups, that is, democratic organizational forms and structures, giving women authority and decision-making power.

We demand that these questions be placed on the agenda of the upcoming plenary session of the Central Committee of the SED and that they be seriously considered in the conceptional planning of the XIIth SED party congress, as well as in the changes being made in political and governmental structures.

On the basis of the conditions already achieved for women, we believe that decisions still outstanding must be made without delay on the following issues:

- Quotas: This means equal distribution among men and women of all functions and positions in the government, in politics, in industry and research, as well as creation of appropriate work and living conditions.

- Restructuring the apparatus of state, political parties, trade unions and social organizations so that the special conditions, needs, and interests of women are voiced and acted upon – for example, through women's divisions and commissions possessing necessary authority and decision making power.

- Reorganization of the DFD and/or tolerance of an autonomous Women's Movement dealing with the interests of women in all facets of their lives.

- Establishment of a Committee for Women's Affairs in the Volkskammer as well as at the highest governmental level.

- Support for the creation of women's spaces (i.e., in the media, clubs, etc.).

- Counteracting assignment of family-related tasks primarily to women, by means of a reorientation facilitating the combination of career and parenting activities; changing related socio-political measures which, up to now, have only minimally included fathers in family issues.

- Qualitative improvement of public services, the welfare system, day care facilities, and the public transportation system, and elimination of existing territorial differences.

Document 5:

The Berlin demonstration, organized by creative artists, was the climax of the socialist movement for change. Not only were there an impressive number of participants – between one half and one million people – but the biting slogans on the banners and the frank, honest speeches were unprecedented.

Christa Wolf, Christoph Hein, and Steffi Spira at the Berlin Demonstration, 4 November 1989

(Source: Initiativgruppe 4 .11. 1989, *TschüsSED: 4.11.1989*, Bonn 1990, 38ff.)

Christa Wolf, Author:

My dear fellow citizens: Every revolutionary movement also liberates the language. Suddenly, that which has been so difficult to say up to now rolls freely from our lips. It amazes us to hear what we have apparently been thinking all along, and what we can now shout out loud: Democracy now or never! And we mean people power. We can remember the attempts in our history which faltered or were beaten down, and we don't want, yet again, to sleep through the opportunity presented by this crisis which has awakened all our productive strength (applause). . . .

I have my problems with the word "turn." I see a sailboat and the captain shouts "Prepare to come about," since the wind has turned or is blowing in his face (applause). And the crew ducks as the boom sweeps across the deck. But does this image still apply today? Does it still apply in this situation, which is moving further each day? I would speak of revolutionary renewal (applause). Revolutions begin at the bottom. Top and bottom are reversed in the value system, turning the socialist society upside-down, back onto its feet. Major social movements are growing (applause); people in our country have never before spoken so much as in the last few weeks. Never before really spoken with each other, with such passion, such anger and sadness, but also with such hope. We want to use each and every day; we are not sleeping much, if at all. We are getting to know people we have never met before. And we are painfully struggling with others whom we thought we knew. So this is called "dialogue." We demanded it, and now we can hardly stand hearing the word. But we have yet to learn what the word "dialogue" really means. We stare distrustfully at hands suddenly outstretched before us, and at faces that used to be so unmoving. Distrust is good, control is better (applause).

We are reversing old slogans which have hurt and oppressed us; they are being returned to sender. We are afraid of being exploited, used. And we are afraid of turning down a genuine offer. Our whole country now faces this dilemma. And we have to practice the art, not to let this dilemma become a confrontation. We will be given these few weeks, these opportunities, only once, and by ourselves (applause).

We are surprised to see the agile ones, the ones now popularly called the wrynecks [*Wendehälse*] (applause). According to the dictionary, they can adapt quickly and easily to any new situation, responding with skill and knowing how to use it to their advantage. It is these opportunists, I believe, who undermine the credibility of the new policies the most (applause). Alas, we are not yet at the point where we can take them with humor, as we can in other situations. "Free-riders, step down!" I have read on banners. And heard the yells of demonstrators to the police: "Take your uniforms off and join us!" (applause). I must say, that's a generous offer. And we are thinking economically as well: "Legal security saves on State Security" (loud applause). And today I saw an absolutely unbelievable slogan on a banner: "No more privileges for us Berliners" (applause).

Indeed, the language is bursting out of the bureaucratic and newspaper German in which it has been wrapped for so long, and recalling its emotional, expressive vocabulary. One such word is "dream." Let us dream with an alert sense of reason: Imagine there was socialism and no one ran away! (loud applause).

But we continue to see pictures of those leaving, and we have to ask ourselves, "What is to be done?" And the answer echoes, Do something! It is a start when demands become rights – and obligations. Fact-finding committees, constitutional court, administrative reform. There's a lot to be done. And all of it during our spare time. And we still need time to read the newspaper (applause)! We won't have any more time to pay official homage or to attend prescribed demonstrations (loud applause).

This is a rally, authorized and nonviolent. If it stays that way until the end, then we will have learned yet more what we are capable of. And then we will insist upon it (loud applause).

I have a suggestion for the First of May: The leaders march past the people (cheers and loud applause)!

All of that is not from me. It is part of the popular literary heritage. Unbelievable transformation. The people of the GDR have taken to the streets to see themselves as such, as a people. And this is the most important sentence of recent weeks – that which we have shouted thousands of times, "We are the people" (loud applause)! A simple observation, and one we won't forget (applause). . . .

Christoph Hein, Author:

Dear fellow citizens who have found your voices: There is a lot for all of us to do, and we have so little time to do it. The structures of this society must be changed if they are to be democratic and socialist. And this is the only alternative. We must speak of the dirty hands and the dirty laundry. Infiltration, corruption, abuse of power, theft of public property – all these things must be cleared up, and this clarification must extend to the very top of the government; in fact, it must start there (applause).

We must beware of confusing the euphoria we have been experiencing in recent days with the changes that still need to be made. Enthusiasm and demonstrations were, and are, helpful and necessary. But they are not a substitute for work. Let us not be deceived by our own enthusiasm. There is still a lot to do. We're not out of the woods yet! (applause). And there are still a lot of people who do not want to see any changes, who fear a new society, and who have good reason to be afraid (applause). . . .

Let us create a democratic society (applause) with a legal foundation of guaranteed rights. A form of socialism which does not make a mockery of the word. A society appropriate for the people, not subordinating them to its structures. This will mean a lot of work for us all, even a lot of detailed work, worse than knitting. And one more thing. As the saying goes, success has many fathers. Apparently, many believe that the changes in the GDR have already been successful, for many fathers have appeared, reporting such success. Strange fathers (applause). All the way up to the very top of the government. But I don't think our memories are so bad that we don't remember who began to break down the omnipotent structures, who ended the sleep of reason. It was the reason of the streets, the demonstrations of the people (applause).

Without these demonstrations, the government would not have changed and the work which we have begun would not have followed (applause).

Most important to mention in this context is Leipzig (applause). I believe that the mayor of Berlin, on behalf of all its citizens – since we are all gathered here together – and the Council of State and the Volkskammer should declare Leipzig the "GDR City of Heroes" (loud applause). . . .

Steffi Spira, Actress:

In 1933 I went alone to a foreign country. I took nothing with me, but I had several lines of "In Praise of the Dialectic," a poem by Bertolt Brecht, in my head:

Things do not stay the way they are.

Those who live never say never.

Those who have recognized their situation,

how can they be stopped.

And that 'never' will yet become 'today'!

I hope that my great-grandchildren will grow up without a military roll-call, without civics (loud applause), and that no blueshirts[*] with torches will march past high officials (loud applause).

And I have another suggestion: We'll make a senior citizens' home out of Wandlitz[**] (loud applause).

Those over 60 or 65 can stay right where they are if they do what I am now doing – stepping down! (Loud, long applause).

Document 6:

The catastrophic state of the environment in East Germany, whose economy had been based on lignite coal, turned ecological recovery into a major issue for the opposition. This concern ultimately led to the founding of a political party that also rejected a consumer-oriented society along Western lines.

Appeal for the Founding of a Green Party, 5 November 1989

(Source: *Neue Chronik DDR*, 2, 70f.)

The Green Party of the GDR supports all those forces dedicated to achieving democracy and freedom through far-reaching reform within our country.

It is ecological, feminist, and nonviolent.

The particular goals of the Green Party are as follows:

Consistent ecological restructuring of our country by radically rejecting both reckless economic growth at the expense of the environment, resulting in a severe waste of natural resources, and a Stalinist way of dealing with the people, the economy, and the environment.

Immediate negotiations regarding, first, the ecological disaster areas of Leipzig/Bitterfeld/Halle, Dresden/Karl Marx City, and Cottbus, and secondly, the preservation of many historical city-centers, cultural landscapes, and castles, for example, in Mecklenburg.

The attainment of peace by means of general and complete disarmament. The dismantling of military alliances, reduction of the National People's Army to the absolute minimum necessary for defense purposes, and elimination of off-limits military areas are necessary to preserve peace and the environment.

We reject violence, national chauvinism, and racism and are dedicated to fighting fascism.

---

[*] Refers to the party youth organization, Free German Youth.

[**] Walled-off residence of high SED officials.

Absolute and unrestricted equality among all men and women at all economic and political levels of society, from local representative bodies up to the Council of State, to oppose the predominantly patriarchal institutional character which still prevails. . . .

The environment is to be protected from unlimited human exploitation. This is the only way to preserve it as a basis for community and culture. In all economic activities, we must constantly ask ourselves: where, for whom, why?

The Green Party is committed to long-lasting development. Most of all, we want to keep the present movement for change in our country from being so pressured by the unreasonable, shortsighted need felt by many to "catch up" in terms of material possessions that it will lead to a dog-eat-dog society with a wasteful, throw-away mentality.

We consider an ecological orientation at all levels of education to be absolutely imperative, including the introduction of ecology and peace studies.

We will work towards constitutional reform on the basis of the present constitution of the GDR.

We demand that the activities of the Green Party of the GDR not be subject to any state intervention.

As regards specific projects, both nationally and internationally, we will work with all individuals, organizations, and groups that support our ideals, either as a whole or in part. . . .

Document 7:

In a major policy speech, West German Chancellor Helmut Kohl promised continued admission of GDR immigrants, advocated reforms in East Germany as the basis for increased cooperation, and pleaded for future self-determination for all Germans.

Kohl on the State of the Nation, 8 November 1989

(Source: *Frankfurter Allgemeine Zeitung*, 9 November 1989)

I. Free self-determination for all Germans – that was, is, and remains the core of our policies on Germany. Free self-determination – that was, is, and remains the wish, even the yearning of our compatriots in the GDR.

Who among us is not deeply moved at the sight of hundreds of thousands of people assembling peacefully in Berlin, Leipzig and Dresden, in Schwerin, Plauen, and other cities? They shout, "We are the People!" – and their cries no longer go unheeded.

Our compatriots who are taking to the streets daily for freedom and democracy – they are evidence of a desire for freedom that has not been extinguished even after forty years of dictatorship. They are thereby writing, before the eyes of the world, a new chapter in the history of our Fatherland, whose tradition of freedom neither war nor violence and dictatorship could destroy.

All of us are also moved by the impression of the mass exodus from the GDR – a depressing event unparalleled in Europe. Actually, images such as those we have seen in Hungary, Czechoslovakia and Poland, as well as at these people's arrival in the FRG, should be a thing of the past in today's Europe. The flight of tens of thousands of mainly young people from the GDR to the free part of Germany is a "vote with their feet" before the entire world; it is a declaration that cannot be ignored, of their belief in freedom and democracy, legality, and an economic and social order that ensures each person a just share of the fruits of his labor.

It is at the same time an unmistakable rejection of a political system that disregards the basic rights of individuals, their freedom, and their personal welfare.

These events have also shown the entire world that the division of our Fatherland is unnatural – that walls and barbed wire cannot last for long. They have made it clear that the German question is not settled, because the people no longer accept the assumed future.

Our compatriots in the GDR demand respect for their basic civil and political freedoms. They insist on their right to self-determination. They are no longer silent about the imposed system of single-party rule. . . .

III. We have every reason to stick to our goals of freedom in our policy on Germany. We have less reason than ever for resignation or permanent acceptance of two German states. . . .

Some of us have difficulty with the new arrivals. It cannot be denied that this flood of people has caused or intensified problems in some areas – for example, in housing availability. On the other hand, we should always recall what it meant to millions of our fellow citizens in the much more difficult conditions of the late forties and early fifties to find bread, a home, and work. This must be an incentive to us. . . .

This is a task of national importance, over which there must be no argument among the parties. As Chancellor, I appeal to all those in positions of responsibility on the federal, state, and local level: Let us join forces for the benefit of our fellow Germans. . . .

IV. The federal government will do everything in its power to support the process of opening up East Germany for the benefit of our compatriots. It therefore remains determined to continue its policy of practical cooperation with the GDR in the interests of people on both sides. In our economic cooperation, we are working for lasting, wide-ranging improvements for the people of the GDR. . . .

V. The federal government will hold unerringly to its course in German policy. It bases its actions, as always, on the familiar principles of constitutional and international law. In particular, it holds firmly to the goal, anchored in the preamble of our constitution, of achieving "by free self-determination the unity and freedom of Germany". . . .

A change is long overdue; that is what the events of recent days and weeks tell us. They contradict all those who tried to convince us in the past that it was not a change in the direction of more freedom, but a cementing of existing conditions, that would lead to greater stability. This view has plainly been proven wrong. We are now seeing that only rapid, extensive reforms can help. . . .

The SED must give up its monopoly of power, legalize independent parties, and agree definitively to free elections. Under these conditions, I am prepared to discuss a new dimension in economic assistance. . . .

It is our national task to encourage fundamental political and economic change in East Germany. . . .

VII. The German question is a question of freedom and self-determination for all Germans. As difficult as it may be for us, and above all for our fellow Germans in the GDR, let us preserve the stubborn patience to follow a path of evolutionary change, at the end of which must lie complete respect for human rights and free self-determination for all Germans.

Let us not forget that the solution to the German problem does not involve only Germans. Let us not disregard the fact that a failure of reforms in Poland and Hungary would have an impact on the chances for change in the GDR.

Let us guard against the assumption that a solution to the German problem can be predetermined according to a script, with a datebook in hand. History does not stick to schedules. Historical developments do not follow a definite timetable. The enormous transformations on the eastern part of our continent prove this impressively.

Thus it is crucial that we remain faithful to our principles:

- freedom and democracy, legality, and the social market economy remain the basic pillars of our political and social system.

- firm and lasting anchoring of the FRG in the Atlantic Alliance and in the community of values of the free peoples of the West is irrevocable. It is a consequence of the bitter lessons of our history, and it corresponds to our choice of domestic freedom, democracy, and legality. . . .

- Germany's active participation in the process of European unity remains a major element of our policies. Home region, Fatherland, Europe: this triad reflects people's yearning for security and familiarity, openness, friendship and community in relation to their neighbors.

- Germany's future lies in a comprehensive peace settlement that brings together the peoples and nations of our continent in common freedom. The European dimension of the German problem means, to us, national unity and European unification. The constitution demands both from us.

At the same time, we are quite aware that the EC is not all of Europe. In the West, we must not forget that Warsaw, Budapest, and Prague, Rostock, Leipzig, and Dresden are of course also a part of it.

As Konrad Adenauer once said, we are striving for both: a free, unified Germany in a free, unified Europe.

Document 8:

The unexpected opening of the Berlin Wall came as a result of an ambiguous announcement of a more liberal travel ordinance by SED District Secretary Günter Schabowski during a press conference. When East German residents tested the decree by crossing the border en masse, the authorities did not intervene to stop the rush.

The Lifting of GDR Travel Restrictions, 9 November 1989

(Source: *Frankfurter Allgemeine Zeitung*, 10 November 1989)

The GDR Opens its Borders to West Germany:

"Temporary Regulation Pending Passage of a Corresponding Ordinance"

West Berlin, 9 November – GDR residents wishing to leave the country can do so at all border crossings of the GDR into the FRG, effective immediately. This resolution by the Council of Ministers was announced Thursday evening in East Berlin by SED Politburo member Günter Schabowski. According to a report by the GDR news agency ADN, the actual text of the resolution was as follows:

"Applications for private travel outside the country can be made without satisfying any prerequisites (reason for travel, family relationships). Permits will be issued on short notice. Permission will be rejected only in exceptional cases. The Passport and Registration Departments of the Volkspolizei district offices have been told to issue visas for permanent emigration without delay, even if the prerequisites for permanent emigration, which are still in effect, are not fulfilled. Applications for permission for permanent emigration remain possible through the Department for Domestic Affairs. Permanent emigration can occur at any border crossing between the GDR and the FRG or West Berlin. This eliminates the need either for temporary issuance of permits in the foreign offices of the GDR, or for permanent emigration [to the FRG] via third countries, using a GDR identity card."

Regarding the Berlin Wall, Schabowski said that a clarification of the travel issue did not answer the question "of the reason for a fortified national border." That would require consideration of additional factors concerning, for example, the FRG and NATO. A positive factor would be firm resolve on the parts of the FRG and NATO to take steps toward disarmament.

Document 9:

Television pictures flashed the celebration on and around the Berlin Wall on the night of 9 November 1989 around the world. Captured by the leftist newspaper *taz*, this moving moment was repeated thousands of times at the newly opened inter-German border.

taz on the Opening of the Berlin Wall, 11 November 1989

(Source: *taz*, 11 November 1989)

"We Want In!"

The Bear Dances on the Border

RIAS, the U.S. radio station broadcasting to the East, reported at midnight that there was still no disruption of traffic. But there was chaos at the border crossing at Invalidenstrasse in Berlin. Cars parked in all directions, their passengers jumping out, racing to the border. The crowds in West Berlin have already engulfed the radio tower of the station Sender Freies Berlin. They are awaiting the breakthrough of the masses from East Berlin. After three seconds even the least sentimental of the *taz* reporters is cheering the nearest Trabi on. The mood hits everyone, like it or not. Even the most rational in the crowd are clapping, cheering, screaming, laughing. Some succeed, within sight of border guards, in climbing over police barriers to the East, though they aren't allowed all the way over yet – visa and money changing are still compulsory.

Halfway between East and West, the East Germans obediently stand in line, waiting to be called. They receive a stamp and are told, "You can go." "What?! I don't believe it." Some have to be pushed over the border into the West. "I'm supposed to cross over now. Where to? I don't have a coin in my pocket." Many are still afraid they will not be allowed back.

Meanwhile, shouts come from the West Berlin side: "We want in!" For a moment, everyone looks westward: [Mayor Walter] Momper has appeared in the crowd. Flashes, microphones, cameras. Then there's no stopping the crowd anymore; the mass from the West pushes further in the direction of East Berlin. At approximately 1:00 A.M. they all start running. A handful of border guards protect their border. Gates open, the barrier is lifted. This is East Berlin.

West Berliners, illegally in the East Berlin central district, without a visa, are ready to put up their hands at any moment, should it prove necessary. But in fact, confusion rules on the other side of the border. Who is East and who is West? The crowds pushing on the sidewalk along Invalidenstrasse are moving in both directions. Amazement on all faces: are you from the other side? Do you want to go over? A green neon sign on the first pub. Where are the nearest toilets? The "Jägerheim" is already closed, all the bars in the East close at midnight. The rows of canned vegetables and apple crates in the store windows stir the imagination: "Soon there'll be bananas there with pineapples on top of them. And the days for quartz crystal watches are numbered."

"We Climbed over the Wall"

"Let's go to the Ku-Damm[*]!" can be heard at the Friedrichstraße[**] border crossing. With champagne glasses in hand, everyone is pushing their way to passport control. Heavily laden with packages, Poles are standing off to the side. On to the Brandenburg Gate; hardly any cars or pedestrians on [the boulevard] Unter den Linden. There's no border crossing here – just the Wall. A French camera team has set up at the first big flower pot blocking off the Brandenburg Gate; there are other journalists from the West, and some families from the East. A woman is calling to her son who is one barrier further than she is. He goes back to get her, but she is afraid: "I don't even want to go over." But the next morning, we see her again, this time on television: "We were on the other side; we climbed over the Wall!"

But at about 1:30 A.M., soldiers of the East German People's Army gather, heavily armed and in no mood to party. Nevertheless, people continue to run toward the Brandenburg Gate. "Go back, you are subject to arrest." Slight hesitation and then, onto the Wall near the camera teams; then they can't shoot! Just one time through the Brandenburg Gate. Nobody wanted anything more!

Back to the East with all the other Wall-climbers. About 2:00 A.M. at Checkpoint Charlie[***]. The border crossing is now closed to motor vehicles. The first control point lets about ten people go by every 20 seconds. At the second control point, they want to see a passport or identity card. A taz business card works too. The third one grimly asks to see my visa. I show the *taz* card again, this time with a bank card. "That's no good! That's no good! Go on through!" To the waiting pack: "We don't want you here, go on back!" and

---

[*] the exclusive shopping street in West Berlin.

[**] the chief down-town crossing point for West Germans.

[***] the main border crossing for Americans and other foreigners.

someone from the West grabs the *taz* reporter by the collar. The next one shakes his hand, thinking he is from the East: "Do you need an apartment? I have a job for you." Those with a green identity card from the West hold it up and are hit and booed. Shortly after 2:00 - for the first time, the first verse of the German national anthem[****] starts to ring through the air. There are Japanese filming, and the [Berlin] bear – brown and real – is dancing.

Document 10:

Ex-Chancellor Willy Brandt, honorary chairman of the SPD, expressed the euphoria surrounding the opening of the Wall, acknowledged German responsibility for the division and welcomed the beginning of European unity.

Willy Brandt on "Growing Together," 10 November 1989

(Source: W. Brandt, *"...was zusammengehört:" Reden zu Deutschland*, Bonn, 1990, 37ff.)

It is a wonderful day after a very long journey. But we are still on the road. We have not yet completed our trip. There is still a lot to be done. . . .

Much depends on whether we Germans – on both sides – prove capable of coping with this historic situation. Germans coming together – that's what it's all about. Germans are coming together differently than most of us expected. And no one should act as though he knew exactly how the people in the two German states will come to have a new relationship with one another. The important thing is that they will indeed develop a different relationship to one another, that they meet in freedom, and that they can grow together.

One thing is certain – nothing in the other part of Germany will ever again be as it was. The winds of change that have been blowing over Europe could not pass Germany by. It has always been my conviction that such a division – with concrete, barbed wire, and a death strip – went against the tide of history. And this summer I put it once again on paper: Berlin will live and the Wall will fall. By the way, I feel that a piece of that horrendous construction could even remain standing as a reminder of that historical monster. Just as we consciously decided, after heated debate here in Berlin, not to destroy the ruins of the Gedächtniskirche[*].

Certainly it is not always easy for those who are still young and those coming of age to understand the historical context in which we live. Therefore, I am

----

[****] because they evoke a greater Germany the first verse, the lyrics *Deutschland, Deutschland, über alles*, are officially frowned upon.

[*] Destroyed by World War II bombs, the ruins of the Kaiser-Wilhelm church were left standing as a memorial against war.

not only saying that a lot lies ahead of us before the division is ended – in August of 1961, I spoke out angrily, yet also with a feeling of helplessness, against the Wall – instead, I also remind us that it did not all begin on 13 August 1961. Germany's misery began with the terrorist Nazi regime and the war it unleashed. That terrible war, which reduced Berlin, and so many other German and non-German cities, to mountains of rubble. The division of Europe, of Germany, and of Berlin developed out of that war and the disunity of the victorious powers. Now, what belongs together is growing together. We are now experiencing, and I thank God that I am able to share in the experience, how the pieces of Europe are growing together.

I am certain that the president of the United States and the head of the Soviet Union will appreciate what is happening here when they meet shortly on a ship in the Mediterranean [at Malta]. And I am also certain that our French and British friends – with the Americans, our reliable protectors during difficult times – understand the significance of this process of change, this new awakening. I know that our European neighbors to the east understand what moves us, and that this is part of a process of finding new ways of thinking and acting which has also taken hold in Central and Eastern Europe. The assurance we can offer our neighbors and the super powers is that we will not seek any solutions to our problems which neglect our obligations to peace and to Europe. We are guided by the common conviction that the European Community must be further developed and the division of our continent slowly but surely overcome. . . .

Document 11:

In mid-November Hans Modrow became head of the GDR government since, as District Secretary in Dresden, he seemed untainted by any Stalinist abuse of authority. His reform program inspired hopes for a renewal of socialism and included close, treaty-based relations with West Germany.

Hans Modrow's Government Program, 17 November 1989

(Source: *Neues Deutschland*, 18/19 November 1989)

We need an advance on trust from anyone willing to give it to us. I know that's a lot to ask. This is why I want to declare that this government will make only promises it can truly keep. . . .

We declare our support of workers' accomplishments throughout the past decades. In the last few days, we have repeatedly expressed our intention to maintain all we have achieved through hard work, not to give anything up, not to let all our efforts during difficult times go up in smoke. . . . The government's most important task is to lead the GDR economy out of its present crisis and bring stability and new impetus for growth. And we will tackle this task.

We are responsible and accountable to the Volkskammer. We understand this to mean that we are accountable to the people. And we welcome anyone who wishes to help us with this task. . . .

In view of this, the government needs new maxims to work by – namely, those considered to be virtues by the people: openness and honesty, order and legality, moderation and thrift, competence rather than slogans or empty speeches. What is required of employees in a business must also apply to the government, and to the state in general – quality work. And if this is not the case, then it must be demanded by the citizens, unrelentingly and publicly. . . .

Our economy has serious problems; the necessary material resources are limited. Its structure must be significantly improved, and fixed assets modernized in many areas. But the economic basis of our socialist state is strong and resilient enough to stabilize in the near future and become capable of gaining the momentum it needs. . . .

The government program requires reforms, as have been proposed, demanded, and drafted by political parties and other social powers and by the citizens at large. . . . Here I will mention the most important of these:

First, political reform, combined with legislative steps to strengthen constitutional security and law. This includes voting legislation, a law pertaining to the Council of Ministers and laws guaranteeing freedom of the press. Drafts for criminal law reform can be completed very quickly. The freedom of movement law, perhaps referred to as a passport law, will be presented following discussion.

Secondly, economic reform will be aimed at increasing the individual responsibility of economic units. This must lead to considerably greater efficiency, minimization of centralized leadership and planning and, perhaps most difficult, promotion of merit pay. I suggest defining such economic reform, including its contents and stages, by means of special consultation between Volkskammer committees and economic experts. Careful, unbiased examination of subsidy and price policies represents a significant task.

Third, educational reform is necessary. . . .

Fourth, we need a long-term program that can be implemented step by step and reviewed each year, dedicated to reconciling economic and ecological interests. I would like to add that, due to unnecessary secrecy, the GDR's record seemed worse than it really is. In the future, no one should be allowed to delete or delay planned environmental protection measures. And a new energy policy is needed which will lead to a reduction in fossil fuel consumption.

Fifth, administrative reform is necessary to democratize state leadership and administration, to make their activities more transparent, and, last but not least, to reduce administrative costs considerably, both financially and in terms of personnel. . . .

The intended political reform already under way has provided a new foundation to preserve and implement a policy of self-determination for the people of the GDR. This gives new strength to the GDR's legitimacy as a socialist state, as a sovereign German state. Not mere claims, but rather a new reality regarding life in the GDR will serve to clearly reject unrealistic and dangerous speculations about reunification.

The two German states, despite all the differences in their social systems, share a centuries-old history. Both states should take this opportunity to lend their mutual relationship a good-neighborly character.

If the two German states show each other unreserved mutual respect, they can create a worthy example of cooperative coexistence. The government of the GDR is willing to expand cooperation with the FRG to new levels. This applies to all issues: securing of peace, disarmament, economics, science and technology, environmental protection, transportation, postal and telephone services, culture, tourism, and a plethora of humanitarian issues.

We are in favor of strengthening the community of responsibility of the two German states through a treaty-based union that goes far beyond that of the Basic Treaty and other previous treaties and agreements between the two states. This government is open to discussion in this regard. . . .

Document 12:

The accelerating unification process triggered widespread fears within and without Germany. Through a classic summary of international concerns the *New York Times* attempted to stop the momentum by calling for action to be postponed indefinitely.

New York Times Concerns about German Unification, 19 November 1989

(Source: *New York Times* editorial, 19 November 1989)

One Germany: Not Likely Now

No one was prepared for the rush of change in East Germany and the abrupt opening of the Berlin wall. So it's not surprising that the good news is being followed by much disquieting conjecture about a feared old topic: German reunification. Even careful Henry Kissinger calls that prospect inevitable.

Surprises can't be discounted – witness not only the holes in the wall but the other changes in the East. But the fears seem highly premature. For many different and sound reasons, hardly anybody wants reunification to happen.

Look first at East Germany. Its communist leaders are firmly opposed to political unification, though they certainly would welcome closer economic ties with West Germany. Closer political ties would jeopardize their grip on power as well as East Germany's identity as a socialist state.

Even opposition leaders don't want unification. They retain a belief in socialism; they want to reform rather than abolish their state, and want to combine free-market elements with a capacious social safety net.

Consider next West Germany, whose people already fear being swamped by a massive exodus from the East. Chancellor Kohl expressed the consensus accurately: "Our compatriots in the German Democratic Republic must be able to decide for themselves which way they want to go in the future." To Mr. Kohl, reunification is not now on the agenda.

Though President Mitterrand says he does not fear German reunification, France doesn't want it. Reunification complicates Paris's priority of moving ahead quickly with Western European economic integration. A new fatherland of 80 million Germans would tip the balance in the European Community even further in West Germany's direction.

Britain shares French concerns about an enlarged Germany becoming the economic superpower in Europe. Prime Minister Thatcher's warning against talking prematurely about reunification springs from the traditional British desire to maintain a balance of power on the continent by resisting the emergence of any outsized rival.

Like Western Europeans, Poles and other Eastern Europeans have bitter historical memories of previous greater Germanys whose drives to the East have been at their expense. And Poland has a very particular concern about a new united fatherland claiming "lost territories" in now-Polish Silesia and East Prussia.

Washington doesn't want reunification because that would end U.S. military presence in West Germany and dissolve NATO without an adequate substitute. Secretary of State Baker, taking his cue from Bonn, pointedly talks about Germany's legitimate wish for unity.

Finally, the Soviet Union, the country that suffered worst from Hitler's war, fears the nationalism that might emerge from German reunification. Mikhail Gorbachev also worries that a united Germany might be more inclined to throw its weight around Eastern Europe than in a united Western Europe.

Perhaps the only spur to serious demands for a reunited Germany would be foolish, provocative statements that Germans have no right to such an aspiration. They do have that right, and one day it may become a reality. For now, however, neither Europeans, Russians, Americans, nor indeed German leaders themselves are ready or eager to see a Fourth Reich.

More likely, the two Germanys will gradually blend their economies. In time, this will open the way for new forms of political association. Meantime, the overriding goal, for Germans and non-Germans alike, remains to integrate West Germany into Western Europe and move toward a Europe with truly open frontiers. What better end to a tormented German history, and what greater hope for Europe?

Document 13:

Fearing a moral and material "sell out" to West Germany, leading East German intellectuals, reform communists, and dissidents appealed for the development of a socialist democracy in the GDR. Well-known left-wing West Germans expressed their support in a subsequent declaration, "For Your Country, For Our Country."

Appeal "For Our Country," 26 November 1989

(Source: *Blätter für deutsche und internationale Politik*, 1990, 123f.)

Our country is experiencing a severe crisis. We can no longer live as we have up to now, nor do we wish to. The leadership of a party took over the government and representation of the people; Stalinist structures permeated all spheres of life. By means of nonviolent mass demonstrations, the people have now set in motion a process of renewal that is progressing at breathtaking speed. But we must act quickly to bring our influence to bear on the various options before us which can lead us out of this crisis.

Either:

We can insist on the sovereignty of the GDR and try, with all our strength and in cooperation with all interested states and groups, to develop a society demonstrating solidarity and guaranteeing peace and social justice, individual liberty, freedom of movement for all, and environmental protection.

Or:

We will have to suffer the start of a "sell out" of our material and moral values, due to the harsh economic realities and unreasonable conditions that influential economic and political circles in West Germany attach to their offers of aid to the GDR, leading sooner or later to a West German takeover of East Germany.

Let us take the first road. We still have a chance to develop a socialist alternative to the FRG, as an equal neighbor to all European states. We can still focus on the anti-fascist and humanistic ideals which once guided us. We call upon all citizens who share our hopes and our concern to join our effort by signing this appeal.

Document 14:

To the surprise of the domestic and international public, the FRG chancellor proposed a flexible plan for unification in a far-ranging speech before the Bundestag. Starting with closer cooperation with a democratizing GDR, Kohl suggested the gradual development of a federation which would be compatible with East-West detente and European integration.

Kohl's Ten-Point Plan for German Unity, 28 November 1989

(Source: German Information Office, New York, 1989)

1. Immediate measures are called for as a result of events of recent weeks, particularly the flow of resettlers and the huge increase in the number of travelers. The federal government will provide immediate aid where it is needed. We will assist in the humanitarian sector and provide medical aid if it is wanted and considered helpful. . . .

2. The federal government will continue its cooperation with the GDR in all areas where it is of direct benefit to the people on both sides, especially in the economic, scientific, technological, and cultural fields. It is particularly important to intensify cooperation in the field of environmental protection. Here we will be able to make decisions on new projects shortly, irrespective of other developments. . . .

3. I have offered comprehensive aid and cooperation, should the GDR bindingly undertake to carry out a fundamental change in the political and economic system and put the necessary measures irreversibly into effect. By "irreversible" we mean that the GDR leadership must reach agreement with opposition groups on constitutional amendments and a new electoral law.

We support the demand for free, equal, and secret elections in the GDR, in which, of course, independent, that is to say, non-socialist, parties would also participate. The SED's monopoly on power must be removed. The introduction of a democratic system means, above all, the abolition of laws on political crimes and the immediate release of all political prisoners.

Economic aid can only be effective if the economic system is radically reformed. This is obvious from the situation in all COMECON states and is not a question of our preaching to them. The centrally planned economy must be dismantled. . . .

4. Prime Minister Modrow spoke, in his government policy statement, of a "treaty community." We are prepared to adopt this idea. The proximity of our two states in Germany and the special nature of their relationship demand an increasingly close network of agreements in all sectors and at all levels.

This cooperation will also require more common institutions. The existing commissions could be given new tasks and new ones created, especially for industry, transport, environmental protection, science and technology, health and cultural affairs. It goes without saying that Berlin will be fully incorporated in these cooperative efforts. This has always been our policy.

5. We are also prepared to take a further decisive step, namely, to develop confederative structures between the two states in Germany with a view to creating a federation. But this presupposes the election of a democratic government in the GDR.

We can envisage the following institutions being created after early, free elections:

- an intergovernmental committee for continuous consultation and political coordination;

- a joint parliamentary body;

- and many others in the light of new developments.

Previous policy toward the GDR had to be limited mainly to small steps by which we sought, above all, to alleviate the consequences of division and to keep alive and strengthen the people's awareness of unity of the nation. If, in the future, a democratically legitimized, that is, a freely elected government, becomes our partner, that will open up completely new perspectives.

Gradually, new forms of institutional cooperation can be created and further developed. Such coalescence is inherent in the continuity of German history. State organization in Germany has nearly always taken the form of a confederation or federation. We can fall back on this past experience. Nobody knows at the present time what a reunited Germany will look like. I am, however, sure that unity will come, if it is wanted by the German people.

6. The development of intra-German relations remains embedded in the pan-European process, that is to say, in the framework of East-West relations. The future architecture of Germany must fit into the future architecture of Europe as a whole. Here the West has shown itself to be pacemaker, with its concept of a lasting and equitable peaceful order in Europe.

In our joint declaration of June this year, which I have already quoted, General Secretary Gorbachev and I spoke of the structural elements of a "common European Home." There are, for example:

- unqualified respect for the integrity and security of each state. Each state has the right freely to choose its own political and social system.

- unqualified respect for the principles and rules of international law, especially respect for the people's right of self-determination.

- the realization of human rights.

- respect for, and maintenance of, the traditional cultures of the nations of Europe.

With all of these points, as Mr. Gorbachev and I laid down, we aim to follow Europe's long traditions and help overcome the division of Europe.

7. The attraction and aura of the European Community are, and remain, a constant feature of pan-European development. We want to and must strengthen them further still.

The European Community must now approach the reformist countries of Central, Eastern, and Southeastern Europe with openness and flexibility. This was also endorsed by the heads of state and government of the EC member states at their recent meeting in Paris.

This of course includes the GDR. The federal government therefore approves the early conclusion of a trade and cooperation agreement with the GDR. This would give it wider access to the Common Market, also in the perspective of 1992.

We can envisage specific forms of association which would lead the reformist countries of Central and Southeastern Europe to the European Community, thus helping to level the economic and social gradients on our continent. This is one of the crucial issues if tomorrow's Europe is to be a united Europe.

We have always regarded the process leading to the recovery of German unity to be a European concern as well. It must, therefore, also be seen in the context of European integration. To put it simply, the EC must not end at the Elbe but must remain open to the East. . . .

8. The CSCE process is a central element of the pan-European architecture and must be vigorously promoted in the following forums:

- the human rights conferences in Copenhagen, in 1990, and in Moscow, in 1991;

- the Conference in Economic Cooperation in Bonn, in 1990;

- the Symposium on Cultural Heritage in Cracow, in 1991;

- and, last but not least, the next follow-up meeting in Helsinki.

There we should also think about new institutional forms of pan-European cooperation. We can well imagine a common institution for the coordination of East-West economic cooperation, as well as the creation of a pan-European environmental council.

9. Overcoming the division of Europe and Germany presupposes far-reaching and rapid steps in the field of disarmament and arms control. Disarmament and arms control must keep pace with political developments and thus be accelerated where necessary.

This is particularly true of the Vienna negotiations on the reduction of conventional forces in Europe, and for the agreement on confidence-building measures and the global ban on chemical weapons, which we hope will materialize in 1990. It also requires that the nuclear potential of the superpowers be reduced to the strategically necessary minimum. . . .

10. With this comprehensive policy we are working for a state of peace in Europe in which the German nation can recover its unity in free self-determination. Reunification – that is regaining national unity – remains the political goal of the federal government. We are grateful that once again we have received support in this matter from our allies in the declaration issued after the NATO summit meeting in Brussels in May.

We are conscious of the fact that many difficult problems will confront us on the road to German unity, problems for which no one has a definitive solution today. Above all, this includes the difficult and crucial question of overlapping security structures in Europe.

The linking of the German Question to pan-European developments and East-West relations, as explained in these ten points, will allow a natural development which takes account of the interests of all concerned and paves the way for peaceful development in freedom, which is our objective.

Only together and in an atmosphere of mutual trust will we be able to peacefully overcome the division of Europe, which is also the division of Germany. This calls for prudence, understanding, and sound judgement on all sides so that the current promising developments may continue steadily and peacefully. This process cannot be hampered by reforms, rather by their rejection. It is not freedom that creates instability but its suppression. Every successful step toward reform means more stability and more freedom and security for the whole of Europe.

In a few weeks' time we enter the final decade of this century, which has seen so much misery, bloodshed, and suffering. There are today many promising signs that the nineties will bring more peace and freedom in Europe and in Germany. Much depends, and everyone senses this, on the German contribution. We should face this challenge of history.

Document 15:

New citizens' movements (Democracy Now, Democratic Awakening, Green Party, the Initiative for Peace and Human Rights, New Forum, SPD, and United Left) and old bloc parties (CDU, DBD, LDPD, NDPD, SED, FDBG, and the Women's Association) formed the Central Round Table. Led by three church representatives, this forum declared it wanted to be a democratic watchdog and an initiator of further reforms.

Goals of the Central Round Table, 7 December 1989

(Source: *Neue Chronik DDR*, 2, 57ff.)

The participants in the Central Round Table are meeting out of deep concern for our country, which is in a serious crisis, and for its independence and permanent development. They demand that the ecological, economic, and financial situation of our country be made public.

Although the Round Table cannot exercise any parliamentary or government functions, it intends to appeal to the public with its proposals for overcoming the crisis.

It demands that the Volkskammer and the government, in timely fashion, inform it of, and include it in, important legal, economic, and financial decisions.

It sees itself as an institution of public monitoring in our country. It plans to continue its activities until free, democratic, and secret elections have been held. . . .

The following agreements were made:

Drafting a new constitution

1. The participants in the Round Table agree to begin to draft a new constitution immediately.

2. They will form a working group with equal representation that will immediately begin its activity and will include other persons as necessary.

3. The participants in the Round Table agree that this new constitution will be approved in a referendum in 1990 following the Volkskammer elections.

4. The constitutional amendments necessary to allow new elections are to be drafted without delay.

5. The participants in the Round Table take note of the offer to participate in a corresponding committee of the Volkskammer, and autonomously decide to participate.

Election dates

The Round Table recommends that elections to the Volkskammer be held on 6 May 1990.

Creation of working groups

The Round Table agrees to create the following working groups and appoints two people each to constitute them:

1. Election law

2. Party and association law

3. New constitution (see resolution above)

4. Economy

On the Rule of Law

In an effort to achieve the rule of law and to protect the interests of our people, the participants in the Round Table demand that the government take immediate measures in the following areas:

1. Any person guilty of abuse of power or corruption must be held responsible on the basis of current penal law. The provisions of the code of criminal procedure are to be applied in carrying out investigations and trials. This may mean issuing arrest warrants, but not decreeing illegal house arrests.

(1) The office of the General Prosecutor of the GDR must in each case immediately ensure that all information, accusations, and reports are followed up on the basis of paragraph 95 of the code of criminal procedure; where there is reason to suspect a crime, it will immediately consider the best means of securing necessary objects and evidence.

(2) The government of the GDR is called upon to create a special investigative unit to investigate cases of abuse of power and corruption. This investigative unit will be directly responsible to the Minister President for as long as it is active. The duties of the investigative unit will be announced publicly.

(3) The GDR state prosecutor's office is called upon to cooperate effectively with the independent investigating commission established on 4 December 1989.

(4) The government of the GDR is called upon to announce an immediate plan for measures to place under the supervision of the security forces of the Ministry of the Interior all departments of the Office for National Security at all levels, so that no documents or evidentiary material is destroyed and the possibility of abuse is eliminated.

2. The government of the GDR is called upon to dissolve the Office for National Security under civilian supervision and to guarantee vocational integration of its employees. The government should inform the public of the provision of any security services that may perhaps become necessary.

3. The government of the GDR is called upon to create a legal framework to support the work of independent citizens' committees.

Document 16:

By electing the uncorrupted lawyer Gregor Gysi as chairman and renouncing its Stalinist past, the SED attempted to regain political credibility by renaming itself as Party of Democratic Socialism. The new old PDS hoped to ensure the survival of the GDR as an anti-capitalist alternative by propagating a "third way."

Gregor Gysi at the SED Congress, 8-9 December 1989

(Source: *Neues Deutschland*, 9/10 December 1989)

The situation in the country and in the party demands holding this early, extraordinary party congress. The party must have leadership in order to counter tendencies towards dissolution and regain its ability to act. Today, the choice of leadership is the most important issue; but that is not possible without a self-assessment and self-determination. From the position paper drafted by the [preparatory] committee, which has been distributed to you and published in the newspapers, and which of course is not yet completely finished, one thing is nevertheless apparent: we need a radical break with the failed Stalinist, that is, administrative, centralized socialism in our country (applause).

This administrative, centralized socialism led to political, ecological, and economic crisis, to corruption and abuse of office. Here and in other socialist countries, it proved incapable of making an effective contribution to the solution of the problems of humanity. The people of the GDR, all their parties, political and social movements today face the decision on which direction the GDR should take. The economic and political crisis has largely limited the chance for us to determine this path ourselves.

It is of decisive importance to the lives of all citizens and of future generations which historical direction we choose. In the coming weeks and months, groundwork will be laid that will fundamentally change the living conditions of every single one of us. Based on their own experiences, many citizens of the GDR are orienting themselves toward the society of the FRG. Can our problems be solved by simply adopting [Western] structures? West European societies, especially that of the FRG, are not pure capitalist systems in the sense of a textbook model, from which one can learn nothing. We appreciate the modern achievements of the society for which the workers of the FRG have struggled. We respect the free forms of economic, political, and cultural competition that attempt to counter the emergence of monopolies in the economy, politics and culture. We can learn especially from the practice of codetermination in industry, from the threefold separation of powers between the executive, legislative, and judiciary, from the growing role of public opinion and the new social and cultural movements, from the high level of scientific and technological development, from the greater significance of local participation, from the federative and public character of many kinds of cultural support.

But at the same time, we must not ignore how limited these achievements are, as strict democrats in these countries would themselves point out. The achievements mentioned are limited by the strategic power interests of capitalist monopolies – in particular the multinational corporations, the international military-industrial complex. This is the border at which West German sovereignty in regard to the USA and NATO ends.

The capitalistically expanding world market may seem attractive at first glance to many accustomed to a bureaucratically planned economy of shortages. But in its monopolistic form, it worsens existing global problems of environmental protection, peacekeeping, and the gap in socio-economic development. It does indeed lead to mass unemployment, existential fears, socially unjust two-thirds societies even in the rich countries, and, even more, to a further impoverishment of the poor countries.

We must not gamble away the democratic awakening and right of self-determination of the people of the GDR. But we would be doing so if we allowed the old regime of "politbureaucrats" to be replaced by a new regime of capitalist magnates (applause). The crisis of administrative, centralized socialism in our country can be resolved only if the GDR follows a third way, beyond Stalinist socialism and the rule of multinational monopolies. We feel we are especially obliged to consider the social concerns of the people in our country. Solidarity of development based on individual freedom and basic rights, equal conditions for individual self-realization, and protection of humanity's natural and cultural heritage. Those are our basic values. With them, and a new program and democratic statute, we should enter a new path for the future of the GDR.

With all our energy, we will struggle for free competition, for the greatest contribution to the development of social wealth. A just recognition of individual and collective achievements must have a place here. Our struggle will be directed against all monopolistic forms of control in the economy, politics, and intellectual life. This socialist-influenced third way we strive for is characterized by radical democracy and the rule of law, humanism, social justice, and environmental protection. Achievement of true equal rights and equality for women. This orientation toward a third way reveals and takes up the democratic and humanist sources and content of our traditions in the German and international workers' movement. These include, above all, social democratic, socialist, non-Stalinist communist, anti-fascist and pacifist traditions. This isn't a question of changing the wallpaper. We want a new party. . . .

I have already expressed my opinion on the German question, as has our Minister President. We also received many questions on that. I would like to add only one thing. At a time when a European house is to be built, in which we see the dismantling of statehood in Europe, the idea of creating a new unified state is absurd. The important issues are cooperation and encounters at all levels, but at the same time preservation of our independence as the German Democratic Republic. . . .

Let us all fight together for this new democratic socialist party, which has finally freed itself from Stalinism for all time, freed itself as of today; let us all fight for this new party; then it will remain strong and will be able to carry out its political responsibilities for the good of our country, the German Democratic Republic.

Document 17:

In response to upcoming government negotiations, members of the civic movement attempted to develop a grass roots unification strategy, based on a "rapprochement through reform" by two demilitarized German states.

Democracy Now's Three-Step Plan for Unity, 14 December 1989

(Source: *Neue Chronik DDR*, 2, 85ff.)

The two German states and the inter-German border emerged and were established as a result of the Cold War. With the end of the Cold War, we have recently experienced the unity of the German people in its most elementary form. Many citizens are now asking how this unity should be shaped in the future. We are convinced that "reunification" through the annexation of the GDR by the FRG cannot solve the German question. We believe the time for a new German political unity is not yet ripe. However, such unity, founded in a cooperative society, is our goal.

This new form of unity can only be the result of a process of mutual encounter and political and social reform in both German states. Such a process must be nonviolent, respect existing treaties and international obligations, and occur in cooperation with the Allied powers and all our European neighbors. . . .

First Stage

Implementation of basic political and social reforms in the GDR, in a reform alliance with our East European neighbors. . . .

Introduction of social and political reforms in the FRG, leading to greater social justice, a clear reduction in unemployment, and greater environmental awareness in production and consumption. . . .

Calling of a German National Assembly composed of citizens of both states to begin a process of rapprochement and democratic opinion-formation on the national question.

Second Stage

Expansion of the Basic Treaty between the FRG and the GDR through a National Agreement.

Merging into a confederation and creation of dual German citizenship. . . .

Initial steps toward creation of economic, financial, and tax union. Preparation of an inter-German referendum on the issue of national unity.

Third Stage

Completion of demilitarization and withdrawal of the Allied powers.

Passage of the CSCE treaty system as a final peace treaty for all European states (European Peace Treaty).

Referendum on political unity in a federation of German States.

Creation of a single German citizenship.

Internationally binding obligations to participate in creating a new, mutually supportive world economic order.

Internationally binding obligations to fully implement ecologically sound means of production.

Document 18:

Welcomed by thousands of people demonstrating for unification, Chancellor Helmut Kohl and Minister President Hans Modrow began discussions in Dresden on comprehensive development of mutual relations and negotiation of corresponding treaties.

Joint Communique by Kohl and Modrow, 19 December 1989

(Source: *Neue Chronik DDR*, 2, 108f.)

Minister President Modrow and Chancellor Kohl agreed that good-neighborly relations between the two states, based on common responsibility for peace and a treaty system within the relationship, were of great significance for European stability and would represent a contribution to a new European architecture. . . .

Chancellor Kohl briefed Minister President Modrow on the development of the European Community. This represents the cornerstone of a new European architecture for the FRG; in its desire for openness, it remains the steadying influence in a future European balance. The FRG will support the conclusion of an agreement on trade and cooperation between the EC and the GDR in the near future. Minister President Modrow informed Chancellor Kohl of further steps to be taken in the democratic renewal of the GDR. He also explained plans for changes in the constitution and a reform of the penal code. In this context, Chancellor Kohl voiced his expectation that political crimes would be eliminated and those convicted of such crimes released. Minister President Modrow announced that all persons affected would be released from prison in the near future. . . . Minister President Modrow further explained that plans were being drafted to deal with those who have left the GDR in recent months which would do justice to these peoples' interests. There was agreement that cooperation between the GDR and the FRG be increased comprehensively and that relations be elevated to a new level and made closer and more long-term. . . . A treaty system should be developed to supplement existing agreements, including institutions to deal with common social problems. . . .

Both sides agreed to form a joint commission to intensify economic relations. West Berlin will be fully integrated into this cooperation.

Both sides wish to contribute to eliminating obstacles to trade relations. . . .

There was agreement that direct investment and joint ventures will have great significance on the positive economic development of the GDR. The GDR will create the necessary legal conditions as soon as possible. . . .

Regional cooperation committees may be formed on regional and local levels as has already been discussed for Berlin and its neighboring districts. A joint commission at the government level will be formed to coordinate this process.

Document 19:

To restore the sinking prestige of the Modrow government, the PDS used the desecration of the Soviet War Memorial in Treptow by rightists slogans as an opportunity for an anti-fascist mass demonstration. But the party's credibility suffered when rumors surfaced that the vandalism had been planned by the Stasi.

Neues Deutschland on the Treptow Demonstration, 3 January 1990

(Source: *Neues Deutschland*, 4 January 1990)

Our Country Now Needs a Broad United Front Against the Right

Gysi: We Will Not Allow the Chance for Democratic Socialism be Destroyed

Berlin, Wednesday evening, at the memorial in Treptow for the Soviet soldiers who fell liberating Berlin from fascism: More than 250,000 people attended the anti-rightist demonstration. Long before the event began, the wide square in front of the monument was full. Only a few days ago, neo-Nazis had desecrated the site with fascist graffiti. To emphasize their disgust and indignation at these acts of vandalism, the SED-PDS, the Committee of Anti-Fascist Resistance Fighters, and the Society for German-Soviet Friendship had called for a protest rally. The initiatives "For Our Country" and the "United Left," the leadership of the DBD, LDPD, NDPD, FDGB, FDJ, the founding committee of the Nelken,* Spartacist groups, the German Trotskyite League, the SEW**, SDAJ***, and many other anti-fascist and democratic movements joined in the appeal. . . .

"Yes to Perestroika – No to Nazis!"

"Down with Nazis – no Third Reich," "Red Front against the right," "Schönhuber and his brown plague don't have a chance with us," "Yes to perestroika – no to Nazis" – the slogans on numerous banners clearly voiced the will of those taking part in the rally: to create a broad coalition against neo-Nazism, racial hatred, and xenophobia. Again and again, they shouted "Down with Nazis!" and "United front!"

In the name of the Society for German-Soviet Friendship, Michael Koplanski condemned the vandalism as neo-Nazi atrocities. The deputy chairman of the DBD emphasized the fact that the graffiti insulted and ridiculed the fallen Soviet soldiers, the people of the Soviet Union, and all anti-fascists. The speaker stated that such provocateurs should not be permitted to break the strong bonds of friendship. On the contrary, these bonds should be strengthened.

The fascist hydra is once again rearing its ugly head, warned Kurt Höfer, chairman of the Committee of Anti-Fascist Resistance Fighters. As a victim of persecution during the Nazi regime and a fighter in the Spanish civil war, he had sworn never to give up the fight against fascism. "Let us join together to nip it in the bud," he cried, to stormy applause.

---

* a leftist splinter group.

** West Berlin Communist Party.

*** West Berlin Communist youth group.

Anti-Sovietism Must Not be Tolerated

"We owe this rally today not only to ourselves, but to the USSR, the CPSU, and Mikhail Gorbachev personally," said the chairman of the SED-PDS, Gregor Gysi. "Not only did the Soviet armies and people liberate us from fascism; but it was also that country, once again, which introduced perestroika." He said the USSR had made the democratic transformation of our GDR possible. Therefore, no anti-Sovietism, which is at the same time chauvinism and nationalism, will be tolerated.

"Our country is being threatened from the right. We must avert this danger; otherwise we need not even begin discussing democratic pluralism and other issues. How do we expect to vote democratically if the neo-Nazis occupy every sphere of freedom?" Words alone, he said, are not enough.

Referring to the Republikaners' intention to enter the GDR by the thousands and establish operations here, Gregor Gysi said: "If we want to protect this country's sovereignty, we must not allow them to enter this country. And wherever these neo-Nazis cross the border – and they have already done so many times – we once again need state authority." Legal, democratic, but decisive action by our security organs is necessary, he said. The right wing must not be allowed to destroy the chance for democratic socialism in the GDR. Our country must not become a refuge for neo-Nazis. "Let us form a united front against the right. Let us fight for democracy and progress in our country, and prevent anything that could undermine this country's anti-fascist principles!" . . .

Document 20:

In the end, renewal of the GDR was blocked by the collapse of its economy. When optimistic statistics could no longer hide the down-turn, the leading party newspaper attributed its reasons with increasing candor to economic planning until there seemed no alternative but to convert to a social market economy.

SED Disclosures of Economic Decline, 11 January 1990

(Source: *Neues Deutschland*, 11 January 1990)

On the State of the GDR Economy

In the past few weeks, there have been countless calls for a thorough disclosure of the economic situation of the GDR. . . . We appealed to the Central State Office of Statistics for information. On the basis of figures withheld from the public until now, we present a survey of central economic issues. . . .

Despite strenuous and industrious efforts, the speed of economic development had slowed perceptibly: planning mistakes in industry, insufficient supplies of consumer goods, an infrastructure that fell far short of satisfying the demands made upon it. Looking at the country as a whole, all this was reflected in the gross national product. While it grew between 1981 and 1985 – as we discovered – by an average of 4.5 percent, the years 1986 to 1989 showed an annual increase of only 3.1 percent. What caused this? What processes characterize the GDR economy?

Accumulation and Investment

Too Little Investment Was Directed Into Production

The slowdown in GNP growth is reflected in the trends of the economy's labor productivity: In the years 1981 to 1985, it increased by 4.3 percent annually. From 1986 to 1989, growth totaled an average of only 3.4 percent annually. Productivity in the GDR was some 40 percent lower than in the FRG.

What processes were responsible for this development? It involved many negative factors, some of which overlap. They include the long-term consequences of insufficient capital accumulation and inadequate returns on investment. . . . At present, the GDR economy has at its disposal a capital stock of approximately 1,750 billion marks. This amount grew by 535 billion marks – that is, 44 percent – in comparison with 1980. . . .

During the same period (1981-1989), the GNP rose by 41 percent. But in the 1980s, this was not enough to achieve a transition to an intensively expanded reproduction of capital stock.

In addition, one of the basic economic relationships of accumulation to consumption was not structured in accordance with the country's needs. Thus necessary capital could not be ensured for the productive sectors. . . .

Effectiveness of the Capital Stock, Maintenance

Machines and Facilities Began to Age

Although the material and technical infrastructure was partially renewed, worn-out equipment could be replaced only to an inadequate extent. In the period from 1981 to 1989, for example, 61 billion marks of equipment was scrapped, compared with 330 billion marks worth of equipment added. Thus much of the equipment too old in almost all sectors of production. While the volume of machines and facilities that had completely depreciated in 1980 totaled some 58 billion marks, by 1989 this had increased to 133 billion marks, or more than double the earlier amount. Twenty percent of all equipment was worn out; in 1980, the figure was 14 percent. . . .

Beginning in 1985, the gap between new and old equipment grew even further. In "general mechanical engineering, agricultural machinery, and motor vehicle construction," for example, the sector experiencing the greatest requirement for capital goods, the amount of new equipment under five years old grew by 7,900 pieces in the period from 1986 to 1989. In the same period, the number of facilities and machines more than twenty years old grew by 11,100 pieces, to over 66,000, because very little worn-out equipment was retired.

This age structure often led to reduced efficiency and capacity, and thus to inconsistencies between suppliers and producers. In comparison with modern machines and facilities, the large amount of outdated equipment ties up considerably more labor power for operation, and above all for maintenance. Maintenance costs increased over the years. . . .

Foreign Trade, International Division of Labor

Imports Grew Faster than Exports

Our worsening competitive position on foreign markets, along with limited opportunities to exploit the advantages of the international division of labor, were among the factors that influenced the dynamics of our GNP negatively. On the one hand, embargo provisions tied the GDR's hands regarding many high-tech items in non-socialist countries. On the other hand, these products were unavailable in the socialist world.

Productive GNP was not available in the volume and proportions necessary for domestic use and for resolving international problems. For these reasons, despite the goals of the plan, imports increased more rapidly than exports. Combined with the ineffectiveness of trade [with] non-socialist economies, this placed an additional burden on the GDR's balance of payments over the last four years. . . .

The main cause of the inadequate volume of exports to the non-socialist economies and the lack of effectiveness in foreign trade lies in the impossibility of making sufficient export goods available. In addition, products did not meet the scientific and technical standards necessary to remain competitive. . . .

In some decisions, the GDR had little choice but to rely on its own capabilities. For example, it decided to follow the costly path of developing and producing its own very extensive, but inadequately structured, line of microelectric components. . . .

Labor Resources, Vocational Recruitment, Living Standard

Ineffective Employment Structures Created

At the end of the eighties, demographic developments in our country created conditions unfavorable for reproduction of labor resources in society. Until 1988, the working-age population grew only slightly. With the mass emigrations of 1989, the labor force shrank decisively. Emigration continues. At the same time, the number of young skilled workers completing vocational training decreased. The course of administrative reforms and other changes in state institutions, parties, and mass organizations revealed an ineffective employment structure. Labor that is becoming available has qualifications different from those needed for the approximately 250,000 jobs presently available.

Social policy consumed a large share of the overall economic product, without sufficiently stimulating production. The population's net income from 1986 to 1989 exceeded the plan. During the same period, retail turnover fell short of the target. Economic production lagged behind income. Supply of goods and services did not correspond in structure, quality, or quantity with buying-power demand. A significant surplus of purchasing power resulted from the disproportionate relationship between savings and available goods. . . .

Regarding monetary income from employment, the incomes of blue- and white-collar employees and collective-farm workers have developed most quickly since 1980. In other employment groups, measures established in 1986 to promote individual crafts were particularly effective. Overall, however, income differences changed only slightly after 1980. The average net household income of blue- and white-collar workers rose 30.6 percent after 1980, totaling 1,946 marks per month in 1988. Per capita net income was 696 marks a month (1988).

Though increasing production of consumer goods made more food and industrial products available to the public, the range and quality of products lagged behind consumer expectations. . . .

Document 21:

With over 85,000 formal employees and 200,000 informal informers, the Stasi seemed an all-powerful instrument of terror. When the PDS-led government only changed its name, the party organ reported that angry crowds stormed the secret police headquarters in Berlin in an attempt to force its dissolution and to save its records.

Neues Deutschland **on the Attack on Stasi Headquarters, 15 January 1990**

(Source: *Neues Deutschland*, 16 January 1990)

First Stormed, Then Ravaged

Calls to Remain Calm Go Unheeded: Hans Modrow Appeals to Reason

Berlin. At 5 P.M., the first demonstrators climbed the gate. Under pressure from the masses, the police opened the steel entry gate to the headquarters of the former Office of State Security in Berlin. Tens of thousands stormed the entrances on Rusche and Normannen streets. On banners and in chants they expressed their indignation at the hesitant dissolution of the state security service in Berlin, crying "Stasi to the mines," "Down with the Stasi," and "No pardon for the Stasi or there'll be trouble."

The New Forum had called for a peaceful "demonstration against Stasi and Nasi[*]" last Thursday during a demonstration at the Volkskammer. But as events progressed on Monday, the organizers gradually lost control.

The first to enter charged to House 18, a block of offices and supply rooms. Stones smashed the glass entrance, clearing the way into the building. A large, howling crowd stormed the multistory building. Papers and furniture flew to the pavement from shattered windows. Rioters destroyed the rooms and plundered anything not tied down in offices, the cafeteria, a book store, and a theater box office.

Appeals for non-violence and calm remained unheeded for a long time. Equally ineffective at first were pleas from members of a citizens' committee who, in a security partnership with the *Volkspolizei* and the military prosecutor's office, had already begun to take charge of rooms in the large complex that afternoon. Committee members profited from experience already gained in dissolving offices in their home districts. Members of the citizens' committee appealed repeatedly for maintenance of the security partnership. They said they intended to have the buildings occupied around the clock by Wednesday.

In House 18, organizers and demonstrators who felt the destruction had gone too far attempted to restore order. They insisted over and over that people leave the building, and stopped the rioters. They confiscated plundered inventory such as books, computer disks, telephones, uniform parts, documents, etc. Those who behaved calmly in this way were subjected to insults such as "Are you the new Stasi?" and "They persecuted us for forty years, now we can smash all this." Others had smeared the walls with oil paint and spray cans. There were also slogans on the outer walls and windows. Side by side on House 21: "We don't need anyone listening in on us" and "The VEB Steremat urgently needs lathe operators. Telephone 27 14/221." Symbolic walls were set up in the inner courtyard and outside both entrances.

Shortly after hearing of the events, GDR Prime Minister Hans Modrow proceeded immediately to the scene of the action along with SPD spokesman Ibrahim Böhme, Pastor Rainer Eppelmann from Democratic Awakening, and the press spokesman of Democracy Now, Konrad Weiss. In front of the complex on Normannen Street, he appealed to the demonstrators to keep order and remain calm. "I came here to carry out my responsibilities as Prime Minister of our country." He said the awakening that began in November should remain nonviolent. He entirely understood, he said, why spies were condemned. But non-violence and level-headedness went together. In every democracy, there will be people who think differently. No one must endanger the democratic awakening. He said all those who destroyed things here should be aware that they were in fact harming themselves.

---

[*]National Security Office, created by Modrow government to replace the Stasi.

4

National Turn and Fears of Germany

In late January 1990, it became increasingly clear that the Soviet Union could no longer stave off the collapse of East Germany. In fact, the disintegration of the Eastern Bloc (Document 1) had in many ways been initiated by USSR perestroika itself. On his return from Moscow, Prime Minister Hans Modrow presented a plan for German unity (Document 2), and Chancellor Kohl announced Gorbachev's explicit consent to unification soon thereafter (Document 3). Because of the impending collapse of the GDR, Bonn refused to shore up Modrow's tottering transition government. Instead, West Germany tried to stop the continuing stream of migrants by proposing a monetary union (Documents 5 and 6). These steps toward unity aroused international reservations and domestic criticism (Documents 8 and 9). At their mid-February meeting in Ottawa the four World War II victors nonetheless cleared the path for settling the international aspects of unification with the Two-plus-Four formula for negotiations (Document 7).

The issue of German unity also dominated the first free election campaign in East Germany. While the PDS and the civic movement remained skeptical, the social democrats favored a gradual transition, whereas middle and right wing parties advocated a quick merger (Document 11). Instead of listening to intellectuals' warnings against precipitous accession, the silent majority of East German citizens chose to believe Chancellor Kohl's promises of "flourishing landscapes" (Documents 4 and 12). The East German public ignored Soviet warnings against incorporation by West Germany (Document 13) as well as social democratic complaints about unfair campaign tactics (Document 15). Aversion against further socialist experiments was the chief reason for the surprising victory of the "Alliance for Germany" which marginalized the very dissidents who had initiated East Germany's democratic transformation (Document 15).

The electoral verdict speeded German unification by providing a popular mandate for self-determination. In Great Britain and France, the Eastern choice of quick unity rekindled old fears of German hegemony (Documents 16 and 17). West German critics like Jürgen Habermas could only warn angrily against economic nationalism (Document 18). The clear vote also ended all attempts to democratize socialism in East Germany through a new constitution (Document 19). The first freely elected GDR government sought to allay rising international fears with a declaration apologizing for the crimes of German history (Document 20). Responding to popular pressure, the de Maizière cabinet pushed ahead with plans for rapid unification with the West (Document 21).

Document 1:

On 30 January 1990, President Mikhail Gorbachev and Prime Minister Hans Modrow met in Moscow. In an interview, broadcast by an (East) Berlin radio station, the Soviet leader hinted that he was beginning to change his mind on German unity.

Gorbachev on His Change in German Policy, 30 January 1990

(Source: *Deutschland Archiv*, 23, 1990, 468)

Reporter: Following the welcome, I took the opportunity to ask Gorbachev about the Soviet strategy for Germany . . . .

Gorbachev: It appears to me that Germans in the West and East agree to a certain extent with the representatives of the Four Powers that German unification should never be fundamentally called into question by anyone. We have always said . . . that history influences the course of events. This will also be the case in the future when the German question is posed in practice.

I believe that the course of current events . . . must be considered carefully. Things have apparently been enormously accelerated.

In European as well as international politics, all of us in the GDR, the FRG, in all European capitals, above all in those of the Four Powers, must now act responsibly.

The issue here is one that affects not only the fate of Germans in the GDR, but also Germans in the FRG. It must be discussed in a responsible manner. It cannot be resolved in the streets.

For me, the starting point is clear. . . . There are two German states, there are the Four Powers, there is the European process, which is proceeding just as turbulently. All of this must be brought into harmony. It is in all our interest. . . .

Under no circumstances can we belittle the interests of the Germans, for I advocate a realistic process. If we say that history determines the course of events, and I have often said so, then it will do so, and I believe history has already begun to make changes.

Document 2:

Upon returning from Moscow, Modrow presented his own plan for unity, containing long forbidden words, such as confederation. Its title, "Germany, United Fatherland," refers to the text of the GDR anthem, prohibited during the Honecker era, which became one of the popular slogans at the 1989/1990 mass demonstrations.

Modrow's Plan for a German Federation, 1 February 1990

(Source: *Deutschland Archiv*, 23, 1990, 471f.)

Europe is entering a new stage of development. The post-war chapter is closing. The conditions for peaceful, good-neighborly cooperation among all peoples are developing. Unification of the two German states has moved onto the agenda.

The German people will find a place in the construction of a new, peaceful order that will overcome the division of Europe into hostile camps and the division of the German nation. The time has finally come to put an end to the World War II, to conclude a German peace treaty. It will settle all problems connected with the aggression of Hitler Germany and the failure of the Third Reich.

A final resolution of the German question can be achieved only through free self-determination by Germans in both states, in cooperation with the Four Powers, taking account of the interests of all European states. It must promote a process throughout Europe that will free our continent once and for all from all military threats. No one should consider the rapprochement between the two German states and their subsequent unification a threat.

In this spirit, I propose a responsible national dialogue. Its aim should be to establish concrete steps leading to a unified Germany that will become a new factor for stability, confidence, and peace in Europe.

As equal negotiating partners in such a dialogue, the representatives of the GDR and the FRG could find the best-possible solutions to issues involving the future of the German nation.

Steps in the direction of German unity could be:

- Conclusion of a treaty on cooperation and good-neighborly relations in a treaty association, which would contain considerable confederative elements such as economic, monetary, and commercial unions, as well as legal adjustments.

- Creation of a confederation between the GDR and FRG with joint organs and institutions, such as parliamentary committees, a chamber of states, joint executive organs for certain areas.

- Transfer of both states' rights of sovereignty to confederative organs of government.

- Creation of a unified German state in the form of a German Federation or German Union by way of elections in both parts of the confederation.

- Meeting of a unified parliament to create a unified constitution and a unified government with its capital in Berlin.

Necessary conditions for this development:

- Each of the two German states must ensure that steps leading to German unity conform to its obligations to other states and groups of states, as well as to necessary reforms and changes. This includes the GDR's transition to a Länder structure. Ensuring domestic stability, rights, and laws is as indispensable a condition as strict fulfillment of prior treaties between the GDR and FRG, which provide, among other things, for noninterference in each other's domestic affairs.

- Ensuring the interests and rights of the Four Powers, as well as the interests of all European peoples in peace, sovereignty, and secure borders. The Four Powers should declare their intention of settling all issues arising from World War II and the post-war period after creation of a unified German state. This would include such issues as the presence of foreign troops on German soil and membership in military alliances.

- Military neutrality of the GDR and FRG prior to federation.

This process of German unification will take place on the basis of agreements between the parliaments and governments of the GDR and the FRG. All parties declare their desire for democratic, nonviolent forms of political participation and will create the necessary guarantees, including referenda.

This strategy supports the democratic, patriotic, progressive ideas and movements aimed at the unification of the German nation, arising from a common history and the recent past. It stands by the humanistic, anti-fascist traditions of the German people.

This strategy is aimed at the citizens of the GDR and the FRG, all European peoples and states, and the international public; it needs their support.

Document 3:

During his visit in Moscow, Kohl met Gorbachev in order to discuss European political and economic questions. The Soviet leader gave his visitor unmistakable assurances on German unification.

Kohl's Report on his Meeting with Gorbachev, 10 February 1990

(Source: *Deutschland Archiv*, 23, 1990, 474)

Tonight I have to covey a single message to all Germans. General Secretary Gorbachev and I agreed that the German people have the sole right to make the decision whether they want to live together in one state.

General Secretary Gorbachev unmistakably promised that the Soviet Union will respect the decision of the Germans to live in one state and that it is up to the Germans to determine the timing and form of unification themselves.

General Secretary Gorbachev and I also agreed that the German question can be solved only on the basis of realities: that means, it must be embedded in the common European architecture and in the entire process of East-West relations.

We must take into account the justified interests of our neighbors and friends as well as partners in Europe and the world.

It is now up to us Germans in the Federal Republic and the GDR to embark upon the common path with prudence and resolution.

General Secretary Gorbachev and I have talked extensively about the fact that European security questions have an outstanding importance on the path to German unity. We want to discuss the issue of membership in different alliances in close coordination with our friends in Washington, Paris, and London, and I am certain we will find a common solution.

I want to thank General Secretary Gorbachev for having made this historic result possible.

Document 4:

In an interview with the left-wing Berlin daily *taz*, novelist Günter Grass opposed what he called a "prohibition on dreaming" about socialist utopias and appealed for a confederation.

Günter Grass Against the Clamor for Unity, 12 February 1990

(Source: *taz*, 12 February 1990)

taz: Günter de Bruyn[*] and Monika Maron[**] accuse many intellectuals in both German states of viewing the GDR as a "national park of socialist utopias." Do you consider that this accusation applies to you?

---

[*]East German writer.

[**] former East German writer.

Günter Grass: I don't think much of such sweeping accusations. Monika Maron is certainly free, using the jargon of the [newsmagazine] *Spiegel*, to join in the trend of over-generalized criticism of intellectuals in the *Frankfurter Allgemeine Zeitung* and elsewhere. It seems to be in style right now.

taz: Günter de Bruyn also made the accusation . . . .

Grass: I don't think so. Besides, my position with regard to the SED was always clear. But I grant people who stood up for their convictions against the SED – like Stefan Heym[*] and Christa Wolf[*] – the right to hold to their dreams. And I ask myself whether everything else coming from the left has to be demolished for practical reasons. After all, the two states also lose something if part of this failed history is simply leveled. There's a mentality behind this which, in the final analysis, says that with the end of the SED, the dream of democratic socialism is over. . . .

taz: You are a vehement proponent of retaining two states, thus ignoring those in Leipzig and elsewhere in the GDR who want unity. Why?

Grass: I'm not a proponent of retaining two states. I assume that there are two states of one nation. I have always spoken of the cultural nation – a concept that must of course be modified. You can't stop at Herder[***]. I am definitely opposed to two states in the sense of two foreign countries. Everything I have said on this in the past implies that the German question must be resolved in a different way, not through reunification. Everything we do in Germany now has to be done with a glance of acknowledgment to our neighbors. They've had experience with us, just as we have had experience with ourselves. We are still dealing with the consequences of that today. I mean National Socialism, the huge crime that can be relativized neither through a historians' quarrel nor through the hullabaloo over unity. This remains a burden that has to be considered when thinking about Germany today.

taz: Do you accuse those in Leipzig who now shout "Germany, united fatherland" of lacking historical consciousness?

Grass: I don't blame anyone living under the economic pressures in the GDR for calling for unity; I blame the politicians, whose responsibility is not to follow the public attitude, which is in itself justified, but to develop a strategy acceptable to us and our neighbors. If they fail to do this and merely follow the trends, we will find ourselves once again on a historical and political slope that does indeed have its precursors, particularly in Germany. That's what I'm afraid of.

---

[*]East German writer.

[***]eighteenth century philosopher and founder of nationalism.

taz: Can we confront the cries of "We are one people!" in Leipzig and elsewhere politically – rather than on the basis of memory or conscience – by referring to Auschwitz[****]?

Grass: No. Politicians must respond to the public: Yes, we are one people. But history has decreed that we live in two states. We must nevertheless attempt to be one people, to find a form that takes account of the burdens placed upon us. And that includes, above all, Auschwitz. Despite Auschwitz, it must be possible – and we can expect our neighbors to understand this – to find an acceptable form. That is why I propose a confederation. It is not a concentration of power; it is something much easier to integrate into a future Europe than the state of eighty million imagined by those in the GDR desperately crying "Germany, united fatherland," and by the politicians here who conjure it, though they should know better. Politicians accede to this pressure; they've even introduced such a promise into the electoral campaign in the GDR. European realities will call them to order. I am quite sure of that. The strategy of a confederation I have proposed for further development will again be a subject of debate. . . .

taz: That sounds nice, but meanwhile more and more people are leaving the GDR.

Grass: Right up front, at the beginning, there has to be something more: the Federal Republic must pay the GDR the financial compensation it owes it for the war. It is absolutely clear – though this is not an excuse for the SED – that this smaller state had to bear the greater share of post-war consequences: reparations, dismantling of industry, oppressive economic contracts still in force today. We must not forget that there was no Marshall Plan for the GDR. We have to keep all this in mind. In addition, decency requires the GDR population to cast off the humiliating role of supplicant

Document 5:

On 13 and 14 February 1990, Hans Modrow visited Bonn with a delegation that included the eight ministers from the Round Table. Instead of promising compensation for war debts, Helmut Kohl proposed a monetary union.

Kohl's Currency Union Proposal, 13 February 1990

(Source: *Deutschland Archiv*, 23, 1990, 475f.)

Ladies and gentlemen, the talks with Prime Minister Modrow and his delegation were matter-of-fact, open, and in general characterized by a mutual desire to send a hopeful signal to the people of the GDR.

[****]infamous extermination camp in Poland.

The talks took place against the background of a situation that has clearly worsened, particularly as a result of the continuing wave of emigrants. In 1989, the number of emigrants reached a total of around 340,000. Since the beginning of this year, an additional 85,000 have joined them. Therefore, I made two things clear in the discussions today: First of all, as we have repeatedly declared, we are willing to help in the short term where this is urgent and necessary, especially for humanitarian reasons. Such support measures are included in the 1990 supplementary budget. I will mention here the key terms: hard currency travel funds; ERP[*] credit program, especially for small and middle-sized businesses; training and technology transfer; and environmental protection and improvement of traffic arteries. . . .

We are going a decisive step further. I suggested to Prime Minister Modrow that we begin immediate negotiations on creation of a monetary union and economic community.

A joint commission will be formed for this purpose; it will begin talks immediately.

How will this offer help concretely?

The offer consists essentially of two parts:

1. On a particular day, the GDR mark will be replaced by the D-mark as monetary unit and legal tender.

2. At the same time, the GDR must create the necessary legal conditions for introduction of a social market economy.

The federal government considers both elements to be inseparably linked.

I would like to add: politically and economically, this offer means that the federal government is prepared to respond to the unusual, in fact revolutionary, events and challenges in the GDR with unusual, in fact revolutionary, measures on our part.

For there can be no doubt about one thing. In a normal political and economic situation, this path would be different – one of step-by-step reforms and adjustment, with a common currency only at a later date.

Against this background, criticism by experts is understandable. But the critical deterioration of the situation in the GDR demands far-reaching, courageous responses.

Political and social transformations have led here to a dramatic contraction of the political time frame, so that the social basis for step-by-step plans has disappeared, whatever their definition and economic justification. In such a situa-

---

[*] Refers to funds from the European Recovery Program.

tion, the issue is more than economics. A clear, unmistakable signal of hope and encouragement must now be sent to the people of the GDR.

For this reason, and only for this reason, we have made a decision that may in fact be termed historic, offering the GDR immediate creation of a monetary union and economic community. For the FRG, this means we are offering our strongest economic asset – the German mark.

We will thus allow our countrymen in the GDR to take immediate and direct part in something the citizens of the FRG have created and achieved through decades of persistent labor. For the D-mark – one of the hardest, most stable and widely accepted currencies in the world – is the basis of our prosperity and economic productivity.

But a monetary union makes sense only if the GDR immediately introduces comprehensive market-economy reforms. This means, concretely,

- taking complete stock of financial data and facts;

- ensuring the Central Bank's proven policy of stability for the entire monetary region;

- convincing, rapid implementation of announced economic reforms under the key headings of commercial freedom, property settlement, competitive order, environmental protection, a market economy wage and price system, and freedom in foreign trade;

- reordering state finances, including the tax system,

- necessary social support measures for these reforms; for example, introduction of unemployment insurance and adjustment of the pension system.

I would like to emphasize that the social and ecological safeguards of this reform policy are of central importance to the federal government. Without them, in our opinion, no economic reorientation in the GDR can succeed.

Therefore, present economic difficulties can be eliminated only by restructuring into a market economy, accompanied by social and ecological reorganization. Only in this way can an influx of private capital be set in motion, and only in this way can new, promising industries and jobs be created.

There is no doubt that this path requires much readjustment and great effort. However, through decisive action, the opportunities far outweigh the risks. This is at least partly due to the unusually favorable economic situation in the FRG.

Above all, however, our high foreign trade surpluses have gained new significance with regard to the GDR. To put it more precisely: If we succeed in rerouting a small amount of our trade surplus, a good 130 billion DM, to the GDR, if we succeed in making a small part of our annual capital export of 100 billion DM available to the GDR, this would be enough to provide a strong economic push.

In short, there is no basic shortage of goods and capital that can be utilized for an economic rebirth in the GDR.

I assess equally positively the great willingness of our industries to become involved in the GDR. I know from many discussions that an abundance of plans for concrete investment and cooperation already exists and can be implemented over the short term.

I would like to add: it is obvious that, in this context, the economic framework in the GDR – determined only there, and not here – will play a decisive role. Ladies and gentlemen, our motto in the months to come will be "national solidarity." Solidarity is, at this hour, our obvious human and national duty.

We are dealing with a great joint effort, with which we can ensure our previously divided fatherland a happy future in a free, united Europe – imbued with the will to serve world peace as an equal member of a united Europe.

May I say for the FRG: We accept this responsibility.

The talks were – and I'd like to repeat this – marked by this spirit of responsibility, even though, understandably, we did not agree on a whole range of issues at this meeting. Therefore, I emphasize that this was not the last meeting. We will have to continue our encounters – especially, of course, once the Volkskammer has been elected and the new GDR government takes office.

Document 6:

According to the GDR wire-service ADN, East German reactions to the talks between Kohl and Modrow in Bonn were mixed. PDS and dissident critics accused Kohl of annexation politics, while moderates of the bloc parties welcomed the currency union offer.

East German Reactions to Bonn's Offer, 13 February 1990

(Source: *Deutschland Archiv*, 23, 1990, 477f.)

In Berlin, the chairmen and spokespersons of parties, organizations, and movements expressed their reactions to the initial results of the talks between GDR Prime Minister Hans Modrow and FRG Chancellor Helmut Kohl, which were announced at a press conference in Bonn. Their varied statements voiced approval of the fact that the two sides were speaking with each other on possible paths to German unity, revealed great expectations of future developments, and also showed some disappointment over achievements thus far.

DBD Chairman Günther Maleuda stated, "The press conference on the initial results of the Bonn visit by Prime Minister Hans Modrow strengthens our expectation that the road to German unity will be taken by both German governments rapidly but rationally." He said it was the DBD's view that binding decisions were now necessary. He noted with satisfaction that requests by the GDR for guarantees on farmers' ownership of land would be included in the negotiations.

For the first time, Prime Minister Modrow had taken the negotiating position of the Round Table seriously. This was shown by the creation of expert commissions rather than premature decisions on an immediate monetary union, the United Left pointed out.

The CDU welcomed the fact that Chancellor Helmut Kohl stood by his offer of a monetary union, stated spokesman Helmut Lück. "The most effective help the Federal Republic can give the GDR is obviously implementation of the monetary and economic union. It will be crucial to do so in a way that guarantees the social rights of the people of the GDR."

"We agree entirely with Prime Minister Modrow that unification of the two German states must not occur at the expense of the public. This is also the expectation and demand of our union members, who will not permit social programs to be dismantled in connection with the announced monetary and economic union," stressed Helga Mausch of the FDGB.

The NDPD spokesman emphasized the fact that the NDPD sees its position confirmed by government head Modrow's assessment of the situation, particularly with regard to practical steps "in the process by which the two German states approach unity." This was particularly true of the necessary maintenance of European security interests.

Democracy Now considers the outcome of the meeting between Modrow and Kohl "inadequate and politically incorrect." In a statement, representatives said that important conditions for German unity, such as disarmament and demilitarization and recognition of the Oder-Neisse border [with Poland], had not received the consideration expected from Chancellor Kohl. "We believe that rapid monetary union poses an unacceptable economic and socio-political risk. We consider the policies of the federal government a threat to the process of democratization and the right to self-determination of the people of the GDR."

In a prepared statement, the Green Party said: "Since today's press conference by Kohl and Modrow, it is clear that there will be no gradual growing-together of the two German states, but only unconditional annexation of the GDR by the FRG. Kohl's conditions for the immediate monetary and economic union he desires apparently include nonrecognition of the Oder-Neisse border and political integration of the GDR into NATO. The Green Party in the GDR firmly declares that the democratic movement in our country did not come into being in order to be suffocated by forced unification."

Democratic Awakening "advocates a rapid assumption of negotiations on a monetary union between the FRG and the GDR," according to press spokeswoman Angela Merkel. "We see this as a step in the right direction." She said the party had long demanded German national unity, for which monetary union was a necessary condition. DA is committed to social guarantees for the citizens of the GDR, especially in the areas of employment, rent control, savings, and property rights.

The deputy spokesman of the SPD in the GDR, Markus Meckel, said there had been no actual results of the talks between Prime Minister Modrow and Chancellor Kohl. However, the event was "not entirely unimportant," as "opposition ministers were also included in the communication process between the governments of the GDR and the FRG." He expressed his regret at Kohl's statement "that no immediate aid could be expected in the coming days, so that additional time will be lost."

Document 7:

During a NATO meeting with the Warsaw Pact on "open skies" in Ottawa, the German foreign minister announced the Two-Plus-Four formula for negotiating about unification. While the Germans would settle the internal aspects directly, international and security questions were to be discussed with the World War II victors Britain, France, the Soviet Union and the United States.

Hans-Dietrich Genscher on the Two-Plus-Four Formula, 14 February 1990

(Source: Bundespresseamt, "Erklärung des Bundesministers des Auswärtigen, Hans-Dietrich Genscher, vor der Presse in Ottawa," 13 February 1993)

Ladies and gentlemen, today we have reached agreement on talks of both German states with the Four Powers about the establishment of German unity. The following communique has been released:

The foreign ministers of the FRG, the GDR, France, the United Kingdom, the Soviet Union, and the US had talks in Ottawa. They agreed that the foreign minsters of the FRG and the GDR would meet with the foreign ministers of France, the UK, the Soviet Union and the US to discuss external aspects of the establishment of German unity, including the issues of security of the neighboring states. Preliminary discussions at the official level will begin shortly.

This clears the way for talks of both German states with the Four Powers, which we have always described with the formula Two-Plus-Four. This is an important date for us, since it allows the process of negotiations to be initiated. . . .

I can, therefore, say that our presence in Ottawa is very important, not only for the future of Europe, but also of Germany. The declaration, made by both German states and the Four Powers, has opened the path for negotiations on the establishment of German unity. The commitment of all states present to the holding of a CSCE summit meeting strengthens our confidence that the processes of European integration and of cooperation in the creation of a European security partnership shall advance decisively during this year. And finally our interest in the uninterrupted continuation of the negotiations for the reduction of conventional forces has also been taken into account. . . .

Today I have directed my remarks not only to the Four Powers but also to the European states represented here and the entire European public, so as to express the view of the FRG that the establishment of German unity shall make an important contribution to the creation of stability in Europe. That means that we do not want to promote German unity at the expense of others but start from the premise that the creation of German unity will also benefit our neighbors and Europe as a whole.

Document 8:

The neighboring countries in Europe reacted ambivalently to the negotiating framework, since this agreement made international approval of German unification more likely.

European Reactions to German Unification, 15 February 1990

(Source: A. Riding, "On Germany, Not All Is Joy," *New York Times*, 15 February 1990)

With the reunification of Germany now accepted as inevitable in Western Europe, governments from Brussels to Rome are bracing for the emergence of a single German nation rich and powerful enough to dominate European affairs.

The issue of German reunification still dominates headlines here, with Western European governments emphasizing that it should take place in the framework of the European Community and the North Atlantic Treaty Organization and should respect the inviolability of current borders.

But in many capitals, the focus is turning to the likely impact on the balance of power in Europe of a Germany that is already the dominant economy in the 12-nation community and is rapidly becoming the main political player in a emerging Eastern Europe.

For France and Britain, the implications are particularly potent. The two have played worried spectators in the fast-moving German drama of recent weeks, and many experts see a single Germany gradually nudging them off the center stage of European politics.

So far, Paris and London have urged a cautious approach to German reunification, but neither appears to have designed a long-term strategy to deal with the new challenge, as if they are counting on their status as Western Europe's only nuclear powers to maintain their political influence.

As the special relationship between Paris and Bonn shows signs of strain, longstanding differences between France and Britain over European integration have stood in the way of a new relationship between Paris and London that might be a counterweight to growing German power.

The result has been mounting frustration in both Britain and France. "I'm very struck by the rise of anti-German feeling that seems to be rather fashionable among the French elites," said Dominique Moisi, deputy director of the French Institute for International Relations.

Writing in *The Independent*, a London daily, a respected columnist, Peter Jenkins, said Britain's voice now counted for little in Europe. "By giving the impression that she is opposed to German unity," he said, "Mrs. Thatcher has condemned Britain to a marginal role in the management of that change."

In contrast, having first reacted with alarm to the prospect of German reunification, many smaller European countries, including several occupied by the Nazis in World War II, now appear to have come to terms with still greater German influence over the European Community.

Jan Sampiemon, a columnist at *NRC Handelsblad* of Rotterdam, said younger Dutch men and women did not view Germany with fear. "People say a united Germany will represent an economic threat, but if anything the Netherlands will profit," he said. "People say we will become an economic extension of Germany, but we already are that."

In Belgium, which has been invaded by Germany twice in this century, time has also healed many wounds. "Germans are members of the European family," said René Raindorf, a 71-year-old retired civil servant who spent the final year of the last war in Auschwitz. "You cannot make children responsible for the sins of their grandfathers. If unification is carried out carefully, I'm for it."

Italy, which has always kept a low profile in European affairs, thinks that German reunification has become, in the words of Foreign Minister Gianni de Michelis, "the only possible way to prevent Central Europe from becoming even more destabilized than it is now."

Document 9:

On 20 February 1990, Prime Minister Modrow informed the Round Table of the outcome of his visit to Bonn. After heated discussion, the Round Table rejected the accession of the GDR under Article 23 of the Basic Law and pressed for future demilitarization.

Round Table Decision on German Policy, 20 February 1990

(Source: H. Herles, ed., *Vom Runden Tisch zum Parlament*, Bonn, 1990, 168)

The Round Table resolves:

1. A future Germany's membership in NATO is in conflict with the aim of German unity within the framework of a peaceful European order and is therefore rejected on principle. Demilitarized status will be sought for a future unified German state.

2. It is possible to end the division of Europe only if existing borders with European neighbors are not called into question. Thus a precondition of German unity is a joint declaration by both German states that unconditionally recognizes existing borders, especially the Oder-Neisse border [with Poland], and guarantees their security from Germany's perspective.

3. Annexation of the GDR or individual states to the Federal Republic under Article 23 through an extension of the territory under the jurisdiction of the Basic Law of the FRG is rejected. . . .

Document 10:

Motivated by electoral concern for expellee votes, Chancellor Kohl's reluctance to recognize the Oder-Neisse frontier created a storm of international and domestic protest. In an interview with a conservative German paper, Prime Minister Tadeusz Mazowiecki demanded secure borders and Polish participation in unification talks.

Polish Demands for Secure Borders, 5 March 1990

(Source: "Polen läßt sich in der Frage der Grenzen auf keine Diskussion ein," *Welt*, 5 March 1990)

Welt: You expect the FRG to recognize Poland's western border. Why are you not content with de-facto recognition, since the frontier divides entire towns like the former Berlin Wall? Should one redraw the final course of the frontier in the spirit of peace?

Mazowiecki: We shall not enter into any discussions on the question of the Polish frontier. I have emphasized several times that, not only for us, the stability of European borders is a precondition for that European stability which no rational person wants to endanger. Concerning the divided towns, I hope that we shall soon succeed in reintroducing local border traffic, restoring the freedom of movement for the inhabitants of those towns; later – though still soon – we shall introduce far-reaching measures to facilitate personal trips. . . .

Welt: Does Poland fear a united Germany, even if it cannot be compared to its predecessors?

Mazowiecki: Poland does not fear a united Germany, in as long as it emerges within the framework of a process which does not disturb the European balance of power and creates a new European security system, a process which will therefore be embedded in European integration. However, Poland would be afraid of a Germany that is only insufficiently tied to Europe as well as a Germany which does not take a completely clear stand on the question of the security of its neighbors. Therefore we also want Poland to be present during that part of the six-power conference which will discuss Polish problems and the safety of its borders. There cannot be any doubt that we have a right to this presence – in Europe too much injustice has sprung from vital interests being decided over the heads of the countries concerned.

Therefore we also want a contractual confirmation of the inviolability of the Polish frontier through a treaty, initialled by both German states and later ratified by a united Germany. . . .

Welt: To what degree does Poland intend to integrate itself in the West? Do you feel attracted by the confederation, a political union, proposed by Mitterrand or would you prefer a potential economic union?

Mazowiecki: We wish the most extensive possible integration of all of Europe. How far this can go, is difficult to judge at present moment. History has accelerated, but the different factors can often not yet be grasped concretely. They are psychological and historical in nature. Concering concrete questions, we have declared we are joining the Council of Europe, and we are striving for association status with the European Community. In the future we aim for full membership in the EC.

Document 11:

The former bloc parties, including the SED successor PDS, the re-founded SPD, the DSU (supported by the West German CSU), and the citizens' movements competed in the election. The political rivals clashed on the path to unity, NATO membership and social reforms.

Synopsis of GDR Election Platforms, March 1990

(Source: H. Müller-Enbergs, *Volkskammerwahlen in der DDR 1990*, Berlin, 1990, 16ff.)

Christian Democratic Union (CDU):

We want a CDU which is a party for Europe. Within the confederative structure of a common European house, we aspire to the unity of the German nation within its existing borders, while guaranteeing the interests of our neighbors. We believe that through disarmament extending to demilitarization and dismantling of the military alliances, Germany can become a bridge between East and West and a stabilizing factor for security and cooperation on our continent.

Democratic Awakening (DA):

We are unable to accept the division of Germany. We wish to overcome this division under the following conditions:

- Recognition of existing borders;

- Right to self-determination for Germans in the GDR and the FRG;

- Exclusively peaceful, joint decisions with our European neighbors and the victorious powers [of World War II].

We see the path to unification leading from a treaty-based union between the two German states through a confederation of states to a federal state. . . .

German Social Union (DSU):

Our task is to achieve freedom and unity for the entire German people. We want to overcome the division of our fatherland in peace, and live together in a united Europe in the future.

We reject the threat and use of force as a political means. We recognize existing power relationships. However, the power of facts also includes the German nation's will to unification; this will has maintained its historical strength. We seek the unification of Germany based on the principle of self-determination.

Berlin will become the capital of a united Germany. . . .

Bündnis 90 [Alliance 90].

Since the Wall fell, the social balance of the GDR and the political balance of the FRG have faltered. The political balance in Europe is threatened.

We recognize these trends and dangers, and do not cover them up with words. Citizens' movements know from their own experience that democracy can exist only if social rights, equal opportunity, nonviolence, and solidarity are guaranteed. This also applies to democracy in Germany. This is why we believe that German unification must be based upon a society showing solidarity, guaranteeing social stability for the GDR population. A prerequisite for German unification is the practice of democratic self-determination in the GDR. Unification in freedom is possible only if unity comes with equality. And this can only happen if we come together in a reciprocal process. We do not see the efforts to achieve a newly united Germany as a hindrance to European unity; instead, we see the aspirations for demilitarization as a motivating force supporting it.

We believe the following comprise a national contribution to a peaceful European order:

• Demilitarization of both German states;

• Passive membership in both the Warsaw Pact and NATO; active support for the transformation of military alliances into political alliances;

• Guaranteeing the Oder-Neisse border with Poland;

• Social welfare and security for all, the right to work, the right to housing in both German states;

• Democratization of the economy; participation in business and local government;

• Just and fair economic relations with the countries of the Third World.

We reject a special solution for Germany leading to NATO membership.

Free Democratic Party (FDP):

Rapid establishment of German unification:

• Immediate economic and monetary union directly following the Volkskammer elections;

• Reestablishment of the Länder of Brandenburg, Berlin, Mecklenburg, Saxony, Saxony-Anhalt, and Thuringia;

• Creation of an all-German national assembly for the purpose of establishing the political and legal foundations for unification within the 1990 borders;

• Inclusion of German unification as a stabilizing factor in the European unification process. . . .

Party of Democratic Socialism (former SED):

The PDS is committed to directing the historical process of German unification towards overcoming the division of Europe and creating a progressive, social, and democratic Germany. . . .

First: The social values and achievements of the GDR must not be sacrificed. We include among them the right to work, our system of facilities for children, free education up to university level, cooperatives and peoples' property in industry, agriculture, and other branches of the economy, and cultural identity, as well as anti-fascism and internationalism. . . .

Second, change must not occur only in the GDR. We do not want mass unemployment and existential fears, exclusion from professions for political reasons, prohibition of the Communist Party, a right to lockouts, "Paragraph 218,"* housing and real estate speculation, reversal of the land reform, authorization of neo-fascist groups, any doubts at all about the inviolability of the Oder-Neisse border, or existence at the expense of other peoples.

Third, it is necessary for the GDR to participate in the unification process as a sovereign state. These goals cannot be achieved if it is annexed to the FRG. . . .

In this spirit, we support proposals to gradually overcome the division of the German nation through:

- a trans-systemic treaty community and an economic, monetary, and social union with links to the common interests of the working class in both states;

- creation of confederative structures while preserving independence;

- gradual transition to a bloc-free, demilitarized German confederation of states within the framework of European unification.

Social Democratic Party (SPD):

Germans, like all peoples, have the right to self-determination. We Social Democrats want to see Germany newly united in a peaceful, free form. A federative German state should emerge in cooperation with our neighbors and the Allies, constituted democratically and committed to the European anti-Fascist tradition. The German unification process should be part of European integration, and should help overcome the division of our continent.

The reserved rights of the Four Powers that apply to Germany as a whole and to Berlin must be replaced with a peace treaty, which will serve simultaneously as a building block in a peaceful European order. A newly united Germany within its present borders, guaranteeing the western border of Poland established in 1950, should promote understanding and balance in the European family of nations. Common historical experience links us with the peoples of Eastern Europe. For this reason, we advocate that Eastern European states newly emerged from the democratization process be able, if they so desire, to become, like ourselves, members of the European Community as quickly as possible.

Demilitarization and eventual dissolution of the blocs are linked to German and European unification. A new European security system should be created through radical disarmament and military reorganization; its remaining weapons should no longer be capable of aggression but only of defense. The principles of the Helsinki Final Act, the CSCE, and the European Council provide the basis and framework for this process. We seek a peaceful common European order on the basis of joint security, inviolable borders, and respect for the integrity and sovereignty of all states in Europe. This order can only be

---

*West German prohibition of abortion.

erected together, working as partners. The German people will occupy an equal place in it.

The aim of Social Democratic policies is a European confederation with open borders, in which freedom, democracy, and social justice have been achieved.

Document 12:

Chancellor Kohl personally campaigned in the East for the "Alliance for Germany," made up of CDU, DA, and DSU. To gain votes, he raised high expectations for prosperity through a monetary union and political unity, promising to protect the weak through social security.

Kohl's Campaign Promises, March 1990

(Source: *Zeitung zur Wahl: Informationen zur Allianz für Deutschland*, March 1990, 2)

The events of the past weeks and months have moved us Germans; in fact, many of us have been overwhelmed by our emotions. We do not need to be ashamed of this, for we are experiencing events of incredible historic dimension.

It is true: Never before since our nation was divided have we been so close to our goal – the political unity of all Germans in freedom. This is the achievement, above all, of the people in East Germany, who, through consistent peaceful protest, forced a Communist dictatorship to its knees. You can truly be proud of this fact. . . .

Peaceful Revolution

This magnificent event confirms what was said by Germans in the East and the West: "We are one people."

What we now need are sobriety and rationality. We must not lose our patience in the coming weeks. The peaceful revolution of the Germans which has been admired throughout the world cannot be called into question.

Freedom and Unity

The important thing is that the first free and secret elections in the GDR will demonstrate the people's wish for democracy, for unity in freedom. The elections must result in a truly free parliament, and this in turn must form a responsible government capable of action.

I am convinced that this will happen. It is all the more important, in the time remaining until the elections, that voters become aware of the historically significant decision before them. The people in East Germany have clearly shown through their demonstrations that they no longer want socialism, that they want freedom and unity, and that they also have concrete ideas about the future economic and social order.

In short, the people in East Germany know that a social market economy can bring them – as in West Germany – freedom, affluence, social security, and a peaceful and secure future.

Herein lies the key to answering the question of which party to vote for. Each and every voter should see whether the commitment to a social market economy is real or merely lip service, and he or she should seriously consider with whom that social market economy should be brought about.

Clear Commitment to a Social Market Economy . . . .

The parties of the "Alliance for Germany," that is, Democratic Awakening (DA), the German Social Union (DSU) and the Christian Democratic Union (CDU), have made a clear, unmistakable commitment to a social market economy. Whoever votes for them will get a strong advocate for what the people in the GDR ardently desire: They want to enjoy a happy future in their ancestral homeland.

The introduction of a social market economy in the GDR is the basic prerequisite for the implementation of the monetary union which I have proposed. This offer means that West Germany is prepared to give its own extraordinary response to the extraordinary events and challenges in East Germany. In the end, much more than mere questions of economic development are at stake. The important thing now is to give a clear, unmistakable signal of hope and encouragement.

The Strongest Asset: The D-Mark

For the FRG, this offer of a monetary and economic union, unparalleled in history, means that we will introduce our strongest economic asset – the D-mark.

In this way we are enabling the people of the GDR to participate directly in what the people of the Federal Republic developed and attained through decades of hard work. This will create the conditions necessary for rapid improvements in the East German standard of living. The D-mark, one of the hardest and most stable currencies in the world, is the basis of the affluence and economic competitiveness of the Federal Republic. In the future, it will also provide this basis for the GDR and for our common and united fatherland.

It is of utmost importance that we maintain the strength of this basis in our common interest.

The Foundation Must Remain Solid

Consequently, the monetary union makes sense only if comprehensive market economy reforms are carried out in the GDR without delay. Without them, economic renewal in the GDR cannot succeed. The flagrant failure of the socialist planned economy in East Germany can only be eliminated by a market economy with a socially and ecologically oriented reorganization of society. . . .

Many people in East Germany are afraid of ending up at the bottom of the social ladder with the introduction of a social market economy. I take these concerns, particularly voiced by senior citizens and people threatened with unemployment, very seriously. I assure you of

Social Balance

A social market economy always means social balance as well. It is, of course, our goal that the retired generation in the GDR, which carried the burden of reconstruction after the war, also be guaranteed security in their old age. It is also our goal to make appropriate compensation and vocational training available to the unemployed. This is not possible without active support from the Federal Republic.

I am convinced that together we can successfully direct further economic and social development in both parts of Germany, and that we will indeed do this. Citizens of East Germany can count on our support and, above all, on mine.

I am aware of the problems this great challenge brings. But we have the strength and the desire to meet this challenge together.

Document 13:

In support of PDS criticism of unity, the Soviet Foreign Ministry intervened in the East German campaign by warning against rapid unification under Article 23 of the West German constitution.

The Soviet Foreign Ministry's Warning Against Annexation, 14 March 1990

(Source: *Blätter für deutsche und internationale Politik*, 1990, 505ff.)

The process of rapprochement between the FRG and the GDR that has recently begun, and the real prospects for a unification of Germany that have emerged, have placed the German question once again at the forefront of world politics. Public attention today concentrates on such central elements as the conclusion of a peace treaty, the military and political status of the future Germany, as well as on its borders, preservation of the current stability and balance of power on the continent, continued development of the pan-European process, and finally, creation of new structures for collective security. Because of their vast implications, each of these problems – both individually and in their entirety – can be resolved only on the basis of agreed-upon principles.

In view of this, it was decided at Ottawa to create an appropriate negotiating mechanism, with the participation of the two German states, the USSR, Great Britain, the USA, and France, within the framework of which all participants would act in accordance with the character and extent of their rights and obligations. Of course, this does not exclude the participation of any other European state in one or another form in the articulation of issues of interest to them that concern a peaceful solution to the German question. Particular attention should be paid to synchronizing the rapprochement and possible unification of the two German states with the overall European process. Such extensive tasks, if they are of course approached with due responsibility, cannot be accomplished all at once even through the efforts of many participants. Therefore, there can be only a step-by-step development, without artificial coercion and without creating an atmosphere of time pressure surrounding the construction of German unity. In fact, this is assumed by the majority of interested states.

Apparently, Bonn also agrees. However, certain groups in the FRG have continually attempted to exclude a number of potential participants from the settlement of the German question and to present the world community, including the Four Powers, with a fait accompli.

Some CDU-CSU politicians see the key to accomplishing this goal in applying Article 23 of the German Basic Law, which makes it possible for the GDR to join the FRG in parts, as individual states, or as an entire republic. In other words, they aim at the usurpation of one German state by the other. . . .

From whichever side one considers application of Article 23, such a procedure would be unlawful and unacceptable. Questions that, in truth, have a fateful significance for all of Europe cannot be resolved on the basis of the constitution or other domestic acts of the FRG, they cannot be the work of Germany alone.

We must not forget that under the Potsdam Treaty, the Soviet Union, France, Great Britain, and the USA still retain their rights and responsibilities for Germany as a whole, and for ensuring that Germany will never again be a threat to peace. It is their direct obligation to implement these basic conditions, together with the FRG and the GDR, in the form of reliable international legal guarantees.

We must also consider that the Potsdam Treaty unmistakably assumed that restoration of German statehood had to proceed within an orderly, democratic framework; that the order and conditions of unification of the two German states would be determined on the basis of an agreement among all interested states, especially the Four Powers. Later, these basic conditions were anchored in corresponding treaties between the FRG and the three western powers, and the GDR and the Soviet Union; these treaties declared that the Four Powers retained the full extent of their rights and responsibilities in regard to Germany as a whole. This was also true for West Berlin, with its special status, which was established by the quadripartite treaty.

Thus it is not incorporation of one German state by the other, not premature, unilateral action dictated by economic calculation, but only united efforts by all interested parties that can guarantee a solution to the highly complicated German question that is acceptable to all sides and includes long-term prospects. It is further undeniable that the overwhelming majority of European states, supported by the conditions of the Helsinki Final Act, see the preservation and consolidation of stability on the continent as the primary goal. . . .

Document 14:

Since Willy Brandt was highly respected as former mayor of Berlin and as the chancellor associated with easing tensions, hundreds of thousands came to his campaign speeches in East Germany. For the SPD, he reviewed the election campaign before the National Press Association in Bonn.

Brandt's Reflection on the Election Campaign, 15 March 1990

(Source: W. Brandt, *"...was zusammengehört": Reden zu Deutschland*, Bonn 1990, 135ff.)

1. No matter what might otherwise separate the parties in Germany, they should have a common interest in seeing democracy emerge as the overwhelming winner in the East German elections. And in seeing the first freely elected government determined in these elections arrange what is necessary in the interest of German unity – without culpable delay and without irresponsible haste.

Precipitous and pretentious references to Article 23 of the Basic Law alone have not proven an ideal way, but entirely the wrong track. The people of the GDR, for whose benefit the aforementioned constitutional stipulation exists, might get the impression that no one cares about their opinions on the process of unification anymore. Allies of West Germany and others throughout the world were annoyed, since they did not feel sufficiently informed (or even felt that they were to be ignored) about the content and timing of German plans. . . .

2. National unity is primarily a concern of Germans, but it is – as we are now being reminded – not only a German matter. It is particularly important to explain, quickly and clearly, how united Germany will be embedded into European and security policies.

In the meantime, it has become clear to many that, leading up to political unification, even the inter-German economic and monetary union raises many questions which cannot be answered without reliable consultation within the European Community, according to the "1 in 12" formula, if that is desired.

Negotiations under the "2 plus 4" formula have begun on procedural issues. They will need to deal primarily with questions of security policy and issues arising due to the lack of a peace treaty. If any authority for Germany as a whole remains, this can only be legally superseded domestically by a constitution and internationally by treaties.

Negotiations and consultation in the Helsinki process (according to the "2 in 35" formula) should not be judged merely as a compulsory exercise but as a necessary contribution to the settlement of European affairs.

I am also in favor of a "2 plus 9" formula which would express the particular significance of a reunified Germany for its immediate neighbors. It need not bother us if certain neighbors take their place at several different tables due to their specific situations and problems, as long as the new state of peace is not harmed or threatened.

Dilettantish or worse treatment of the issue of the German-Polish border has made us recognize once again the weight of certain problems, even 45 years after the war has ended. The citizens of the GDR have been very active regarding this question.

3. I do not feel it was necessary to export so many bad West German campaign habits into, as far as voting is concerned, "virgin" East German territory. I believe, for example, that it was totally inappropriate to try to intimidate East German voters by implying that West German aid would depend on their behavior in the voting booth ("no Kohl, no dough"). And the repeated insinuation that Social Democrats are very close to the Communists formerly in power (or that they have even been infiltrated by them!) can only leave behind a feeling of bitterness. Especially when we recall the thousands of fellow party members imprisoned by those in power at the time, and the hundreds who died. . . .

Aside from all other concerns, the chances for the parties running in the GDR elections were particularly unequal. Especially for those who couldn't even count on publicity for their campaign events in the newspapers of the former bloc parties. One-sided West German media broadcasting was also criticized.

I cannot rule out that some feel inhibited by procedures of which I am not aware at present. We should have an objective discussion on this. And I do not mean a discussion which aims to explain away rioting during a colonial war. The intention must be to give more consideration in the future to the fact that, in the transition phases before us, the self-esteem of the people of the GDR should not be damaged; instead, a feeling of equal partnership is to be strengthened.

Document 15:

The Volkskammer election returns revealed overwhelming support for unification and a clear majority for a rapid monetary union. The Alliance for Germany, led by the CDU, won a surprising victory, particularly in the south and among blue-collar workers.

Results of the Parliamentary Elections in East Germany, 18 March 1990[*]

(Source: taz, *DDR Journal*, 2, Berlin, 1990, 154f.)

Party	Percent	Seats
SPD [Social Democrats]	21.84	87
PDS [ex-Communists]	16.33	65
Alliance for Germany (total)	48.15	193
CDU [Christian Democrats]	40.91	164
DA [Democratic Awakening]	0.92	4
DSU [German Social Union]	6.32	25
Bündnis 90 [Civic Movement]	2.90	12
Liberal Bloc [LDPD and FDP]	5.28	21
Greens/Independent Women's Association	1.96	8
others[**]	3.57	16

Document 16:

To discuss German unification, Prime Minister Margaret Thatcher invited Foreign Minister Douglas Hurd and well known authorities like Gordon Craig and Timothy Garton Ash to her residence at Chequers. The publication of the secret protocol in July created a scandal, because it documented British prejudices against Germany.

---

[*] preliminary official returns of 19 March 1990; voter turnout: 93.22 percent

[**] fifteen smaller groups, including farmers' associations, nationalists and the United Left.

Charles Powell on the Chequers Meeting, 24 March 1990

(Source: H. James and M. Stone, eds., *When the Wall Came Down: Reactions to German Unification*, New York, 1992, 233ff.)

Introduction

The Prime Minister said that Europe had come to the end of the postwar period. Important decisions and choices about its future lay ahead. . . . We needed to reach an assessment of what a united Germany would be like. History was a guide, but one could not just extrapolate. We also had to devise a framework for Europe's future, taking account of German unification and the sweeping changes in the Soviet Union and Eastern Europe. It was important to get the balance right between the lessons of the past and the opportunities of the future. She would welcome the wisdom and advice of those present.

Who are the Germans?

We started by talking about the Germans themselves and their characteristics. Like other nations, they had certain characteristics, which you could identify from the past and expect to find in the future. It was easier – and more pertinent to the present discussion – to think of the less happy ones: their insensitivity to the feelings of others (most noticeable in their behavior over the Polish border), their obsession with themselves, a strong inclination to self-pity, and a longing to be liked. Some even less flattering attributes were also mentioned as an abiding part of the German character: in alphabetical order, Angst, aggressiveness, assertiveness, bullying, egotism, inferiority complex, sentimentality. Two further aspects of the German character were cited as reasons for concern about the future. First, a capacity for excess, to overdo things, to kick over the traces. Second, a tendency to over-estimate their own strength and capabilities. . . .

Have the Germans Changed?

It was as well to be aware of all these characteristics. But there was a strong school of thought among those present that today's Germans were very different from their predecessors. It was argued that our basic perception of Germans related to a period of German history running from Bismarck until 1945. This was the phase of imperial Germany, characterized by neurotic self-assertiveness, high birth-rate, a closed economy, a chauvinist culture. . . . But 1945 was quite different and marked a sea-change. There was no longer a sense of historic mission, no ambitions for physical conquest, no more militarism. Education and the writing of history had changed. There was an innocence of and about the past on the part of the new generation of Germans. We should have no real worries about them.

This view was not accepted by everyone. It still had to be asked how a cultured and cultivated nation had allowed itself to be brain-washed into barbarism. If it had happened once, could it not happen again? Apprehension about Germany did not relate just to the Nazi period but to the whole post-Bismarckian era, and inevitably caused deep distrust. The way in which the Germans currently used their elbows and threw their weight about in the European Community suggested that a lot had still not changed. While we all admired and indeed envied what the Germans had achieved in the last 45 years, the fact was that their institutions had not yet been seriously tested by adversity such as a major calamity. We could not tell how Germans would react in such circumstances. In sum, no one had serious misgivings about the present leaders or political elite of Germany. But what about 10, 15 or 20 years from now? Could some of the unhappy characteristics of the past re-emerge with just as destructive consequences?

What will be the Consequences of Reunification?

We looked more closely at two particular aspects of the future: the consequences of unification and Germany's role in Eastern Europe.

Even those most disposed to look at the bright side admitted to some qualms about what unification would mean for German behavior in Europe. We could not expect a united Germany to think and act in exactly the same way as the Federal Republic which we had known for the last 45 years – and this would be true even though a united Germany would almost certainly inherit the FRG's institutions. The Germans would not necessarily think more dangerously, but they would think differently. There was already evident a kind of triumphalism in German thinking and attitudes which would be uncomfortable for the rest of us. Reference was also made to Günter Grass's comment: in the end reunification will get everyone against us, and we all know what happens when people are against us.

Then, too, there were reasons to worry about the effects on the character of a united Germany of bringing in 17 million predominantly Protestant north-Germans brought up under a mendacious orthodoxy. How would this alter the basically Catholic Rhineland basis of the post-war FRG, with its political and economic center of gravity increasingly in the south and west? We could not assume that a united Germany would fit quite so comfortably into Western Europe as the FRG. There would be a growing inclination to resurrect the concept of *Mitteleuropa*, with Germany's role being that of broker between East and West. It was noticeable that Chancellor Kohl now spoke of German's partners in East *and* West.

That tendency could be strengthened by the effect of unification on Germany's party system. The vote for the conservative alliance in East Germany could be seen as a vote for quick unification rather than for the values and policies of the West German CDU. There was a strong pacifist, neutralist, anti-nuclear constituency in East Germany, which could have a considerable effect on the views of a united Germany. That effect could be to make a united Germany both less "Western" and less politically stable than the FRG. At worst, the extremes at both ends of the political spectrum could grow in influence, leading to a return to Weimar politics (although no one argued this with any great conviction). . . .

Conclusions

Where did this leave us? No formal conclusions were drawn. The weight of the evidence and the argument favoured those who were optimistic about life with a united Germany. We were reminded that in 1945 our aim had been a united Germany shorn of its eastern provinces but under democratic and non-Communist government, with the states of Eastern Europe free to choose their own governments. We had failed to get that in 1945, but had won it now. Far from being agitated, we ought to be pleased. We were also reminded that Anglo-German antagonisms since the fall of Bismarck had been injurious to Europe as a whole and must not be allowed to revive once more. When it came to failings and unhelpful characteristics, the Germans had their share and perhaps more, but in contrast to the past, they were much readier to recognize and admit this themselves.

The overall message was unmistakable: we should be nice to the Germans. But even the optimists had some unease, not for the present and the immediate future, but for what might lie further down the road than we can yet see.

Document 17:

In an interview with a Bonn paper, political scientist Alfred Grosser tried to calm French elite fears of losing leadership in Europe. Worried about dealing with a larger neighbor, the Paris government insisted on the europeanization of German unity.

Alfred Grosser on French Fears, 28 March 1990

(Source: T. Klau, "Angst or dem bösen "Boche" geht in Frankreich wieder um," *Bonner Rundschau*, 28 March 1990)

During the last weeks the press in France has rediscovered an ancient topic: the French fear of the Germans. "Some politicians have lost all sense; the German colors wave on the title pages of magazines like on military command-posts; caricatures of the fat Mr. Kohl fill newspaper pages," the liberal paper *Le Monde* described the sudden mood-swing. In French fantasies, the *Boche*, the bad German, has returned.

The most prominent German specialist in France, political scientist Alfred Grosser, denies that such headlines adequately mirror French feelings towards the rapid unification of their neighbors. "The French elite lags forty years behind the mood of the population," grumbles Grosser, who escaped as an eight-year-old with his parents from Hitler's Germany and nonetheless works tirelessly for Franco-German reconciliation.

The professor, who lives in Paris, emphasizes that for some time surveys have named the Germans the most popular neighbors of the French. Yet French elites continue to be schooled in "absurd and outdated foreign-political thought patterns" and still see in today's Germany the Prussian bogeyman of yesterday: "Instead of opening their eyes and figuring out that the GDR is turning west, they speak about the eastward drift of Germany." . . . .

The political scientist considers it inevitable that the importance of France will decline in comparison to its German neighbor. Bonn is becoming less handicapped by the German past, German economic power is growing, and in the age of disarmament France's *force de frappe*, its coddled nuclear force, can no longer make up for this loss of influence. The restoration of a German national state only adds momentum to this trend. . . .

Yet Grosser and many other commentators criticize the manner in which Chancellor Kohl promotes the unification process and surprises France, its politically most important neighbor, time and again by unannounced plans and statements.

"With boorish unconcern," the chancellor forgets that Germany's fate also involves its neighbors and that so far consultation with Paris had been the highest political imperative. After the GDR election, *Le Monde* complained about this in an analysis which also attacked the German policy of François Mitter and for omissions and superfluous ambiguities. The feeling between the Elysee-Palace and the Chancellor's Office in Bonn resembles a "marital crisis, one of those silent alienations which grow and feed on themselves."

Document 18:

Frankfurt sociology professor Jürgen Habermas is one of West Germany's best-known intellectuals, respected far beyond left-wing circles. After the disappointing GDR election outcome, he attacked economic nationalism and called for a new constitution.

Jürgen Habermas's Critique of D-mark Nationalism, 30 March, 1990

(Source: *Die Zeit*, 30 March 1990)

Three months after the democratic revolution in East Germany, they are shaking hands – the politicians, who have blossomed into business people, and the intellectuals, who have become the singers of German unity. Günter Grass is denounced in the literary pages, and the mere sight of a left-wing economics professor on a talk show is enough to turn friendly middle class ladies and gentlemen into a mob. The self-tormenting and superfluous issue is now gaining attention: What will become of German identity? Are economic problems steering the unification process down a rational path? Or has the D-mark taken on a libidinal connotation, emotionally overrated in such a way that a type of economic nationalism is overwhelming republican consciousness? The question is still open but demands an answer, in view of the psychological damage which the campaigns of West German parties have already caused in the eastern territory.

It is difficult to refrain from writing a satire on the first blossoms of such chubby-cheeked D-mark nationalism. The crowing Chancellor [Kohl] let the frail Prime Minister [de Maizière] know the conditions under which he would be prepared to buy the GDR. Using monetary politics, he encouraged the blackmailed voters of the "Alliance for Germany." He used constitutional politics to set the stage for annexation under Article 23 of the Basic Law. His foreign policy consisted of protecting the expression "Victorious Powers" and not responding to the question of Poland's western border. . . . [There is] only one unit of account for all issues. German interests are weighed and implemented in D-marks. To be sure, this code isn't as bad as the language of dive bombers. But in any case, the mere sight of this German show of muscle is obscene.

I. In order to understand how things could get to this point, one has to recall the internal situation of West Germany, caught totally unprepared by a wave of refugees across the Hungarian border, and the response to it, the opening of the Wall. For all the rhetoric, who would have expected anything like reunification any longer, and who would have wanted it anyway?

Karl Jaspers[*] put it clearly in 1960: "The history of the German nation-state is over." This creed was not shared only by liberals and left-wing intellectuals at the time. Wolfgang Mommsen[**] offered a diverse picture of the "shifts in the national identity of the Germans" in West Germany, in an article published in 1983. While first-generation politicians, the "fathers of the Basic Law," still believed they could perpetuate the nation-state tradition of the Weimar Republic, thereby sustaining the lesser-German Bismarckian Reich without any far-reaching consequences, the broad mass of the population developed a more pragmatic sense of itself in the 1950s and 1960s, one that put the question of national identity on a back burner.

According to Mommsen, this consciousness is shaped by four elements: (1) no longer making an issue of the recent past and defining one's own location in a rather ahistorical manner; (2) fiercely disassociating one's own system from those of Eastern Europe, i.e. perpetuating the historically rooted anti-commmunist syndrome; (3) continuing an orientation toward the values and behavioral

---

[*] leading post-war philosopher.

[**] prominent liberal historian.

patterns of Western civilization, especially the "protecting power," the USA; and last, but not least, (4) pride in one's economic achievements. Mommsen suspected that the heart of the sense of political identity lay in this element, the self-confidence of a successful economic nation. And that it provided a substitute for the largely absent sense of national pride. . . .

From an all-German perspective, the barrier which hindered the national identity from taking on the repressed component of West German economic pride has been removed [by the fall of the wall]. With the inter-German monetary union, all Germans can now identify with the potency of the expanded imperium of the D-mark. The "Alliance for Germany" seems to have tapped this unexploited emotional territory, in which nationalistic blossoms sprout from the arrogance of economic supremacy. . . .

III. The alternative to this variety of economic nationalism is to strengthen that component of our self-image whereby "even West German citizens approached the standard Western form of national identity" in the 1980s. Identifying with the principles and institutions of our constitution demands an agenda for the unification process that gives priority to citizens' non-mediated right of self-determination. That means priority over a cleverly introduced annexation that is, in the end, purely administrative and totally disregards an essential condition for establishing any civic nation namely, the public act of a carefully considered democratic decision, in both Germanies, by the citizens themselves. This founding act can only be implemented intentionally and consciously, assuming we forego unification under Article 23 of the Basic Law (which provides for annexation of the "other part of Germany"). . . .

Not until it is possible to choose freely among alternatives can we gain an awareness of something that is widespread, in any case, among youth – namely, that the establishment of one single civic nation on the former territories of the Federal Republic and the GDR can by no means be prejudged through pre-political conditions of language, culture, or history. This is why people want at least to be asked.

I consider the arguments of my friend Ulrich Oevermann[***] to be totally off the mark. He supports the theory that "the revolutionary processes in the GDR have virtually posed anew the incomplete task of the political constitution of a nation-state." It is supposed to be a case of a "catch up" revolution, but not in terms of society and democratic legal order; rather, in terms of a delayed nation which finally achieves its true form as a nation-state. Especially if you decidedly reject the "transposition of the political onto the level of culture and intellect," as Oevermann does, it is inconsistent to blur M. R. Lepsius's[****] distinction between a civic nation and an ethnic nation.

[***] conservative literary critic.

[****] well-known sociologist.

Unlike the classical nation-states of the West, in the successor states of the Old German Reich or Bismarck's lesser-German Reich, the political socialization of the citizens never corresponded exactly to the pre-political conditions of an "historic, material existence of a unified nation." Strong tensions existed, as Lepsius noted, between the "political frame of reference of the people as supporters of the political rights of the rulers" and the pre-political "frame of reference of the people as an ethnic, cultural, and socioeconomic unit." "The recognition of this tension is the basis by which a civil society legitimizes itself democratically. Any attempt to equate the 'demos,' or populace, as a supporter of political sovereignty, with a specific 'ethnos' will lead to repression or forced assimilation of other ethnic, cultural, religious, or socioeconomic segments of the population within a political unit." . . .

Auschwitz can and should remind Germans, on whatever state territories they may establish themselves, that they cannot count on the continuity of their history. With that monstrous break in continuity, Germans have forfeited the chance to base their political identity on something other than universalistic civic principles. In light of these principles, the national tradition can no longer be adopted indiscriminately, but rather critically and self-critically. The post-traditional identity then loses its substantial, uninhibited character; it exists only in the mode of public, discursive debate on the interpretation of constitutional patriotism which, depending on the historical conditions, must be put in concrete terms.

In his article "The National Illusion," Reinhard Merkel[*****] hits the nail on the head: "Up to now, German nationalist intellectuals have rejected the lessons of the Enlightenment, the French Revolution, and Ernest Renan that the concept of 'nation' in democratic states – if it means anything at all – cannot mean cutting oneself off from the outside behind ethnic peculiarities; instead, it must be the symbol of an internal 'daily plebiscite' for democratic participation in political organization."

Document 19:

The draft constitution produced by the Round Table was completed on 4 April 1990. Among those contributing to the text were Ulrich Preuss (Bremen), Rosemarie Will (East Berlin), and author Christa Wolf. The working group suggested far-reaching guarantees of basic social rights and the rights of citizens' movements.

Round Table Draft of an East German Constitution, 4 April 1990

(Source: *Blätter für deutsche und internationale Politik*, 1990, 731ff.)

[*****] left-wing journalist, writing in *Die Zeit*.

Preamble

Based on the humanist tradition contributed to by the best women and men from all classes of our people, considering the responsibility of all Germans for their history and its consequences,

in the desire to live as peaceful, equal partners in the community of nations, involved in the process of European unity

in which the German people will also achieve national unity, convinced that the opportunity for self-determined, responsible action is the highest form of freedom, based on revolutionary renewal,

determined to develop a democratic community based in solidarity that ensures the dignity and freedom of the individual, guarantees equal rights for all, ensures equality of the sexes, and protects our natural environment,

the citizens of the GDR grant themselves this constitution.

Chapter I: Human and Civil Rights

Article 1: (1) Human dignity is inviolable. The highest duty of the state is to respect and preserve it.

(2) All people owe one another recognition as equals. No one may be disadvantaged due to race, origin, nationality, language, gender, sexual orientation, social position, age, disability, religion, world view, or political convictions. . . .

Article 3: (1) Women and men enjoy equal rights.

(2) The state is obligated to take measures to ensure equal rights for women in the workplace and education, in the family, and in the area of social welfare.

Article 4: (1) All people have the right to life, physical autonomy, and respect for their right to a dignified death. The right to physical autonomy may be limited only by law. . . .

(3) Women have the right to self-determined pregnancy. The state protects unborn life through the availability of social assistance. . . .

Article 27: (1) All citizens have the right to work or to assistance in finding work.

(2) The citizen's right to freely dispose of his or her labor and freely choose a job is guaranteed. Public work and service obligations are permitted only for special purposes to be established by law. They must be equal for all. Women may be obligated to perform public service only in emergency situations. Military conscription is abolished. . . .

Article 33: (1) Protection of the natural environment as the basis of the existence of present and future generations is the duty of the state and all its citizens. National environmental policies must take preventive measures against the emergence of harmful environmental impact and work toward achieving sparing use and recycling of nonrenewable resources and limited energy consumption. . . .

Article 35: (1) Organizations devoted to public service that seek to influence public opinion (citizens' movements) enjoy special constitutional protection as promoters of independent social action, criticism, and supervision. . . .

Chapter II: Principles and Organs of the State

Article 41: (1) The GDR is a legally based, democratic, social federal state consisting of states. . . . Its goal is to create a peaceful order throughout Europe, in order to overcome the situation created in Germany through World War II on the basis of reconciliation with all nations persecuted and oppressed by Germans. Within this framework, the German people will itself determine how to structure the German state.

(2) The GDR declares its commitment to the goal of ensuring the unification of the two German states. . . .

Article 43: (1) The state flag of the GDR contains the colors black, red, and gold. The country's coat of arms is a depiction of the motto "Swords into Plowshares". . . .

Article 45: (1) The GDR calls for all efforts and measures aimed at balanced disarmament.

(2) Preparing for or carrying out a war of aggression is prohibited.

(3) Weapons may only be produced, transported, or brought into circulation with permission of the government. They may be exported only to countries involved in the same system of collective security. . . .

Article 132: (1) If unification is carried out by accession to the FRG, the conditions under which the Basic Law of the FRG will be applied to the present territory of the GDR must be determined by agreement. Fulfillment of the GDR's international, legal, and economic obligations must be ensured.

(2) To become valid, the agreement must be approved by a two-thirds majority of the Volkskammer and by plebiscite.

(3) This agreement shall include regulations on accelerated equalization of the economy of the part of the country presently comprising the territory of the GDR and of the standard of living of its population with conditions existing in the present area of the FRG. To implement the right of citizens of the GDR to participate in the democratic self-determination of the German people, an all-German constitutional assembly shall be the goal.

(4) The agreement shall further provide that the human and civil rights guaranteed in this constitution continue to apply on the present territory of the GDR, even if they are not contained in the Basic Law. . . .

Article 136: This constitution ceases to be in force on the day a constitution determined by an all-German constitutional assembly and approved by plebiscite goes into force, or on the day it ceases to be in force when the conditions of Article 132 are met.

Document 20:

On 12 April 1990, the newly elected East German parliament issued a declaration on the responsibility of Germans in East Germany regarding several dark chapters of German history.

Volkskammer Declaration on German History, 12 April 1990

(Source: *Deutschland Archiv*, 23, 1990, 794f.)

We, the first freely-elected representatives of the GDR, acknowledge the responsibility of Germans in the GDR for their history and their future, and unanimously declare to the world:

During the period of Nazi rule, Germans inflicted immeasurable suffering upon the peoples of the world. Nationalism and racial chauvinism led to genocide, particularly of the Jewry throughout Europe, of the peoples of the Soviet Union, the Polish people, and the Roma and Sinti peoples.

We must not permit this guilt to be forgotten. From it we derive our responsibility for the future.

1. The first freely elected parliament of the GDR acknowledges, in the name of the citizens of this country, that it shares responsibility for the humiliation, persecution, and murder of Jewish women, men, and children. We feel grief and shame in accepting responsibility for this historical burden on Germany.

We ask the world Jewry for forgiveness. We ask the people of Israel for forgiveness for the hypocrisy and animosity of official GDR policy toward the State of Israel and for the persecution and degradation of Jewish citizens in our country, which continued even after 1945.

We declare we will do everything possible to contribute to healing the physical and emotional suffering of survivors, and to speak out for just compensation of material losses. . . .

2. We, the representatives of the first freely elected parliament of the GDR, perceive an intense need to make the following declaration to the citizens of the Soviet Union:

We have not forgotten the horrendous suffering that the Germans inflicted upon the people of the Soviet Union during World War II. This violence which emanated from Germany also finally engulfed our own nation. We want to continue intensively the process of reconciliation between both peoples.

Therefore it will be our goal to integrate Germany into a common European security system in such a way that peace and security are guaranteed for our peoples. . . .

3. The Volkskammer of the GDR acknowledges the GDR's joint responsibility for suppression of the "Prague Spring" in 1968 by Warsaw Pact troops.

The illegal military intervention subjected the people of Czechoslovakia to great suffering, interrupting the democratization process in Eastern Europe for 20 years. The invasion by the *Volksarmee* took place in violation of Article 8 (2) of the constitution of the GDR. Fear and resignation kept us from preventing this violation of international law.

The first freely elected parliament of the GDR apologizes to the peoples of Czechoslovakia for the injustice committed.

4. Through a peaceful revolution in the fall of 1989, the people of the GDR eliminated the divisive, inhuman, inter-German border. Now the two parts of Germany are to grow together, supporting the creation of a peaceful order throughout Europe as part of the CSCE process. We recognize our particular responsibility to bring our historical relationship to the peoples of Eastern Europe into the European unification process.

In this context, we happily reiterate our unconditional recognition of German borders with all neighboring states, established after World War II.

In particular, the Polish state should know that its right to live within secure borders will never be challenged by any territorial claims by Germany, now or in the future.

We confirm the inviolability of the Oder-Neisse border with the Republic of Poland as the foundation for peaceful coexistence of our peoples in a common European house.

This will be reaffirmed by treaty by a future all-Germany parliament.

Document 21:

As Minister President of the GDR, Lothar de Maizière (CDU) led a Grand Coalition government made up of the CDU, DA, and DSU, as well as the Social Democrats and Liberals. In his government program he articulated the goal of reforming the GDR so as to eliminate it and move toward unification.

Lothar de Maizière's Government Program, 19 April 1990

(Source: *Deutschland Archiv*, 23, 1990, 795ff.)

The renewal of our society grew from the chant "We are the people!" The people have become conscious of themselves. For the first time in many decades, the population of the GDR has indeed developed itself into a people. The elections that led to formation of this parliament were elections of the people. For the first time, the Volkskammer does justice to the word *Volk* in its name.

And the chant "We are the people!" grew into "We are one people!" The people of the GDR considered itself part of a people, part of the German people, which is to grow together once again. Our voters clearly voiced their political wish in the elections of 18 March 1990. We are under an obligation to this wish. It is our joint responsibility to fulfill it as best we can. . . .

The task given the government by the voters demands the establishment of German unity in an undivided, peaceful Europe. This demand includes conditions regarding the speed and quality with which it is established.

Unity must come as quickly as possible, but under conditions as good and reasonable as necessary to provide a promising future.

The debate on a monetary conversion at 1:1 or 1:2 has made us extremely aware of the context here, and that we must agree upon conditions which ensure that GDR citizens do not feel they are second-class citizens of the Federal Republic. Both goals, speed and quality, can best be guaranteed if we implement unity via a path based on an agreement under Article 23 of the Basic Law.

Since the summer of last year we have experienced many wonderful signs of friendship, helpfulness, and openness from the citizens of the Federal Republic. But we are also concerned to see a trend of decreasing willingness to sacrifice and to show solidarity.

For this reason, we extend a warm request to the citizens of West Germany: Please remember that we have had to carry the heavy burden of German history for 40 years. As is known, the GDR did not receive any support from the Marshall Plan; instead, we had to make reparations. We do not expect you to make any sacrifices. We expect mutuality and solidarity. The division can in fact only be eliminated by sharing.

We will work hard, but we need your continued support and solidarity, as we felt it last fall.

We are asked, Don't we have anything to bring to German unification? And we answer, Yes, we do!

We have our land, our people, the values we have created and our diligence, our training, and our ability to improvise. Necessity is the mother of invention.

We can bring the experience of the past decades, which we share with the countries of Eastern Europe.

We bring our sensitivity to social justice, solidarity, and tolerance. In the GDR, there was education against racism and against hostility toward foreigners, even if there was little opportunity to live it in practice. We dare not and do not wish to yield to racism.

We can bring our bitter and proud experiences of the fine line between conformity and resistance. We bring our identity and our dignity.

Our identity is our history and culture, our failures and our achievements, our ideals and our suffering. Our dignity is our freedom and our human rights, based on self-determination.

But the issue is more than the last 40 years. Germany has a lot of history with which we need to come to terms, especially that which we have more often passed on to others, therefore taking too little responsibility upon ourselves. But whoever lays claim to the positive aspects of German history must also accept its guilt, regardless of when he was born or when he started taking an active role in this history. . . .

Ms. President, honored representatives,

The coalition government which has been formed faces great, difficult, and very concrete tasks that require clear and strategic decisions.

The economic goals of the coalition government involve converting the previously state-controlled economy into an ecologically oriented social market economy.

The conversion from state planning to a social market economy must proceed quickly, yet in ordered steps. In the coming months, both forms will have to exist side by side, whereby we need to work according to the formula "as much market as possible and as much state as necessary." In this context, competition among all enterprises plays a significant role. It is the most important regulating factor in a market economy.

The coalition government will pass laws supporting stability and growth of the economy, an anti-trust law, revision of the banking law; most important, it will introduce a law on breaking up of state mongolies and large concerns to create competitive business units typical for the respective branches.

In this context, the tasks and structures of the Trusteeship Agency need to be defined so that an instrument is created with which to effect the breakup of state-owned enterprises and the transition to appropriate legal forms. Dismantling the planning system in its previous form should be largely completed by the time the monetary union takes effect.

Based on the offer of the government of the FRG to the government of the GDR to create a monetary, economic, and social union, the coalition government has the task of guaranteeing the necessary legal prerequisites. In negotiations with the federal government of the FRG, we assume the firm principle that the monetary, economic, and social union must comprise an inseparable unit, all parts of which will take effect simultaneously. This includes start-up financing, especially in the area of social welfare.

We confirm the statement already made several times that the introduction of the D-mark to the territory of the GDR shall proceed as follows:

- for salaries and wages, at a rate of 1:1;

- for pensions, also at a rate of 1:1, with a stepwise increase up to a net pension level of 70% after 45 years of insurance payment;

- for savings and insurance with effective savings, also at a rate of 1:1, whereby there should be a differentiated exchange procedure.

The domestic debts of the state-owned enterprises, cooperatives, and private companies are to be handled in a more differentiated way.

The monetary conversion is to be based in principle on the productivity difference between the FRG and the GDR. The government will tend in this regard to widespread write-offs of domestic debts, particularly in the private and cooperative sectors, in order to strengthen their competitiveness, and to convert the VEB domestic debt at a rate of at least 2:1. Conversion aid will also be given to competitively structured enterprises, for example, by eliminating debt within the scope of typical EC business rehabilitation regulations.

Just as with the transition regulations, applied over several years in the cases of Greece, Portugal, and Spain, comparable protective mechanisms must be agreed upon with the FRG.

Upon assuming the economic and social legislation system of the Federal Republic, it must be taken into consideration that special regulations are necessary for a transition period. In this context, we refer to the Saarland model. At the same time, discriminatory economic and trade restrictions should be eliminated. . . .

5

Economic Union and Diplomatic Breakthrough

After the creation of a democratically legitimate East German government, domestic discussions shifted from civil society (Document 2) to economics. Though Eastern intellectuals feared a Western takeover (Document 13), the majority of the population continued to desire the rapid completion of unification. Following clarification of the conditions of a monetary union (Document 3), GDR citizens once again voted for Kohl's coalition in local East German elections (Document 4).

The first product of the unification process was the treaty on monetary, economic, and social union (Document 7). Supplementary agreements on a "German Unity Fund" (Document 6) and the settlement of property questions (Document 9), sought to ease the transition. Moreover, a trusteeship agency (*Treuhandanstalt*) was created to privatize state-owned property (Document 10) and thus transform the planned economy into a competitive market structure. The introduction of not only the D-mark but essentially the entire West German economic and social system inspired great hopes as well as sharp criticism (Document 8). The commemoration of the revolt of 17 June 1953 (Document 11) allowed a moment for reflection on the challenges of growing together.

The implementation of monetary union on 1 July 1990 was the beginning of the end of the division of Germany. While a currency reform had deepened the partition in 1948, this time it brought the country together again. On the occasion of the monetary union, Chancellor Kohl repeated his promise that no one would be worse off than before, and many would do better (Document 14). With the introduction of the D-mark into East Germany, border controls and barriers were removed.

However, rejoicing about free physical movement and new economic opportunities was marred by serious social fears (Document 15).

The currency union also speeded up the completion of the international negotiations about unification. The European Community welcomed the inclusion of East Germany (Document 1), and the Two-plus-Four negotiations were making surprising progress (Document 5). Assurances that the post-war borders, especially those with Poland, would be recognized helped speed the final settlement (Documents 12 and 17). In personal negotiations, Gorbachev and Kohl compromised with surprising ease on the remaining questions. In exchange for German disarmament and economic assistance, the Soviet Union acquiesced on future NATO membership (Document 16).

The economic and political disintegration of the GDR accelerated during the summer of 1990. After interminable controversy, the Volkskammer agreed in late August to join the Federal Republic under Article 23 of the Basic Law on October 3 (Document 19). This parliamentary decision meant that all-German elections could be held in December (Document 18). For supporters the accession vote was a "day of joy," but for critics it signalled the "end of the GDR" (Document 20).

Document 1:

The rapid developments in Germany led the Commission of the European Community to prepare a statement to the special summit on 28 April 1990, favoring accession of the GDR to the FRG under Article 23 of the Basic Law.

The EC Commission on the Integration of the GDR, 28 April 1990

(Source: *Blätter für deutsche und internationale Politik*, 1990, 759ff.)

Introduction

1. At the Council of Europe session in Strasbourg from 8-9 December 1989, heads of state and government emphasized their commitment to German unification within the scope of a peaceful and democratic process, i.e., in keeping with all existing agreements and treaties as well as all principles laid down in the Helsinki Final Act, within the context of a dialogue and East-West cooperation, and on the basis of free self-determination. . . .

2. The gradual integration of more than 16.5 million citizens into a united Germany and an expanded Community represents a great challenge for the German authorities and the Community. . . .

All in all, the GDR seems at first sight to be a relatively efficient economy with a per capita GDP well above that of other COMECON member states and not far below the European Community average. An in-depth analysis, however, reveals considerable structural deficiencies and inadequate means of production. At the same time, there is a real development potential which can be quickly stimulated to competitive levels by the existing desire for modernization. . . .

Methods of Unification

3. According to German constitutional law, unification can occur in various ways. . . . From the perspective of the Community, unification according to Article 23, which is clearly less complicated, is the preferred procedure. . . .

Integration of the GDR into the Community by means of German unification does not, therefore, represent a formal accession. Problems associated with such a procedure are nevertheless comparable to those which arose in the most recent cases in which the Community expanded. In this case, integration into the Community will also take place in stages. This necessitates transitional measures to facilitate the gradual application of Community law.

One significant difference from a classical accession to the Community is the fact that the first phase of integration of the GDR into the Community will take place within the framework of the German unification process, that is, before formal integration of the territory of the GDR into the Community. A second difference involves the exceptional quality of the German case, i.e., the lack of negotiations on the conditions of accession, as would normally take place. At the Community level, both analogous and special aspects must be considered in order to guarantee, even in the interim phase, optimal integration of the GDR into the Community. . . .

Integration Scenario

4. Integration of the GDR into a united Germany and thus into the Community will take place in several phases, according to the Commission:

- The initial, or interim, phase starts with the introduction of an inter-German monetary union supported by a number of social and economic reforms in the GDR (economic and social union).

- The second, or transitional, phase starts with formal unification of the two German states.

- Not until this time, in the final phase, will the law of the Community be applicable in its entirety.

During the interim phase, the GDR will introduce the legal regulations necessary for its gradual incorporation into the system of law of the FRG and the Community. . . .

Conclusion

Introduction of the GDR into the community of democratic nations, along with the approaching unification of the FRG and the GDR, are among the most significant events in post-war history. They should be welcomed whole-heartedly and without reservation. The Community shares the German people's joy as it finds a new place within a united Germany and within the EC. . . .

Document 2:

As legal advisor to the Round Table, the leftist lawyer Ulrich Preuss appealed for a new constitutional order for a united Germany. His aim was to expand the Basic Law in a post-materialist direction in order to approach the goal of a civil society.

Ulrich Preuss on Civil Society, 28 April 1990

(Source: *Frankfurter Allgemeine Zeitung*, April 28, 1990)

The end of the GDR is foreseeable; it has been given at most another two years to live. Under these circumstances, it must seem somewhat remarkable that the Round Table leaves behind as its political legacy, of all things, a "Constitution of the GDR"; it thereby gives the impression of wishing to reawaken a political community whose unloved remains were to be liquidated as quickly as possible following the results of the plebiscite-like Volkskammer elections of 18 March. . . .

Nevertheless, the whole thing does make sense. An initial, quite practical reason for a new GDR constitution lies in the fact that the constitution of 1968/74, never officially annulled, is now worthless as a constitution, despite elimination of offensive references to the Marxist-Leninist party dictatorship and its metaphysics of history and progress. . . .

There is a second reason, which directly affects us in the Federal Republic. Independent of all consequences to international law if the GDR joins the Federal Republic, a new political order will emerge within a united Germany, with new economic and social conditions and contrasts, as well as more diverse cultural and political orientations, traditions, and forms of behavior. A new political body will emerge; its unity can no longer be protected through simple absorption, as was the case with the integration of ethnic Germans and East German emigrants up to now, but instead requires a new constitution. It does not matter whether this occurs through a change in the Basic Law or the creation of a new constitution. What is important is that it is not each individual East German citizen who declares, in an individual declaration of will, a desire to "join" the Federal Republic, whose territory is at the same time extended; instead, a state is ending its existence through fusion with another state, with binding effect on the totality of its citizenry. A constitution, which alone can create this totality, acts as a sort of collective memory that stores a society's bitter, as well as pleasant, experiences, reflects its hopes and fears, and protects it from the danger of falling victim to the immediacy of spontaneous impulses. Through collective self-mediatization, it creates room for political reflection, increases the leeway for options, and thus strengthens the ability of a community to act politically. . . .

The political elites in the Federal Republic need not be afraid. The Round Table's draft constitution is not to be considered an alternative to the Basic Law. Above all, it is an extension – though conscious of the problems – of the Basic Law's democratic, legal, social, and federal possibilities, as developed in decisions of the Federal Constitutional Court and constitutional legal doctrine; however, some of its sections can be considered a response to deficits and shortcomings in the Basic Law. Overall, a constitution with an independent image has emerged. Its most constant feature is that, more consistently than the Basic Law, it is conceived as a social as well as a state constitution. Guarantees of the integrity of state institutions lie in free forms of intercourse among citizens – not surprising in a society that suffered for decades under almost total statism, and in which revolutionary renewal arose out of independent social initiatives. One small detail is typical: in the preamble, it is not "the people," an a priori unit, that declares its will to create a constitution, but "the citizens of the GDR" who declare themselves the constitution-giving subjects. The constitution is not conceived as a sovereign's authoritative statute but as a mutual promise by citizens, who thereby constitute themselves as a "civil society," with a constitution that defines their way of life. With inner consistency, the draft constitution also attempts to develop the Basic Law's extremely hesitant efforts to recognize a sphere of political society that would bring together the individual citizen and the state. In the form of mass media, associations, unions, parties, and churches, this makes up, actually but not always constitutionally, the robust infrastructure of West German society's democratic life. This section of the draft constitution, covering the rights, duties, and internal order of essential actors in political society, was originally entitled "Groups, Interests, Responsibility" (it was replaced by "Social Groups and Organizations"). This was an attempt to apply the standards of rule of law, democracy, and protection of minorities and individual rights to the bearers of collective, interest-based power, whose semi-corporative strength has become a significant threat to individual freedom. . . .

Certain basic rights whose absence from the Rights Section of the Basic Law is unimaginable to us, such as the right to legal protection of rights against state interference or the right to asylum, are by nature "positive"; that is, they depend on state action and policy, or, like the right to free choice of an education, have become dependent upon such state policy through decisions by the Constitutional Court. In other words, liberal and social rights are not mutually

exclusive but simply describe gradual variances on a scale upon which negative and positive rights depend equally on political and administrative preconditions. As Ernst Benda[*] recently put it, even if the right to work does not create
a single job, this does not mean such a right must remain a nonbinding recommendation. If that were the case, basic legal guarantees of property would
also be superfluous, for they, too, create no property, and, contrary to widespread belief, they also depend on extensive state action – from laws on contracts, land registry, business, and securities, to a productive infrastructure.

Document 3:

Before the local elections, the two German governments responded to
the concern of GDR citizens regarding the exchange rate, issuing a declaration on the principles governing the introduction of the West
German D-mark to East Germany.

Two German Governments on a Currency Union, 2 May 1990

(Source: *Blätter für deutsche und internationale Politik*, 1990, 764ff.)

The governments of the GDR and the FRG, in full awareness of the joint tasks
of the two German states on the path toward German unity, plan to conclude
an international treaty for the introduction of monetary, economic, and social
union. This treaty is to take effect on 1 July 1990.

Part of this treaty concerns conversion of the GDR-mark to the D-mark. Both
sides have agreed on the essential points of this currency conversion. They
were guided in their decision making by the goal of improving living and
working conditions of the people. This assumes that:

- the stability of the D-mark and the solidity of state finances continue to be
  guaranteed; and

- through the introduction of a social market economy, the economy of the
  GDR will quickly become competitive and capable of modernization.

1. The currency conversion is to take place on 2 July 1990, after the inter-
German treaty goes into effect.

2. Salaries, wages, scholarships, rents, leases, and pensions, as well as other
recurring welfare payments (such as maintenance benefits), will be converted
at a rate of 1:1. Salaries and wages will be based on gross pay as of 1 May 1990.

3. The pension system of the GDR will be adjusted to the pension system of
the FRG. This means that most pensions in D-marks will be higher than the
current pensions in GDR-marks. In certain cases in which a lower amount is

---

[*] former Chief Justice of the Federal Constitutional Court.

calculated than the pension up to now in GDR-marks, it is assured that this previous amount will be paid in D-marks.

4. Hardship cases which arise because of the legal provisions to be laid down in the GDR, particularly people receiving low pensions and college students, will receive compensation. The GDR will regulate these payments within the framework of individual financial accountability and in consideration of his or her overall financial situation.

5. Other claims and obligations will be converted at a rate of 2:1.

6. Persons with permanent residence in the GDR can convert the following amounts (cash and bank balances) at a rate of 1:1:

- Children up to their 15th birthday: 2,000 Marks;
- Persons from 15 years of age until their 60th birthday: 4,000 Marks;
- Persons past their 60th birthday: 6,000 Marks.

Amounts exceeding these limits will be converted at a rate of 2:1, subject to the conditions listed under point 9 below.

After taking stock of state-owned assets and their potential yield, and after their priority utilization for structural adaptation of state-owned industry and rehabilitation of the state budget, the GDR will attempt, at a later date, to provide those with savings converted at a reduced rate of 2:1 with attested interest rights in state-owned assets for the amount converted at the reduced rate.

7. Balances of persons or legal entities or offices having permanent residence or location outside of the GDR will be converted at a rate of 3:1, provided the balance originated after 31 December 1989.

8. Conversion is possible only via accounts at financial institutions in the GDR. Payments of converted cash amounts are to be made only into such accounts.

9. Appropriate measures will be taken to prevent circumvention and abuse of these regulations, e.g. by setting qualifying dates.

10. The exchange rate of 1:3 for conversion of D-marks into GDR-marks which has been in effect since 1 January 1990 is changed to 1:2, effective immediately.

11. The conditions for monetary conversion are hereby established. Further details of the planned inter-German treaty will be clarified in subsequent talks.

12. Obligations of the GDR toward other countries continue in force.

Document 4:

Though it received a smaller share of the votes than before, the CDU-led coalition repeated its victory in the East German local elections on May 6, 1990. This result confirmed the unification course of the government, despite some local particularities.

Results of the Local Elections in East Germany, 6 May 1990

(Source: *Neues Deutschland*, May 8, 1990)

Election Returns in Percent

Party	Percent	
	18 March 1990	6 May 1990
CDU	40.91	34.37
SPD	21.84	21.27
PDS	16.33	14.59
Liberal Bloc	5.26	6.65
DSU	6.32	3.41
DBD	2.19	3.67
Bündnis 90	2.90	2.41
Bauernverband*	1.98	
DFD	0.33	1.23
Others**	3.92	10.43

Document 5:

At the Bundestag session on 10 May 1990, West German Foreign Minister Hans-Dietrich Genscher outlined his policies regarding NATO membership and the resolution of other diplomatic difficulties.

(Source: *Bulletin des Presse- und Informationsamtes*, 11 May 1990)

Hans-Dietrich Genscher on the Two-Plus-Four Talks, 10 May 1990

The first foreign minister meeting within the framework of the Two-Plus-Four talks, which took place in Ottawa, has given political form to this [negotiating] process.

The foreign ministers of the FRG and the GDR are equal participants in these talks. This contrasts with the situation in the 1950s. The chair is rotated alphabetically, according to the German alphabet. . . .

An encouraging message is being conveyed by this meeting in Bonn; namely, that the long-time German wish for peaceful unification is becoming reality.

---

* the Bauernverband (Farmers' Union) did not participate in the Volkskammer elections.

** in May the category of "Others" was swelled by the success of new regional groups that proved ephemeral.

In agreement with the five other foreign ministers, I was able to make the following assessment at the conclusion of the meeting:

The will of the German people to implement unification, properly and without delay, was recognized by all participants. German unification should be beneficial for all countries. The goal of the talks is to attain an international settlement to end the Four Power rights and responsibilities. . . .

Our policy aims to discontinue the rights of the responsible powers over Germany as a whole, thereby establishing the full sovereignty of the united Germany. This is to be concluded by an international agreement.

Several times the Soviet government has stressed the importance of closing the book on post-war history. Foreign Minister Shevardnadze announced in Bonn, and I quote: We believe that discrimination against Germany can no longer be a matter of discussion – on neither a legal nor a psychological level.

Who would not agree with that?

As a sovereign country, a united Germany also must have the right, guaranteed by the Helsinki Final Act, "either to become a contracting party of an alliance or not."

We view united Germany's membership in the Western alliance as offering a significant contribution to stability in Europe.

Here we are in agreement not only with our allies, but also with our neighbors directly to the east.

Because we already know the impact of our alliance in terms of furthering peace and security, we cannot consider a united Germany which does not belong to any alliance as favorable for Europe.

A united Germany treated in a manner equivalent to the rest of Europe, neither discriminated against nor receiving special treatment, will become an important factor for stability in Europe and an indispensable component of a *united* Europe. German unification does not create a problem for Europe; rather, it solves a serious and smouldering European problem. Treating the united Germany in a special way would merely replace one problem with another. . . .

We are aware that the Soviet Union – as well as the other countries of Europe – has legitimate security interests.

The federal government and our allies have from the very beginning considered it possible for Soviet troops to remain stationed on the territory that is now East Germany for a limited transition period.

Our government is also aware that external factors related to German unification can be solved only within the European framework This is why the

CSCE process and disarmament are key factors in establishing the unity of Germany and of Europe.

There was remarkable agreement at the Two-Plus-Four talks on the necessity of extending and deepening the scope of the CSCE process. In the past, it was most important to enforce the protection of human rights throughout Europe and facilitate cooperation among different, even opposing, political systems; the important thing today is to create the foundation for a united Europe. . . .

It is of great significance that at the Two-Plus-Four talks there was full agreement on Poland's role. As chair of the first foreign minister meeting, I sent a letter to the Polish foreign minister inviting him to the third meeting of foreign ministers in Paris in July, where he can make a statement on issues concerning the Polish border. . . .

We informed the "Four" that the united Germany will conclude an international treaty with Poland to resolve the border issue. The treaty will recognize, once and for all, the existing German-Polish border, as it is defined in the treaties of Görlitz and Warsaw and supplementary documents. . . .

The German people are entitled to German unity. They also have a right to demand that external aspects of that unity be clarified without delay.

We do not want to burden the united Germany with unsettled questions, not even in cases requiring transitional arrangements, such as the agreement allowing Soviet troops to remain temporarily stationed on the territory that is now East Germany.

We are especially pleased that the developments in Germany have provided positive stimuli for developments in all of Europe.

This will accelerate the development of the European Community into a European union. New, pan-European structures will emerge in the CSCE process. . . .

The united Germany will be a free democracy governed by the rule of law. The economic, monetary, and social union represents a significant step, but we want total unity. And that means far more than the introduction of the D-mark to East Germany.

The position for which we are striving for the united Germany is prescribed by the Basic Law. Its preamble expresses the wish of the German people "to serve the peace of the world as an equal partner in a united Europe."

The gate to German unity has been opened. And it was the yearning of the people of East Germany for freedom that kicked it open.

Serious problems still lie ahead of us, as we know. We will need clear goals and a lot of imagination to solve them. This will require accountability and perceptiveness. But we can be sure of one thing: We will attain the unification of Germany.

Document 6:

To finance the costs of unification, the West German government and states created a "German Unity Fund." Underestimating the likely burden, the Kohl coalition refused to raise taxes to pay for unity.

The Creation of the "German Unity Fund," 16 May 1990

(Source: F. Protzman, "Germans in Accord on Financing Unity," *New York Times*, 17 May 1990)

West Germany's federal and state governments agreed today to create a "German unity fund" totaling $70 billion to finance the reconstruction of East Germany's decrepit economy and crumbling infrastructure.

While the ultimate price tag for reunification cannot yet be calculated, the new fund should allay, at least temporarily, West Germans' fears that the expense will be paid out of their pockets: the fund does not call for a new rise in income tax. . . .

The financial package of 115 billion marks, or $70 billion, was approved at a meeting in Bonn this morning between Chancellor Kohl and the premiers of West Germany's 11 federal states.

"A German unity fund will be set up in which the federal Government and the states will take part with 50 percent each," said the West German Finance Minister, Theo Waigel. "It will finance the investment needed for German unification in the following years, especially 1990 and 1991."

Mr. Waigel said that $12.2 billion for the fund would come from Government savings and that the rest would be borrowed on capital markets between now and 1994. He said the savings would gradually be squeezed from existing West German Government subsidies to West Berlin and other border areas whose economies were damaged by the division of Germany in 1949.

The fund is to finance anticipated expenditures over four years. The planners of the fund said money would be used to finance the East German budget deficit.

Heavy costs are likely to be incurred by the rebuilding of East Germany's aged and obsolete industries and infrastructure; a switch of the economy from the East German mark to the West German mark; adapting to the West German tax system; and cleaning up the nation's badly polluted environment. The fund might also be used to cover social costs like unemployment benefits, pensions and social welfare programs for residents of what is now East Germany.

East and West German officials estimate that the East German deficit will total 30 billion West German marks, or $18.3 billion, in the second half of this year and 50 billion marks, or $30.5 billion, next year. Even under monetary union, East Germany will maintain budget autonomy until full political unity. Mr. Waigel said the East Germans would be expected to pick up about a third of those costs, while the fund would cover the remaining two-thirds.

The Bonn Government insists that it will finance unity without tax increases. West Germany's opposition Social Democratic Party had accused Mr. Kohl, a strong advocate of speedy reunification, of trying to hide the costs of unity from West German voters and of secretly planning tax increases to pay for it. . . .

Document 7:

The treaty on monetary, economic, and social union authorized the integration of the GDR into the social market economy of the FRG. It stipulated the introduction of the D-mark into the East on 2 July 1990 and hastened the internal unification of the two Germanys.

Treaty on the Creation of a Monetary, Economic, and Social Union, 18 May 1990

(Source: German Information Office, *Treaty Between the FRG and the GDR, Establishing a Monetary, Economic and Social Union*, Bonn, 1990)

The High Contracting Parties,

Owing to the fact that a peaceful and democratic revolution took place in the GDR in the autumn of 1989,

Resolved to achieve in freedom as soon as possible the unity of Germany within a European peace order,

Intending to introduce the social market economy in the GDR as the basis for further economic and social development, with social compensation and social safeguards and responsibility towards the environment, and thereby constantly to improve the living and working conditions of its population,

Proceeding from the mutual desire to take an initial significant step through the establishment of a monetary, economic and social union towards national unity in accordance with Article 23 of the Basic Law of the FRG as a contribution to European unification, taking into account that the external aspects of establishing unity are the subject of negotiations with the Government of the French Republic, the Union of Soviet Socialist Republics, the United Kingdom of Great Britain and Northern Ireland and the United States of America,

Recognizing that the establishment of national unity is accompanied by the development of federal structures in the GDR,

Realizing that the provisions of this Treaty are intended to safeguard the application of European Community law following the establishment of national unity,

Have agreed to conclude a Treaty establishing a Monetary, Economic and Social Union, containing the following provisions.

CHAPTER I: Basic Principles

Article 1: Subject of the Treaty

(1) The Contracting Parties shall establish a monetary, economic and social union.

(2) Starting on 1 July 1990 the Contracting Parties shall constitute a monetary union comprising a unified currency area and with the Deutsche Mark as the common currency. The Deutsche Bundesbank shall be the central bank in this currency area. The liabilities and claims expressed in Mark of the GDR shall be converted into Deutsche Mark in accordance with this Treaty.

(3) The basis of the economic union shall be the social market economy as the common economic system of the two Contracting Parties. It shall be determined particularly by private ownership, competition, free pricing and, as a basic principle, complete freedom of movement of labour, capital, goods and services. This shall not preclude the legal admission of special forms of ownership providing for the participation of public authorities or other legal entities in trade and commerce as long as private legal entities are not subject to discrimination. It shall take into account the requirements of environmental protection.

(4) The social union together with the monetary and economic union shall form one entity. It shall be characterized in particular by a system of labour law that corresponds to the social market economy and a comprehensive system of security based on merit and social justice.

Article 2: Principles

(1) The Contracting Parties are committed to a free, democratic, federal and social basic order governed by the rule of law. To ensure the rights laid down in or following from this Treaty, they shall especially guarantee freedom of contract, freedom to exercise a trade, freedom of establishment and occupation, and freedom of movement of Germans in the entire currency area, freedom to form associations to safeguard and enhance working and economic conditions and, in accordance with Annex IX, ownership of land and means of production by private investors.

(2) Contrary provisions of the Constitution of the GDR relating to its former socialist social and political system shall no longer be applied. . . .

CHAPTER II: Provisions Concerning Monetary Union

Article 10: Prerequisites and Principles

(1) Through the establishment of a monetary union between the Contracting Parties, the Deutsche Mark shall be the means of payment, unit of account and means of deposit in the entire currency area. To this end, the monetary responsibility of the Deutsche Bundesbank as the sole issuing bank for this currency shall be extended to the entire currency area. The issuance of coin shall be the exclusive right of the FRG.

(2) Enjoyment of the advantages of monetary union presupposes a stable monetary value for the economy of the GDR, while currency stability must be maintained in the FRG. The Contracting Parties shall therefore choose conversion modalities which do not cause any inflationary tendencies in the entire area of the monetary union and which at the same time increase the competitiveness of enterprises in the GDR.

(3) The Deutsche Bundesbank, by deploying its instruments on its own responsibility and, pursuant to Section 12 of the Bundesbank Law, independent of instructions from the Governments of the Contracting Parties, shall regulate the circulation of money and credit supply in the entire currency area with the aim of safeguarding the currency.

(4) Monetary control presupposes that the GDR establishes a free-market credit system. This shall include a system of commercial banks operating according to private-sector principles, with competing private, cooperative and public-law banks, as well as a free money and a free capital market and non-regulated interest-rate fixing on financial markets. . . .

(7) The Deutsche Bundesbank shall exercise the powers accorded it by this Treaty and by the Law concerning the Deutsche Bundesbank in the entire currency area. It shall establish for this purpose a provisional office in Berlin with up to fifteen branches in the GDR, which shall be located in the premises of the State Bank of the GDR.

CHAPTER III: Provisions Concerning Economic Union

Article 11: Economic Policy Foundations

(1) The GDR shall ensure that its economic and financial policy measures are in harmony with the social market system. Such measures shall be introduced in such a way that, within the framework of the market economy system, they are at the same time conducive to price stability, a high level of employment and foreign trade equilibrium, and thus steady and adequate economic growth.

(2) The GDR shall create the basic conditions for the development of market forces and private initiative in order to promote structural change, the creation of modern jobs, a broad basis of small and medium-sized companies and liberal professions, as well as environmental protection. The corporate legal structure shall be based on the principles of the social market economy described in Article 1 of this Treaty, enterprises being free to decide on products, quantities, production processes, investment, employment, prices and utilization of profits.

(3) The GDR, taking into consideration the foreign trade relations that have evolved with the member countries of the Council for Mutual Economic Assistance, shall progressively bring its policy into line with the law and the economic policy goals of the European Communities. . . .

Article 12: Intra-German Trade

(1) The Berlin Agreement of 20 September 1951 concluded between the Contracting Parties shall be amended in view of monetary and economic union. The clearing system established by that Agreement shall be ended and the swing shall be finally balanced. Outstanding obligations shall be settled in Deutsche Mark. . . .

Article 13: Foreign Trade and Payments

(2) The existing foreign trade relations of the GDR, in particular its contractual obligations towards the countries of the Council for Mutual Economic Assistance, shall be respected. They shall be further developed and extended in accordance with free-market principles, taking account of the facts established by monetary and economic union and the interests of all involved. Where necessary, the GDR shall adjust existing contractual obligations in the light of those facts, in agreement with its partners. . . .

Article 15: Agriculture and Food Industry

(1) Because of the crucial importance of the European Community rules for the agriculture and food industries, the GDR shall introduce a price support and external protection scheme in line with the EC market regime so that agricultural producer prices in the GDR become adjusted to those in the FRG. The GDR shall not introduce levies or refunds vis-a-vis the European Community, subject to reciprocity. . . .

Article 16: Protection of the Environment

(1) The protection of human beings, animals and plants, soil, water, air, the climate and landscape as well as cultural and other material property against harmful environmental influences is a major objective of both Contracting Parties. They shall pursue this objective on the basis of prevention, the polluter

pays principle and cooperation. Their aim is the rapid establishment of a German environmental union.

(2) The GDR shall introduce regulations to ensure that, on the entry into force of this Treaty, the safety and environmental requirements applicable in the FRG are the precondition for the granting of authorizations under environmental law for new plant and installations on its territory. For existing plants and installations the GDR shall introduce regulations to bring them up to standard as quickly as possible. . . .

CHAPTER IV: Provisions Concerning the Social Union

Article 17: Principles of Labour Law

In the GDR freedom of association, autonomy in collective bargaining, legislation relating to industrial action, corporate legal structure, codetermination at board level and protection against dismissal shall apply in line with the law of the FRG. Further details are contained in the Protocol on Guidelines and in Annexes II and III.

Article 18: Principles of Social Insurance

(1) The GDR shall introduce a structured system of social insurance, to be governed by the following principles:

1. Pension, sickness, accident and unemployment insurance shall each be administered by self-governing bodies under public law subject to legal supervision by the state.

2. Pension, sickness, accident and unemployment insurance including employment promotion shall be financed primarily by contributors. Contributions to pension, sickness and unemployment insurance shall, as a rule, be paid half by the employee and half by the employer in line with the contribution rates applicable in the FRG, and accident insurance contributions shall be borne by the employer.

Article 19: Unemployment Insurance and Employment Promotion

The GDR shall introduce a system of unemployment insurance including employment promotion which shall be in line with the provisions of the Employment Promotion Act of the FRG. Special importance shall be attached to an active labour market policy, such as vocational training and retraining. Consideration shall be given to the interests of women and disabled persons. . . .

Article 20: Pension Insurance

(1) The GDR shall introduce all necessary measures to adapt its pension law to the pension insurance law of the FRG, which is based on the principle of wage and contribution-related benefits. Over a transitional period of five years

account shall be taken of the principle of bona fide rights protection in respect of persons approaching pensionable age. . . .

(3) Upon conversion to Deutsche Mark current pensions from the pension insurance fund shall be fixed at a net replacement rate which, for a pensioner who has completed 45 insurance or working years and whose earnings were at all times in line with average earnings, shall be 70 per cent of average net earnings in the GDR. For a greater or smaller number of insurance or working years, the percentage shall be correspondingly higher or lower. . . .

(4) Pensions from the pension insurance fund shall be adjusted in line with the development of net wages and salaries in the GDR. . . .

Article 21: Health Insurance

(1) The GDR shall introduce all necessary measures to adapt its health insurance law to that of the FRG. . . .

Article 22: Public Health

(2) While provisionally continuing the present system, which is necessary to maintain public medical services, the GDR shall gradually move towards the range of services offered in the FRG with private providers, particularly by admitting registered doctors, dentists and pharmacists as well as independent providers of medicaments and remedial aids, and by admitting private providers of independent, non-profit-making hospitals. . . .

Article 23: Accident Insurance Pensions

(1) The GDR shall introduce necessary measures to adapt its accident insurance law to that of the FRG. . . .

Article 24: Social Assistance

The GDR shall introduce a system of social assistance which shall correspond to the Social Assistance Act of the FRG.

Article 25: Initial Financing

If, during a transitional period, contributions to the unemployment insurance fund of the GDR and both the contributions and the government subsidy to the pension insurance fund of the GDR do not fully cover expenditure on benefits, the FRG shall provide temporary initial financing for the GDR within the framework of the budgetary aid granted under Article 28 of this Treaty.

CHAPTER V: Provisions Concerning the Budget and Finance

Article 26: Principles underlying the Fiscal Policy of the GDR

(1) Public budgets in the GDR shall be drawn up by the relevant national, regional or local authorities on their own responsibility, due account being

taken of the requirements of general economic equilibrium. The aim shall be to establish a system of budgeting adapted to the market economy. Budgets shall be balanced as regards revenue and expenditure. All revenue and expenditure shall be included in the appropriate budget.

(2) Budgets shall be adapted to the budget structures of the FRG. The following in particular shall be removed from the budget, starting with the partial budget for 1990 as of the establishment of monetary union:

- the social section, in so far as it is wholly or mainly financed from charges or contributions in the FRG,

- state undertakings by conversion into legally and economically independent enterprises,

- transport undertakings by making them legally independent, the management of the Deutsche Reichsbahn and the Deutsche Post, which will be operated as special funds.

Government borrowing for housing shall be allocated to individual projects on the basis of their existing physical assets.

(3) National, regional and local authorities in the GDR shall make every effort to limit deficits in drawing up and executing budgets. As regards expenditure this shall include:

- abolition of budget subsidies, particularly in the short term for industrial goods, agricultural products and food. . . .

- sustained reduction of personnel expenditure in the public service,

- review of all items of expenditure, including the legal provisions on which they are based, to determine whether they are necessary and can be financed,

- structural improvements in the education system and preparatory division according to a federal structure (including the research sector). . . .

(4) An inventory shall be made of publicly owned assets. Publicly owned assets shall be used primarily for the structural adaptation of the economy and for the recapitalization of the budget in the GDR.

Article 27: Borrowing and Debts

(1) Borrowing authorizations in the budgets of the local, regional and national authorities of the GDR shall be limited to 10 billion Deutsche Mark for 1990 and 14 billion Deutsche Mark for 1991 and allocated to the different levels of government in agreement with the Minister of Finance of the FRG. A borrowing limit of 7 billion Deutsche Mark for 1990 and 10 billion Deutsche Mark for 1991 shall be established for the advance financing of proceeds expected to

accrue from the realization of assets currently held in trust. . . .

(3) After accession, debt accrued in the budget of the GDR shall be transferred to the assets held in trust in so far as it can be redeemed by proceeds expected to accrue from the realization of the assets held in trust. The remaining debt shall be assumed in equal parts by the Federal Government and the Länder newly constituted on the territory of the GDR. Loans raised by Länder and local authorities shall remain their responsibility.

Article 28: Financial Allocations granted by the FRG

(1) The FRG shall grant the GDR financial allocations amounting to 22 Billion Deutsche Mark for the second half of 1990 and 35 billion Deutsche Mark for 1991 for the specific purpose of balancing its budget. Furthermore, initial financing shall be made available from the federal budget, in accordance with Article 25, amounting to 750 million Deutsche Mark for the second half of 1990 for pension insurance as well as 2 billion Deutsche Mark for the second half of 1990 and 3 billion Deutsche Mark for 1991 for unemployment insurance. Payments shall be made as required. . . .

Article 29: Transitional Regulations in the Public Service

The Government of the GDR shall guarantee, with due regard for the first sentence of Article 2 (1), that in collective bargaining agreements or other settlements in the public administration sector the general economic and financial conditions in the GDR and the exigencies of budget consolidation are taken into account, with any new service regulations being of a transitional nature only. The Federal Representation of Staff Act shall be applied mutatis mutandis.

Article 30: Customs and Special Excise Taxes

(1) In accordance with the principle set out in Article 11 (3) of this Treaty, the GDR shall adopt step by step the customs law of the European Communities, including the Common Customs Tariff, and the special excise taxes stipulated in Annex IV of this Treaty. . . .

Document 8:

In their first joint statement, the Bündnis 90/Green delegates in the Volkskammer and the Green delegates in the Bundestag criticized the agreement on the creation of a monetary, economic and social union from an alternative and ecological perspective.

Green Criticism of the Currency Union, 6 June 1990

(Source: *Blätter für deutsche und internationale Politik*, 1990, 882ff).

Preamble

I. With the fall of totalitarian regimes in the countries of

Central and Eastern Europe, the division of Europe and Germany is coming to an end. Because of our history, we bear particular responsibility for our own destiny and that of our neighbors, who follow developments in Germany with concern.

We approve of German unity. At the same time, we emphasize: if Germany hopes to earn trust rather than spreading fear, it must recognize the Oder-Neisse border and integrate itself into a cooperative security system growing out of the CSCE process and replacing the old military blocs. . . .

II. We reject the agreement because of serious constitutional, political and economic reservations and because of the grave social consequences of the irresponsible deadline for monetary union:

- The GDR surrenders important aspects of its sovereignty before state unity is settled in substantive or temporal terms. The citizens of the GDR and their parliament will be exposed to a legal system upon which they had, and have, no influence.

- The agreement will be a shock to the economic system, with mass unemployment and unforeseeable social and domestic political consequences. The social net and effective representation of interests are underdeveloped, and insufficiently ensured, in the agreement.

- The agreement leads to a sellout of the productive capacities and the real estate of the GDR.

- Women, who in the past also bore the brunt of aberrant development, will again be among the losers. Protecting their interests is not an issue in the agreement.

- Assuming West German environmental laws may be an improvement for the GDR, but it also means the danger of repeating mistakes made in the Federal Republic. A policy of unlimited growth produces increasing ecological costs and undermines the basis of our existence.

Given the economic strength and prosperity of the Federal Republic, the majority of the GDR population considers the only alternative to be an assumption of the West German economic system as completely as possible. We believe the failure of the "real socialist" planned economy should not keep us from seeing and seeking alternatives to the shortcomings and risks of a growth- and prosperity-oriented society lacking solidarity.

III. Against the background of our fundamental criticism of the agreement as presented, we demand:

1. An agreement between the two German states to call a constitutional assembly and a referendum in the FRG and GDR on a draft constitution;

2. Large-scale cancellation of the debts of GDR enterprises to the GDR State Bank; the remaining debts should be individually revalued and their repayment scheduled realistically.

3. To counterbalance the GDR's agreed-upon loss of sovereignty in monetary and currency policy, the GDR State Bank should be granted five provisional voting seats on the Central Bank Council of the German Central Bank, pending creation of central state banks in the GDR.

4. Real estate and public housing in the GDR should not be included in sales for the purpose of structural adjustment and balancing the budget.

5. In order to guarantee broad distribution of wealth, all citizens of the GDR should receive legally enforceable rights to shares in East German state-owned property; through special share rights, employees should have the opportunity to acquire ownership of their enterprises, thus implementing democratic models of workers' participation.

6. To eliminate acute dangers to life and the environment, immediate abandonment of nuclear energy is absolutely necessary. To protect the atmosphere, a structural assistance program is necessary for a decentralized, local energy system, with preference given to energy-saving and renewable energy sources.

7. To deal with the foreseeable social plight of many in the GDR, it will be necessary to introduce needs-oriented basic insurance and a dynamically adjusted minimum pension. . . .

Document 9:

Following lengthy talks, the two German governments formulated joint principles for settling open property questions. The declaration was a compromise between Eastern demands for protection of existing property rights and Western claims for restitution.

Joint Declaration on the Settlement of Open Property Questions, 15 June 1990

(Source: *Blätter für deutsche und internationale Politik*, 1990, 880ff.)

The division of Germany, the related migration from East to West, and the different legal systems in the two German states have led to numerous problems involving property rights; they affect many citizens of the GDR and the FRG.

In resolving existing property issues, both governments base their views on the assumption that it is possible to balance the various interests in a socially acceptable manner. Legal certainty and clarity, as well as the right to property, are the principles guiding the governments of the GDR and the

FRG in resolving the property issues facing them. Only in this way can peace under the law be permanently assured in a future Germany.

Both German governments agree on the following basic premises:

1. Expropriation on the basis of occupation law or occupational jurisdiction (1945 to 1949) cannot be reversed. The governments of the Soviet Union and the GDR see no possibility of revising measures taken at that time. The government of the FRG acknowledges this in view of historical developments. It is of the opinion that the right to make a final decision on possible state compensation must be reserved for a future all-German parliament.

2. Trusteeship administration and similar measures limiting use of real estate, businesses, and other property must be rescinded. In this way, citizens whose property devolved to state administration as a result of flight from the GDR or for other reasons will regain control of their property.

3. In principle, confiscated real estate will be returned to former owners or their heirs, taking account of the cases listed in a) and b):

a) Restitution of property rights to real estate and buildings whose use or function was changed, in particular through public use in construction of complex housing and settlement, employment for commercial purposes, or inclusion in a new commercial unit, is not possible by its nature. In such cases, compensation will be paid to the extent it has not already been compensated for under regulations applying to citizens of the GDR.

b) Where a citizen of the GDR has lawfully obtained ownership or rights of, or usage to, property to be reconveyed, a socially acceptable settlement is to be made with the former owner through exchange of property of comparable worth or through monetary compensation. This also applies to property sold to third parties by state trustees. Details remain to be clarified.

c) Where former owners or their heirs have a claim to restitution, compensation may be chosen instead. The issue of compensation for changes in value will be dealt with separately.

Document 10:

On 17 June 1990, the Volkskammer passed the Trusteeship Law, which created a Trusteeship Agency (*Treuhandanstalt*) to privatize East German public property and prepare it for world market competition.

The Charter of the Trusteeship Agency for GDR State Property, 17 June 1990

(Source: *Deutschland Archiv*, 23, 1990, 1301ff.)

Based on the intention

- to restore the state's commercial activity as quickly and extensively as possible through privatization,

- to make as many businesses as possible competitive, thus protecting existing jobs and creating new ones,

- to provide real estate for economic purposes,

- to make it possible, after taking stock of state property, its productivity, and its priority usefulness for structural adaptation of the economy and stabilization of the national budget, to grant investors a vested right to shares in state property for a sum reduced through the monetary conversion of July 2, 1990, the following law is passed:

Article 1: Transfer of Property

(1) State-owned property is to be privatized.

In certain cases to be determined by law, state-owned property can also be conveyed to the ownership of local governments, cities, districts, and states, as well as to the public.

State-owned property serving local needs or providing local services is to be conveyed by law to local governments and cities.

(2) The Council of Ministers bears responsibility for privatization and reorganization of state-owned property and is accountable to the Volkskammer.

(3) The Council of Ministers appoints the Trusteeship Agency to implement the necessary measures.

(4) The Trusteeship Agency is, under the provisions of this law, owner of shares in capital corporations that will be created, or that have already been created before this law takes effect, through transformation of state monopolies, enterprises, institutions, and other legally independent economic units (hereinafter "economic units") registered as state-owned property.

(5) The provisions of this paragraph do not apply to state-owned property if its legal owner is:

- the state,

- the German Post Office and its general management, the German Railways, the waterways administration, the management of public highways, and other state enterprises,

- enterprises or institutions answerable to local governments, cities, districts, and states,

- an economic unit for which, at the time this law takes effect, a liquidation notice has been entered in the registry of state-owned property.

(6) For privatization and reorganization of state-owned property in agriculture and forestry, the trusteeship is to be organized to take account of economic, ecological, structural, and property-law particularities in these areas.

Article 2: Status and Responsibilities of the Trusteeship Agency

(1) The Trusteeship Agency is a public-law agency. It is responsible for privatizing and utilizing state-owned property under the principles of the social market economy.

(2) The Trusteeship Agency is supervised by the Prime Minister.

(3) The Trusteeship Agency statute is to be presented to the Prime Minister for approval.

(4) The Trusteeship Agency's commercial rules must be approved by the Council of Ministers.

(5) Regulations under Paragraph 96 Sections 2 and 3 of the Republic's Budgetary Law on management of businesses in the form of a legal person at public law, and on managing their participation, are to be applied to the Trusteeship Agency.

(6) The Trusteeship Agency is to promote structural adaptation of the economy to the requirements of the market, in particular by exercising an influence on the development of reorganizable enterprises into competitive businesses and privatizing them. It is to work toward creating competitive enterprises by effectively separating business structures, thus allowing an efficient economic structure to emerge.

(7) In anticipation of future profits from privatization, the Trusteeship Agency may take out loans and issue promissory notes for purposes of reorganization within the framework and under the provisions of Article 27 of the State Treaty between the FRG and the GDR.

(8) The headquarters of the Trusteeship Agency is Berlin. . . .

Article 8: Responsibilities of the Trusteeship Stock Corporation

(1) The Trusteeship Stock Corporation, in collaboration with business consultants, sales corporations, banks, and other enterprises, will guarantee that the following tasks are carried out, decentrally and entrepreneurially, in its area of operations:

- privatization through sale of shares in business or property,

- ensuring the efficiency and competitiveness of enterprises,

- closure and utilization of the property of businesses or parts of businesses no longer amenable to reorganization.

(2) The Trusteeship Stock Corporation is to inform the Trusteeship Agency on the progress of privatization. . . .

Document 11:

On 17 June 1990, the Bundestag and the Volkskammer held a joint cere-mony to commemorate the workers' revolt of 1953. On this moving occasion, Protestant Church leader Manfred Stolpe welcomed unifica-tion but warned against rushing into it.

Manfred Stolpe's Plea for a Slow Approach to Unity, 17 June 1990

(Source: *Blätter für deutsche und internationale Politik*, 1990, 858ff.)

People have often wondered about the Germans. Their national cohesion has been questioned, even more so within the country than outside it. Official GDR policy attempted to eliminate it. Clever references to language, history, and cul-ture attempted to recall German ties. But a nation is more than a collection of key sociological data. The facts, the flesh, must be accompanied by a soul. And that is the consciousness of, and will to, unity. This was preserved; the German nation lives!

Four essential factors contributed to this end: First, the desire of East Germans for participation, freedom, and better living standards. We can thank the citizens of the Federal Republic for creating a free, democratic, legally based order in the larger part of Germany, and for constructing a productive, socially supervised economic system. Once citizens of the GDR were able to compare the systems directly after November 1989, the majority opted for the social sys-tem of the Federal Republic and against attempts to improve the GDR.

Second, the policies of all parties in the German Bundestag kept the door to national unity open. They fruitfully utilized the tension between necessary peace policies, which required reserve in [using] the German language, and protection of the interests of the German people for the sake of peace and the Germans. The nuances in their political positions were, I am convinced, of sec-ondary importance, given the fundamental political will common to all, which we observed from the GDR with respect, hope, and thanks.

Third, artists and writers made an important contribution to German cohesive-ness. Heinrich Böll and Günter Grass, Christa Wolf and Stefan Heym, and many others who described the sensibilities of the German people, like musicians, painters, sculptors, and other cultural figures, continued to develop German culture and keep it cosmopolitan. I am convinced they did us an inestimable service. They could help us greatly in forming a peace-loving, tolerant and free-dom-loving national consciousness. We should be grateful to them!

Fourth, tens of thousands of messengers of unity held the Germans together. These were visitors from the Federal Republic who braved all harassment to keep human contacts alive. Visits by relatives in both directions cemented this unity. Journalists kept inter-German interest alive. The churches organized such contacts on a large scale. And through joint services, Bible readings, hymnals, and socio-political statements, they cemented not only the church's spiritual unity but also a German consciousness. Hosts in Hungary, Poland, and Czechoslovakia made German encounters possible. Friends in many other countries helped the Germans to maintain their ties. We should thank all those who helped us stay together. . . .

Germans are coming together. In contrast to many people's fears, no national euphoria or German megalomania has broken out. Instead, one hears skepticism. There are reasons for this. Germany is becoming Germany out of two different parts. The differences do not divide, but growing back together will be more difficult if they are not taken into account.

There are, for one, old regional associations that have been rediscovered here. During the past four decades they affected people more than the people themselves realized and will undoubtedly very much revitalize German federalism.

Then there are the differences emerging from social conditions. They influenced people in different ways. A society based on achievement and competition encourages different characteristics than a society that is not free and is characterized by shortages. East German citizens face a total social transformation. Many fear it like the deluge. Many take the cliche of the capitalist dog-eat-dog society and its law of the jungle seriously. People must learn to live with freedom, with its opportunities and its dangers. The days of overprotection, when the state told us what to do, are over. No longer is everything taken care of; one must think for oneself. Waiting no longer helps. The role of money must be recognized.

Following the transformation from dictatorship to democracy, the GDR is now experiencing a transformation from a patriarchal, need-satisfying society with a pronounced system of connections and distinct elements of a barter economy to a modern monetary economy with a consistent, individually formed system that rewards achievement. This is a cultural transformation that threatens people's self-esteem and requires much sympathy.

For citizens of West Germany, the approaching unity is a disturbance of familiar routine. Social and political fears can be observed; West German identity is being called into question. The younger generation knows only their Germany; they shaped their lives aligned toward the West and are now forced to deal with East Germans, even to encourage future competition. The property controversy is another clear indication of inter-German tension. The louder fears coming from the GDR should not conceal the apprehensions in the Federal Republic.

The West is now coming to the GDR, but the GDR is also coming to the West!

Germans have to learn how to treat each other. After four decades of separation, a broad social consensus for the future common Germany must be found. We can assume a fundamental consensus grounded in the Basic Law. But a common constitution must not remain an abstract, unknown quantity. Therefore, after an all-German parliament is elected, it should declare its willingness to consider changes in the Basic Law, making the results clear to the people. The necessary debate will not be possible without vehement differences of opinion. . . .

The question of the hour for Germans is how and when German national unity will occur. There are significant reasons for speed, although a transition period of a good two years would have made sense. Though we do not have that much time, the problems remain. Two years of solid work after the fact should be a compulsory requirement, during which urgent economic and social matters can be dealt with humanely.

The complex of problems is long. But one issue has, to my mind, the highest priority. It will set the standard for the credibility of the social market economy. Hundreds of thousands will have to change their jobs. On the other hand, there is work, and the people want to work. They do not want to be consoled with high unemployment benefits; they want to find a place as equally valued workers in a new, common Germany. The most important issue for internal social peace is job creation without interim unemployment. People will understand that their wage levels depend on efficiency. However, in this transitional situation, their acceptance of the new order will depend on whether they are given a chance. Therefore I ask those with political responsibility in both German states to organize rapid, extensive job-creation measures and provide them with financial backing.

The approaching German unity is the will of the people and a result of the relaxation of tensions in Europe. Without the European peace process, June '53 could not have been repeated in October '89. In the meantime, the German unification process has begun to overtake the European peace process. Great diplomatic skill will be necessary to ensure that German unity promotes rather than disrupts peace. With thanks and respect, we observe the willingness of the four victorious powers and our neighboring states to approve German unity. This is an advance on trust that we cannot take for granted, after everything Germans have done to other people. We will prove worthy of this trust. For the future Germany will remain firmly integrated in the European Community.

That is not threatened by the GDR's accession to the FRG. A European consciousness is already widespread here.

For years, the GDR was the model pupil of the eastern alliance; it is now the favorite candidate for Western Europe. We bring to a common Germany the moral obligation to stand by the countries of Eastern Europe and the Soviet Union on the road to better living standards, including more humane environmental conditions. Support for Eastern Europe will help awaken the reserves there that are necessary in order to take on the unresolved problems of humanity. Because of our history and our geography, we Germans must be prepared to be especially sensitive to the burdens of others. This is true above all for the growing social catastrophes in the developing countries. . . .

Document 12:

On 21 June 1990, the West German Bundestag and the East German Volkskammer, following public criticism, issued identical resolutions that clearly recognized the existing German-Polish border.

Declaration of Both German Parliaments on the Polish Border, 21 June 1990

(Source: *Deutschland Archiv*, 23, 1990, 1138)

The German Bundestag,

- aware of its responsibilities in light of German and European history,

- absolutely determined to contribute to the achievement of unity and freedom in Germany, in free self-determination, so that Germany will serve justice and human rights, peace and world freedom as an equal partner in a united Europe,

- in an effort, through German unification, to contribute to the establishment of a peaceful order in Europe, in which borders no longer divide and all European nations are guaranteed the ability to coexist in trust and work together in all areas for the general good and for lasting peace, freedom and stability,

- aware that horrendous suffering was inflicted upon the Polish people through crimes committed by Germans and in the name of Germany,

- aware that millions of Germans who were driven from their ancestral homeland suffered a great injustice,

- in hopes that, in commemoration of the tragic and painful chapters in their history, a united Germany and the Republic of Poland will resolutely continue their policy of understanding and reconciliation between Germans and Poles, looking toward the future and setting a good example in the development of neighborly relations,

- convinced that involvement of the younger generation will play a significant role in reconciling these two nations,

- in the expectation that the freely elected Volkskammer of the GDR will simultaneously pass an identical resolution, expresses its resolve that the border between united Germany and the Republic of Poland finally be confirmed by means of a treaty, binding under international law, as follows:

The border between united Germany and the Republic of Poland is established under the Agreement between the GDR and the Republic of Poland on the Designation of the Established Existing German-Polish State Border of 6 July 1950, as well as supplements executing and extending this agreement (Treaty between the GDR and the People's Republic of Poland on the Delimitation of Water Areas in the Oder Bay, 22 May 1989; Act Marking the State Border between Germany and Poland, 27 January 1951) as well as the Treaty between the FRG and the People's Republic of Poland Normalizing their Mutual Relations of 7 December 1970.

Both sides assure the inviolability of the present border between their two states, now and in the future, and obligate themselves to mutual and unconditional respect for sovereignty and territorial integrity.

Each side declares that it has no territorial claims on the other and that no such claim will be raised in the future.

The government of the FRG also officially declares herewith to the Republic of Poland that this resolution represents an expression of its convictions.

Document 13:

In an article for the West Berlin newspaper *taz*, the GDR architect Wolfgang Kil criticized media tendencies of an "intellectual colonization" of East Germany.

Wolfgang Kil on the Intellectual Colonization of East Germany, 29 June 1990

(Source: *taz*, 29 June 1990)

Now that the economic aspects of annexation have been just about settled by international treaty, overwhelming the "superstructures" is next on the agenda, just to be safe. In terms of categories that still sound familiar, that means economic changes are to be followed by a "cultural revolution."

Along a wide (Western) media front, East German culture is being convinced that it never really existed. Attacks on East German authors (above all, the disputes over Christa Wolf and Heiner Müller,[*] which, though perhaps overdue, are nevertheless arrogant) represent only a symptom. Whether film, art or the-

---

[*] leading East German playwright.

ater, everything which could be seen as a necessary, unique cultural development in GDR intellectual history is being retrospectively eliminated. The survival of traditional East-West solidarity groups, such as the discussion group
on city development, "9th of December," is precarious, since Western participants accuse their partners from the East of stubbornly insisting on their own
ideas, developed in a long, hard process. Yet all along, the Westerners had
eagerly followed the growth of "Eastern" approaches and solutions with supportive interest. East German intellectuals who are open to discussion are confronted more and more with hegemonic condescension at all levels whenever
they assume equality in an East-West exchange of ideas. Even the *taz* conflict
regarding the publishing of addresses of Stasi informants was perceived in this
way within the East German editorial office by many of those involved: it was
a struggle for the right to one's own history, one's own life experiences and the
resulting individual political action. But questioning the right to deal with
one's history in a self-determined manner represents a general attack on the
identity of a social community. And wherever this is deliberate and purposeful,
it must be regarded as intellectual colonization. The ruling "powers that be"
have a well-tuned feel for potential resistance and are prepared to lead such
attacks mercilessly. The sweeping suppression of East German radio and television is evidence of this. East German media not only struggled and succeeded
in creating totally new mass media structures within only a few months (from
which even West German facilities could learn something), but could also have
served, (like a reformed FDGB [trade union], which was shut down in time) as
a factor in mobilizing a GDR identity. But ARD and ZDF[**] were bound to
oppose it!

When feelings of superiority start to strike and subvert even left-wing circles,
a new low is reached in the catastrophic inability of the left to react to the conservative and nationalistic state takeover efforts. By suppressing the claims of
East Germans to recognition and respect – at the very least of their unique, difficult identity – the Western intelligentsia shows that it is apparently struggling
with its own problems of repression: Is this supposed to correct their earlier
ambitions in retrospect? Or were the critical spirits back then already "all-
German", but they just didn't notice?

Document 14:

On the day the Treaty on Monetary, Economic and Social Union went
into effect, FRG Chancellor Kohl promised on radio and TV that no one
would be worse off, and many would be better off, than before.

Kohl's Celebration of the Currency Union, 1 July 1990

(Source: German Information Office, *Informationen*, 1990, No. 12, XIIf.)

[**] national West German public television channels.

My dear fellow Germans: a few weeks ago, the State Treaty on Monetary, Economic, and Social Union was signed by the FRG and the GDR, here in the Schaumburg Palace, the seat of former chancellors of the FRG.

Today it goes into effect.

This is the crucial step on the road to the unity of our Fatherland, a great day in the history of the German nation. Unity has now become a perceptible reality for the people of Germany in important areas of daily life.

The State Treaty is an expression of solidarity among Germans. Germans in the Federal Republic and the GDR are once again linked indissolubly. They are linked, first of all, by a common currency, by the common system of the social market economy. They will soon also be linked in a free, united state.

Germans can now come together unhindered. As of today, free travel prevails at the border. We are glad of it; we Germans have waited forty years for this moment. . . .

There will be much hard work before we achieve unity and freedom, prosperity, and social equality for all Germans. Many of our compatriots in the GDR will have to adapt to new, unfamiliar conditions – and to a transition period that will certainly not be easy. But no one will be expected to endure undue hardship. I can say to Germans in the GDR what Prime Minister de Mazière has already emphasized: No one will be worse off than before, and many will be better off.

Only the monetary, economic, and social union offers the chance, yes, even the guarantee, of improving living conditions rapidly and thoroughly.

Through our joint efforts, we will soon succeed in transforming Mecklenburg-Vorpommern and Saxony-Anhalt, Brandenburg, Saxony, and Thuringia into flourishing landscapes where it is worthwhile to live and work.

Of course, many people ask what this unparalleled process means for them personally – for their jobs, their social welfare, their families. I take these concerns very seriously.

I ask our compatriots in the GDR: Seize the opportunity; do not let yourselves be put off by the difficulties of the transition. If you look confidently to the future, and if everyone lends a hand, you and we will make it together. For the great goal of the unity of our Fatherland, we in the Federal Republic will also have to make sacrifices. A nation unwilling to do so would have long ago have abandoned its moral strength.

I call on Germans in the Federal Republic to continue to stand by our compatriots in the GDR. Remember that the people of the GDR have been cheated of the fruits of their labor for four decades by a socialist dictatorship. The have earned our support.

For the people of the Federal Republic, the following is true: No one will have to do without anything because of German unification. At most, it is a question of making available to our compatriots in the GDR part of any additional revenue earned in coming years, to help them help themselves. For me, this is an obvious imperative of national solidarity.

At the same time, it is an investment in our common future. An economic upswing in the GDR will benefit everyone – Germans in East and West, our allies in Europe and around the world.

When were we ever better equipped for the common tasks of German unity than today? The economy is flourishing; the economic upswing is in its eighth consecutive year, with no end in sight. When was this ever before the case?

We will make it – if we recall the abilities with which we built the FRG forty years ago, in an incomparably difficult situation, out of the ruins of our destroyed cities and countryside. Then, the people erected a stable democracy with their courage and stubborn determination, with industry and imagination, and last but not least, with the consciousness of a common task.

They achieved peace and freedom, prosperity and a high degree of social justice – for part of Germany. We want all this, finally, to become reality for all of Germany.

Today I ask all of you: Let us set to work without hesitation. Our common future is at stake – in a united Germany and a united Europe.

Document 15:

East German journalists wrote a skeptical report on popular reaction to the monetary union in the weekly *Sonntag*. Evoking Hans Fallada's popular novels, they quoted from newspaper articles in the *Berliner Zeitung*, *Neues Deutschland* and *Berliner Morgenpost*.

Jutta Voigt and Detlev Lücke on the Coming of Capitalism, July 1990

(Source: *Sonntag*, 1990, No. 28, 3)

Work and guaranteed bread: Once upon a time. Poverty is not only misery, poverty is also criminal. Poverty is stigma, poverty is suspicion.

I've made 25,000 DM in the last six weeks; it will continue until July 7th, sums up the black-marketeer wearing shining leather pants. Everyone has to be a speculator, which means harvesting where no seeds were sown, getting rich at someone else's expense, counting on the bad luck of others, or turning chance to your own advantage. Will there be a Western department store in our backyard tomorrow? four-year-old Karl asks his father. Incognito, dressed in a flowered summer dress, Ingrid Matthäus-Meier, mother of the monetary union, is at the Kaufhof[*] inspecting the largest social experiment ever conducted on people. What do the Westerners think, anyway; were we too stupid or too lazy to work? I can't bear to hear it any more. . . .

The revolution continues. Unlimited low coffee prices at Tschibo[**]! The monetary union made it all possible. Written on the wall at commuter station Wollankstrasse: "And can no one take this sad dream out of my mind?" A stranger in one's own land, extras in an open-ended party game. They are saying goodbye to Utopia, arriving in nowhereland, and clinging desperately to the principle of hope. Remolded as quickly as new coins are minted, they search for themselves just as they search for their old coins. In Werder on the Havel River, ripe tomatoes are being plowed under. A greengrocer on Husemann Street doesn't have enough to sell. He's still waiting for the delivery; it isn't so easy, he explains, to supply 16 million more people. Wholesalers are just looking on. Their own production is paralyzed, and Western industry is holding back investment. They can make money faster through sales. Capital is horrified by little or no profit the way nature abhors a vacuum. Yesterday communist, today capitalist; in any case, a dictator. The director is self-appointed – we have no say. Ex-comrade Abraham[***], resign! Waiters strike. The employees of the fancy restaurants around the Gendarmenmarkt have locked the doors and gone to the steps of the theater with their banners. They call 208 02 27, the telephone number of the former director of the state restaurant chain, now its corporate director. Supposedly Abraham made his former party secretary and his girlfriend shareholders. Manchester-style capitalism, yells a waitress, they're driving a Mercedes already. A West German tourist strolls lightheartedly across the square. Collect East German money, he says. It'll be as valuable as a blue Mauritius stamp.

Document 16:

Personal talks between Kohl and Gorbachev on 15 and 16 July 1990 in the Caucasus mountains helped eliminate Soviet resistance to united Germany's membership in NATO. In return for the withdrawal of the Red Army, Bonn offered disarmament and economic aid.

Kohl on His Caucasus Meeting with Gorbachev, 17 July 1990

(Source: German Information Office, *Informationen*, 1990, No. 13, Iff.)

---

[*] five and dime department store.

[**] national coffee retail chain.

[***] controversial manager of privatized cafe at the Zeughaus.

Thanks to intensive, candid talks and consultation at all levels – unprecedented in their number and frequency – we can now speak of a breakthrough in regulating the external aspects of German unification. We also begin to see clearly the contours of a future European architecture. . . .

Today I can announce to all Germans the good news that all other external aspects have been agreed upon by the Soviet Union and ourselves.

We want forward-looking agreements, extensive cooperation, trust, and, last but not least, a broad-based meeting of our peoples, particularly the younger generation.

We also want this to be a contribution to lasting, peaceful development in Europe.

This provides a model – and on this point, President Gorbachev and I are in full agreement – for a comprehensive treaty of cooperation between united Germany and the Soviet Union, to be concluded as soon as possible following unification.

This treaty will be based on a solid foundation and in the mutual understanding that German-Soviet cooperation, together with our firm position in the West, will provide an essential contribution to stability in Central Europe and beyond.

Based upon these common philosophies – as President Gorbachev also stated – we have resolved the practical problems that still lie ahead on the path to German unification.

I would like to review the most important points here:

1) The unification of Germany includes the FRG, the GDR, and all of Berlin.

2) With unification of Germany, the rights and responsibilities of the Four Powers with respect to Germany as a whole and Berlin will be terminated. Starting at the time of unification, united Germany will receive total and unrestricted sovereignty.

3) United Germany, in exercising its total and unrestricted sovereignty, can freely and autonomously decide whether and to which alliance it wishes to belong. This corresponds to the spirit and text of the CSCE final acts.

I have declared the view of the federal government that united Germany would like membership in NATO, and I know that this corresponds to the wishes of the GDR. Minister President de Maizière made this clear in his comments yesterday. We reconfirmed our decision in this respect when we spoke early this morning.

4) United Germany will conclude a reciprocal treaty with the Soviet Union

on the withdrawal of troops from the GDR. The Soviet leadership has declared that the withdrawal process will be completed within three to four years.

What I have just so simply announced, "three to four years," ladies and gentlemen, means that Soviet troops will have left German territory by 1994 at the latest. And I would like to emphasize this once more: this means that, 50 years from the day on which Soviet troops first set foot on what was then territory of the German Reich, during World War II, the last Soviet soldiers will have left Germany.

Further, a transitional treaty on the effects of the introduction of the West German mark will be concluded for this period.

5) As long as Soviet troops are still present on the territory of the present GDR, no NATO structures will expand into this area. As of the time of unification, Articles 5 and 6 of the NATO treaty will apply to the entire territory of united Germany.

6) Starting immediately upon unification, nonintegrated units of the Bundeswehr, i.e., territorial defense units, will be permitted to be stationed within the territory of the present GDR and Berlin.

7) As long as Soviet troops are still present on territory of the present GDR, we feel that troops of the three Western powers should remain in Berlin. The federal government will request this of the three Western powers, proposing an appropriate treaty. A legal basis for the presence of Western troops must be created by treaty between the government of the united Germany and the Three Powers. We assume that the amount of troops and equipment will, of course, not exceed its present level.

8) Upon withdrawal of the Soviet troops from the territory of the present GDR and Berlin, NATO troops will also be permitted to be stationed in this area of Germany, though no launching facilities for nuclear weapons will be permitted. Foreign troops and nuclear weapons may not be moved there.

9) The federal government is willing to submit a declaration during the Vienna talks currently in progress, [which obliges it] to reduce the size of the army of a united Germany to 370,000 troops within three to four years. This reduction will begin when the first Vienna Agreement takes effect. This means that the military of united Germany will have 45 percent fewer troops than the combined authorized size of the Bundeswehr and the Nationale Volksarmee.

10) United Germany will not produce, own, or possess ABC weapons, and will remain a member of the nonproliferation treaty.

I assume, of course, that the three Western powers as well as the government of the GDR, whose representative, the Minister President, I have already spoken to today, will also support these ideas for unification. Ladies and gentlemen, a further focus of my talks with President Gorbachev, and of the talks between [German] Federal Finance Minister Theodor Waigel and his Soviet counterpart, was forward-looking economic and financial cooperation. . . .

As you have noticed, I have not mentioned another very important date: namely, that of the Bundestag elections, the all-German elections to take place in December. I assume that it will be the first Sunday in December, according to current discussion. You will certainly understand when I close by expressing by intention to win this election.

Document 17:

During their Paris meeting of 18 July 1990 the foreign ministers of the World War II victors and both German states agreed upon five principles, defining "the final character of the German borders."

Two-Plus-Four Resolution on German Borders, 18 July 1990

(Source: D. Rotfeld and W. Stützle, eds., *Germany and Europe in Transition*, Oxford, 1991, 182)

The five principles on the final character of the borders of Germany, on which the participants of the Paris Summit meeting agreed and which will be included in the concluding document of the Two-Plus-Four talks, are the following:

1. The united Germany will comprise the territory of the FRG, the GDR, and all of Berlin. Her external borders will definitely be the borders of the FRG as they are on the day when the final arrangement comes into force. The confirmation of the character of the borders of Germany is a substantial contribution to the peaceful order in Europe.

2. The united Germany and the Republic of Poland will confirm the border existing between their states in a treaty binding under international law.

3. The united Germany has no territorial claims against other states and will not raise any in the future.

4. The government of the FRG and the GDR guarantee that the constitution of the unified Germany will not contain any regulations which are not compatible with these principles. This applies correspondingly to the provisions that are set down in the preamble and in articles 23, paragraph 2, and 146 of the Basic Law for the FRG.

5. The governments of the USSR, the USA, the United Kingdom, and France formally receive the corresponding obligation and declaration of the governments of the FRG and the GDR and emphasize that with their implementation the definite character of the borders of Germany will be confirmed.

Document 18:

For the first election, the GDR and FRG agreed that parties could join forces in one common list and would have to receive more than 5 percent of the vote. To improve chances for Easterners, the Constitutional Court later decided that ballots would be counted separately for the five new states plus East Berlin and the former FRG.

Agreement on All-German Parliamentary Elections, 2 August 1990

(Source: *Frankfurter Rundschau*, 3 August 1990)

The FRG and the GDR,

- bearing in mind the wish, expressed by the implementation of monetary, economic and social union, to create a united state according to Article 23 of the constitution of the FRG;

- and intending to prepare for the election of the German Bundestag by the entire German people, as an important step toward establishment of German unification;

- in consideration of the fact that the election of the German Bundestag must take place within the time period laid down in Article 39, Section 1, Sentence 3 of the constitution of the FRG;

- in the desire that the upcoming election be carried out as an all-German election on the basis of uniform voting rights and, therefore, that the scope of the Federal Voting Law be extended to include the area of the GDR;

- in the knowledge that changes and adaptations are necessary to this end, agree to conclude an agreement on the preparation and execution of the first all-German elections to the German Bundestag, under the following regulations:

Article 1: For the first all-German election, the jurisdiction of the Federal Voting Law of the FRG in the version of 1 September 1975 (*BGbl*. I, 2325). . . will be extended to include the areas of the Länder Mecklenburg-West Pomerania, Brandenburg, Saxony-Anhalt, Saxony, and Thuringia, and the area of East Berlin. The Federal Voting Law applies, with the amendments and stipulations listed in the Appendix. . . .

Appendix I.

The Federal Voting Law in the version of 1 September 1975. . . will be amended as follows:

2. Lists of various parties for a federal Land which do not submit parallel lists of candidates in any Land – except Berlin – may be joined for this election by means of a declaration to the federal election chairperson. . . .

Document 19:

After heated debate throughout the night, the Volkskammer decided, early in the morning hours of 23 August, to join the Federal Republic on 3 October 1990. For Chancellor Kohl, this was cause to declare "a day of joy for all Germans."

East German Decision in Favor of Accession, 23 August 1990

(Source: *Frankfurter Allgemeine Zeitung*, 24 August 1990)

In a government declaration before the Bundestag on Thursday, Chancellor Helmut Kohl called the decision of the Volkskammer that the scope of the Basic Law be expanded to include the area of the GDR, the GDR thereby becoming part of the FRG on 3 October, a "memorable event in German history." "Today is a day of joy for all Germans. Wednesday, 3 October, 1990, will be the date of reunification. It will be a great day in the history of our people. After over forty years, that which the preamble of the constitution demands for `the entire German people' will come to pass: `To achieve by free self-determination the unity and freedom of Germany'," said the Chancellor.

Kohl continued that it was a day to give thanks as well as a day to offer respect and appreciation to colleagues in the Volkskammer and the government of the GDR for carrying out the task assigned them by the voters on 18 March.

Deputy SPD chairman Oskar Lafontaine also welcomed the Volkskammer resolution as representing a foundation upon which the people of East Germany would be able to live their lives in freedom. Lafontaine reminded listeners that political unification was a prerequisite for "real unity" – namely, the establishment of uniform living standards throughout Germany. At the same time, he referred to Carlo Schmid's demand for a European nation, and spoke out for a new national concept, one that could be realized in a United States of Europe. Lafontaine also called for the creation of a constitutional council to prepare a new constitution based on the present one, on which a referendum would then be held in Germany.

The Bundestag approved an election agreement that evening, establishing the basis for the all-German Bundestag elections to be held on 2 December.

The long list of those to whom Kohl expressed thanks started with the former Hungarian Minister President Laszlo Nemeth, who a year ago, opened the border for the refugees in the embassy, thereby cutting the "first stone out of the Berlin Wall." Kohl then thanked the Germans in East Germany. He said their courage, composure, and love of freedom were to thank for the unity in freedom that would be completed in several weeks.

Kohl then included the Western partners in his expression of thanks, mentioning Presidents Bush and Mitterrand, the Eastern human rights movements in Poland, Hungary, and Czechoslovakia, and above all, Soviet President Mikhail Gorbachev. Kohl said that it was Gorbachev's reform policy which made the far-reaching changes in Germany and Europe possible.

The Chancellor particularly acknowledged the contribution of his predecessor, Konrad Adenauer, to the presently completed unification of Germany. What Adenauer described in his memoirs is finally being achieved, said Kohl. . . .

In the second part of his government declaration, Chancellor Kohl discussed the economic problems in East Germany, referring to numerous positive signs that had received little attention so far. One of these, according to Kohl, is the fact that in the first six months, 100,000 new companies were founded in East Germany, 35,000 of them in July alone. . . .

The present situation is marked by the transition from a planned to a market economy. The problems that arose in forty years of mismanagement could not be corrected in eight weeks, Kohl said. The reconstruction of East Germany remains a question of months and years, not one of days, according to the Chancellor. Further, success depends on everyone's contributing to a great common effort at this turning point in German history. Kohl pointed out that for the first eighteen months, 57 billion German marks had been designated for support of the GDR budget. The federal government would push for quick payment of these funds. In addition, approved liquidity aid would have to be paid out faster and more efficiently. Kohl announced that the government would provide "extensive additional support" for the export of agricultural commodities from East Germany. . . .

Lafontaine acknowledged the individuals and groups that had made the German unification process possible. . . . Without the citizens' rights groups in East Germany and without the churches there, the democratization process would not have been possible. Lafontaine recalled the contributions made by the Polish [union] "Solidarity," by the Czechoslovakian [group] "Charter 77," by Gorbachev and Mitterrand. . . .

The SPD candidate for Chancellor said the process of uniting Germany must be done in a democratic and European fashion. The people must decide on their constitution. To this end, a constitutional council should submit a draft to a referendum.

Lafontaine warned that the unification of Europe should not be lost sight of in the wake of German unification. One day, according to Lafontaine, a European nation should exist. The "national concept" should orient itself toward that of the United States. The values of the French Revolution, "Freedom, Equality, and Brotherhood," should not be limited to a national perspective but rather be understood in universal terms. In view of "poverty migration" from Eastern Europe, Lafontaine advocated the establishment of social conditions necessary to integrate such people.

He demanded once again that the costs of unification be clarified and that military service and community service receive equal treatment. Lafontaine accused Kohl of wanting to direct the unification process "alone," which he considered a mistake. He also felt it was a mistake for the federal government to tell the people in the Federal Republic that no sacrifices would be necessary in the course of German unification. That eliminated the "prerequisite of solidarity." Lafontaine announced that there would be social hardship in East Germany and that in West Germany people "will have to do without, to some degree."

Document 20:

The PDS daily lamented the hasty decision of the Volkskammer to become part of the FRG. The paper quoted PDS chair Gregor Gysi who commented wistfully on the "demise of the GDR."

Neues Deutschland on the Demise of the GDR, 24 August 1990

(Source: *Neues Deutschland*, 24 August 1990)

"Parliament has just resolved nothing more and nothing less than the demise of the GDR on 3 October," declared Gregor Gysi Wednesday evening in a personal statement following the announcement of the result of the vote on extending the scope of the FRG constitution to include the GDR under Article 23. The minutes of the 30th Volkskammer session noted at this point: "Exuberant applause by the CDU/DA, DSU, and some of the SPD."

Two-hundred ninety-four representatives voted in favor of the joint proposal by the CDU/DA, DSU, FDP and SPD. Sixty-two voted against. Seven abstained. The motion to vote, called by Lothar de Maizière (CDU), was preceded by a special session which, according to Gregor Gysi, resembled "an ambush." The Minister President said the vote was necessary to put an end to the incessant game of setting a date to become part of the FRG. Even though all speakers repeatedly and verbosely declared their desire to finally concentrate on issues of concern to GDR citizens, many different of dates were proposed. In the course of the special session, de Maizière's preferred date of 14 October was joined by 22 August (proposed by the DSU), 3 October, which – as expressed by Secretary of State Günter Krause – was the "compromise offered by the Volkskammer parties," and 15 September, favored by the SPD. The lot finally went to October 3rd. All other possibilities were defeated in balloting by an alliance of former and present governing parties. This included the proposal by Bündnis 90/Greens to decide on the fastest possible date for joining the FRG at a Volkskammer session on October 3rd.

The date finally set was the subject of numerous declarations on Thursday. Bündnis 90/Greens characterized the late night decision as "extremely undemocratic" and "obviously based on instructions from Bonn." The former chair of the SPD parliamentary group, Richard Schröder, admitted he had held the weaker position in the discussion on the date. Now, he said, campaigning will start, which is "the agony of democracy."

"The most important thing is that the debate is over," said Antje Vollmer, the Green Party's spokesperson in the Bundestag. Jochen Vogel and Oskar Lafontaine [SPD] issued a joint statement that the Volkskammer decision had ended an unbearable uncertainty not only for people in the GDR but for those in the FRG as well. Chancellor Helmut Kohl declared in the cabinet that this decision represented the completion of the task stated in the preamble of the Basic Law – to bring about the unity and freedom of Germany in free self-determination. The government of the Federal Republic was aware of the great responsibility it would bear as the first all-German government, which it would indeed become in several weeks, Kohl said.

6

Unification Treaties and Accession

The final steps in the accession of East to West Germany under Article 23 of the Basic Law began in the fall of 1990. The GDR divided itself into five new federal Länder, with East Berlin becoming part of the already existing state of (West) Berlin. The actual conditions of the merger were regulated by the lengthy unification treaty of 31 August 1990 (Document 3). The declaration of full German sovereignty by the four former occupying powers and the CSCE Charter for a New Europe fit the national process into an international framework (Documents 6 and 13). Despite considerable criticism of the unequal bargaining position of the two states, the treaties became binding under German as well as international law.

In a ceremony in Berlin on 3 October 1990, the East German states became part of the Federal Republic of Germany (Document 9). The merger of the five new with the old Länder was completed with the election of democratic parliaments in Mecklenburg-West Pomerania, Saxony-Anhalt, Brandenburg, Saxony, and Thuringia on 14 October (Document 10). During the subsequent all-German electoral campaign, Oskar Lafontaine, the Social Democratic candidate for Chancellor, continued to criticize the speed and conditions of the merger, showing the Left's difficulties in dealing with unification (Document 15). The results of the federal election on 2 December revealed that a majority of voters did not share his reservations (Document 17). Accordingly, the outcome was a vote of confidence for the unification course steered by West German Chancellor Helmut Kohl and Foreign Minister Hans-Dietrich Genscher (Documents 16, 18, and 19).

The completion of unification stimulated debate about its meaning and implications. Critics predicted that the Eastern states would be Germany's poorhouse for some time to come (Document 2). Apologists wondered whether the old Federal Republic would not disappear as well (Documents 1 and 4). Conservative Western critics also denounced the collaboration of East German intellectuals with the regime, focusing their attacks on the symbolic figure of Christa Wolf (Document 5). Though there was much international acclaim, fears of a greater Germany lingered, especially in Poland (Document 7). In East Germany many people also worried about how they would survive the economic transition (Document 8).

Due to its breathtaking speed, the recovery of German unity left open a number of political issues. One point of symbolic and practical dispute was the location of Germany's future capital (Documents 11 and 12). The question of whether to amend the existing constitution of the FRG or to draft a new document also created much controversy (Document 14). Finally, many commentators were concerned that the psychological integration of East and West Germans might take more time than the actual achievement of political union (Document 20).

Document 1:

Impressed with the rapid disappearance of the GDR, the well-known West German sociologist Niklas Luhmann wondered whether, and in what way, the FRG would change as well.

Niklas Luhmann's Obituary for the Federal Republic, 22 August 1990

(Source: "Dabeisein and Dagegensein. Anregungen zu einem Nachruf auf die Bundesrepublik", in *Frankfurter Allgemeine Zeitung*, 22 August 1990)

Though less than in the case of East Germany, there is a lot of talk that West Germany will soon come to an end. In the case of East Germany, the changes are obvious, clearly perceptible, and therefore everybody is conscious of them. Regarding West Germany, however, they appear to be more an expansion of size – that is, changes in the form of numbers and costs. Thus it is easy to think that things have been good up to this point, and that they will continue to get better. But will future historians judge in the same way? Or will the epoch of two German states be seen merely as a particular era in German history? And if so, shouldn't we today, on an occasion that is also the end of West Germany, at least make the effort to write an obituary. . . ?

Even in terms of intellectual development, the most important chapter has perhaps been destruction – destruction in the sense of being unable to identify specifically German traditions. The Nazis ruined them with their "blood and soil, tradition and kinship." All that remained was a zealously demonstrated shame. And the chance to start something new – like American sociology or analytical philosophy.

In other words, a phoenix rising from the ashes. An obvious historical discontinuity. But nothing that could last. And nothing worth preserving. In a time of newly emerging ethnic nationalism, one should insist upon that. The history of the FRG (with the notable exception of Bavaria) could lead us to participate in this drama of ethnicity, clan, language, and special cultures merely as spectators. In any case, we have none of the ethnic identification gone wild that provides for so many problems elsewhere.

This ability to disassociate oneself should be appreciated and maintained. In other respects, however, the demise of West Germany cannot be taken lightly. Its heirs do not have the chance to base their views on [post-war] destruction (we aren't talking about the GDR). And it may well be, in fact it is to be expected, that well-rehearsed attitudes will be perpetuated without reflection.

I'd like to demonstrate this with two particularly striking examples that show the aftereffects of the Federal Republic phase of German history. The first deals with the economy, the second with the tradition of protest.

We have become accustomed to using the expression "market economy" as a label for, and in celebration of, the success of a highly diversified money economy. We add the qualifier "social" in order to stress the fact that a humanitarian component can also be financed. The same can be said of ecological considerations.

The collapse of the socialist economic order, and I mean particularly its economic failure, is seen as a triumph of the market economy. And the more "facts" that come to light, the more apparent it becomes that the economic, social, and ecological "facts" in the two economic orders diverge. But does that justify triumphalism?

Perhaps we tend to affirm this all too quickly, especially here on West German soil. In addition to the successful implementation of a democratic constitution, it is primarily this economic success that will be remembered in the history of the FRG. . . .

It could very well be that the socialist idea of ethical and political economic control was so far off course that it would even be wrong to want to use it as a contrast. One might think it was indeed so absurd that it means nothing to declare the following: "We avoided going astray." Just as farm animals do not discover anything meaningful about themselves when they realize one day that they do not live and die as fish in water do. The question is rather: "What categories, forms, distinctions, etc. do we use to interpret our economic system?" And it is possible that we are motivated, by our confrontation with socialism and the result of this confrontation, to choose the wrong or, in any case, a short-sighted and inflexible scheme in this important question for the future – simply because we can then declare ourselves the winners in the market economy versus planned economy debate?

The tradition of protest holds an even firmer place in the history of the Federal Republic than does our profession of belief in a social market economy and its democratic dividends. And we are famous around the world in this regard. The issues have changed, and indeed so rapidly that generational gaps in the protest cohorts would have been unavoidable had it not been possible to move on from protest to protest. Protests against remilitarization and nuclear weapons were followed by Easter marches and opposition to the state of emergency, the student movement and neo-Marxism, grass roots initiatives, the campaign against banning leftists from professions, the peace movement, the women's movement, self-help groups and, most successfully, the environmental movement. New social movements are symbolized by a value shift, finding converts in the Marxist camp who can be recognized only by their accents. Issues of distribution are supplemented, if not replaced, by issues of risk. Alternative culture will always be alternative culture, dedicated to opposition. And the need to replace old issues with new ones – the secret dictate of the mass media – makes a significant contribution to keeping consciousness up-to-date. The French see it as a series of typically German neuroses. That may well be. But in the context of a functioning democracy it also has an early-warning effect, particularly where environmental problems and issues of possible political resistance are concerned.

Market economy and protest – if these were the accomplishments, one could ask at the end of the Federal Republic, if they should be preserved. But no one will want to give them up, nor will they be able to. Maybe the naiveté with which affirmation and rejection are assigned in the FRG could be reduced to some extent. The challenges of the future have different magnitude.

Document 2:

Following the monetary union, critics warned increasingly of the social consequences of the upcoming unification. One of these leftist intellectuals was West Berlin political scientist and economist Elmar Altvater.

Elmar Altvater on the GDR as the Poorhouse of Germany, 29 August 1990

(Source: *Prinz*, 29 August 1990, 26)

Prinz: What was the biggest mistake of the hasty monetary union?

Altvater: The currency of a different economy cannot be introduced without taking social relationships into account. And that's only possible in a process lasting several years.

Prinz: Didn't the politicians know that?

Altvater: They consciously decided to carry out the experiment. As Brecht said, it is possible to "kill someone with an apartment." It's also possible to destroy an entire society with someone else's money.

Prinz: Can it be that West German companies consciously accepted the collapse of their competitors as a consequence of their decision to implement the monetary union in the way it was done?

Altvater: Definitely. It's easier to take over bankrupt companies than stable ones.

Prinz: Would reform in East Germany have been possible without untenable hardship?

Altvater: If more time and more thought had been given to it, chances for reform in East Germany could have developed which would have made the process less expensive and involving less social hardship, as well as being more democratic.

Prinz: Can the hardship cases be considered individual fates?

Altvater: In light of the figures available that approximately 1.2 million people in East Germany are unemployed with the trend rapidly rising, it is obviously a mass fate. The West German federal budget will be faced with enormous costs.

Prinz: Will East Germany make up the bottom third of a two-thirds society[*] in a combined Germany?

Altvater: Unfortunately, that danger definitely exists. East Germany will become Germany's poorhouse. A new division will emerge as the price of unification.

Document 3:

The Unification Treaty regulated the chief steps toward unity beyond monetary union. The public heatedly debated such issues as the social consequences of the merger, the control of Stasi files, and the continuation of choice in abortion. After last-minute compromises, a broad majority of CDU, FDP, and SPD supported the agreement while the PDS, Greens, and Bündnis 90 rejected it.

The Unification Treaty, 31 August 1990

(Source: German Information Office, *Treaty Between the FRG and the GDR on the Establishment of the Unity of Germany*, September 1990)

The Federal Republic of Germany and the German Democratic Republic,

- Resolved to achieve in free self-determination the unity of Germany in peace and freedom as an equal partner in the community of nations,

---

[*] a society in which the rich two-thirds live at the expense of the poor third.

- Mindful of the desire of the people in both parts of Germany to live together in peace and freedom in a democratic and social federal state governed by the rule of law,

- In grateful respect to those who peacefully helped freedom prevail and who have unswervingly adhered to the task of establishing German unity and are achieving it,

- Aware of the continuity of German history and bearing in mind the special responsibility arising from our past for a democratic development in Germany committed to respect for human rights and to peace,

- Seeking through German unity to contribute to the unification of Europe and to the building of a peaceful European order in which borders no longer divide and which ensures that all European nations can live together in a spirit of mutual trust,

- Aware that the inviolability of frontiers and of the territorial integrity and sovereignty of all states in Europe within their frontiers constitutes a fundamental condition for peace,

Have agreed to conclude a Treaty on the Establishment of German Unity, containing the following provisions:

Chapter I: Effect of Accession

Article 1: Länder

(1) Upon the accession of the GDR to the FRG in accordance with Article 23 of the Basic Law taking effect on 3 October 1990 the Länder of Brandenburg, Mecklenburg-Western Pomerania, Saxony, Saxony-Anhalt and Thuringia shall become Länder of the FRG.

(2) The 23 boroughs of Berlin shall form Land Berlin.

Article 2: Capital City, Day of German Unity

(1) The capital of Germany shall be Berlin. The seat of the parliament and government shall be decided after the establishment of German unity.

(2) 3 October shall be a public holiday known as the Day of German Unity.

Chapter II: Basic Law

Article 3: Entry into Force of the Basic Law

Upon the accession taking effect, the Basic Law of the FRG . . . shall enter into force in the Länder of Brandenburg, Mecklenburg-Western Pomerania, Saxony, Saxony-Anhalt and Thuringia and in that part of Land Berlin where it has not been valid to date, subject to the amendments arising from Article 4, unless otherwise provided in this Treaty.

Article 4: Amendments to the Basic Law Resulting from Accession

The Basic Law of the FRG shall be amended as follows:

1. The preamble shall read as follows:

"Conscious of their responsibility before God and men,

Animated by the resolve to serve world peace as an equal partner in a united Europe, the German people have adopted, by virtue of their constituent power, this Basic Law.

The Germans in the Länder of Baden-Württemberg, Bavaria, Berlin, Brandenburg, Bremen, Hamburg, Hesse, Lower Saxony, Mecklenburg-Western Pomerania, North Rhine-Westphalia, Rhineland-Palatinate, Saarland, Saxony, Saxony-Anhalt, Schleswig-Holstein and Thuringia have achieved the unity and freedom of Germany in free self-determination. This basic Law is thus valid for the entire German people."

2. Article 23 shall be repealed.

3. Article 51 (2) shall read as follows:

"(2) Each Land shall have at least three votes; Länder with more than two million inhabitants shall have four, Länder with more than six million inhabitants five, and Länder with more than seven million inhabitants six votes." . . .

5. The following new Article 143 shall be inserted in the Basic Law:

"Article 143

(1) Law in the territory specified in Article 3 of the Unification Treaty may deviate from provisions of this Basic Law for a period not extending beyond 31 December 1992 in so far as and as long as no complete adjustment to the order of the Basic Law can be achieved as a consequence of the different conditions. . . .

(2) Deviations from sections II, VIII, VIIIa, IX, X and XI are permissible for a period not extending beyond 31 December 1995. . . .

6. Article 146 shall read as follows:

"Article 146

This Basic Law, which is valid for the entire German people following the achievement of the unity and freedom of Germany, shall cease to be in force on the day on which a constitution adopted by a free decision of the German people comes into force."

Article 5: Future Amendments to the Constitution

The Governments of the two Contracting Parties recommend to the legislative bodies of the united Germany that within two years they should deal with the questions regarding amendments or additions to the Basic Law as raised in connection with German unification, in particular- with regard to the relationship between the Federation and the Länder in accordance with the Joint Resolution of the Minister-Presidents of 5 July 1990,

- with regard to the possibility of restructuring the Berlin/Brandenburg area in derogation of the provisions of Article 29 of the Basic Law by way of an agreement between the Länder concerned,

- with considerations on introducing state objectives into the Basic Law, and

- with the question of applying Article 146 of the Basic Law and of holding a referendum in this context. . . .

Article 7: Financial System

(1) The financial system of the FRG shall be extended to the territory specified in Article 3 unless otherwise provided in this Treaty.

(2) Article 106 of the Basic Law shall apply to the apportionment of tax revenue among the Federation as well as the Länder and communes (associations of communes) in the territory specified in Article 3 of this Treaty. . . .

The entire Land portion of the turnover tax will therefore be divided into an East and West portion so that as a result the average turnover tax share per capita of the Länder Brandenburg, Mecklenburg-Pomerania, Saxony, Saxony-Anhalt and Thuringia shall amount to

1991   55 percent

1992   60 percent

1993   65 percent

1994   70 percent

of the average turnover tax share per capita of the states Baden-Württemberg, Bavaria, Bremen, Hesse, Hamburg, Lower Saxony, North Rhine-Westfalia, Rhineland-Palatinate, Saarland and Schleswig-Holstein. . . .

Chapter III: Harmonization of Law

Article 8: Extension of Federal Law

Upon the accession taking effect, federal law shall enter into force in the territory specified in Article 3 of this Treaty unless its area of application is restricted to certain Länder or parts of Länder of the FRG and unless otherwise provided in this Treaty, notably Annex I.

Article 9: Continued Validity of Law of the GDR

(1) Law of the GDR valid at the time of signing of this Treaty which is Land law according to the distribution of competence under the Basic Law shall

remain in force in so far as it is compatible with the Basic Law, notwithstanding Article 143, with the federal law put into force in the territory specified in Article 3 of this Treaty and with the directly applicable law of the European Communities, and unless otherwise provided in this Treaty. . . .

Article 10: Law of the European Communities

(1) Upon the accession taking effect, the Treaties on the European Communities together with their amendments and supplements as well as the international agreements, treaties and resolutions which have come into force in connection with those Treaties shall apply in the territory specified in Article 3 of this Treaty. . . .

Chapter IV: International Treaties and Agreements

Article 12: Treaties of the GDR

(1) The Contracting Parties are agreed that, in connection with the establishment of German unity, international treaties of the GDR shall be discussed with the contracting parties concerned with a view to regulating or confirming their continued application, adjustment or expiry, taking into account protection of confidence, the interests of the states concerned, the treaty obligations of the FRG as well as the principles of a free, democratic basic order governed by the rule of law, and respecting the competence of the European Communities. . . .

Chapter V: Public Administration and the Administration of Justice

Article 13: Future Status of Institutions

(1) Administrative bodies and other institutions serving the purposes of public administration or the administration of justice in the territory specified in Article 3 of this Treaty shall pass under the authority of the government of the Land in which they are located. Institutions whose sphere of activities transcends the boundaries of a Land shall come under the joint responsibility of the Länder concerned. . . .

(3) Institutions under paragraphs 1 and 2 above shall also include such

1. cultural, educational, scientific and sports institutions,

2. radio and television establishments as come under the responsibility of public administrative bodies. . . .

Article 15: Transitional Arrangements for Land Administration

(1) The Land spokesmen in the Länder named in Article 1 (1) of this Treaty and the government plenipotentiaries in the districts shall continue to discharge their prior duties from the time of accession until the election of the minister-presidents under the supervision of the Federal Government and are subject to its directives. . . .

Article 17: Rehabilitation

The contracting parties reaffirm their intention to create immediately a legal basis for the rehabilitation of all persons, who became the victims of a politically motivated criminal persecution or other decision running counter to legality and constitution. The rehabilitation of these victims of the iniquitous SED regime shall be accompanied by appropriate arrangements for compensation. . . .

Article 20: Legal Status of Persons in the Public Service

(2) The exercise of public responsibilities (state authority as defined in Article 33 (4) of the Basic Law) shall be entrusted as soon as possible to professional civil servants. Public service law shall be introduced in accordance with the agreed arrangements set out in Annex I. . . .

Chapter VI: Public Assets and Debts

Article 21: Administrative Assets

(1) The assets of the GDR which are used directly for specific administrative purposes (administrative assets) shall become federal assets unless their designated purpose as of 1 October 1989 was primarily to meet administrative responsibilities which, under the Basic Law, are to be exercised by Länder, communes (associations of communes) or other agencies of public administration. Where administrative assets were primarily used for the purposes of the former Ministry of State Security/National Security Office, they shall accrue to the Trusteeship Agency unless they have already been given over to new social or public purposes since the above-mentioned date. . . .

Article 22: Financial Assets

(1) Public assets of legal entities in the territory specified in Article 3 of this Treaty, including landed property and assets in agriculture and forestry, which do not directly serve specific administrative purposes, shall, unless they have been handed over to the Trust Agency or will be handed over by law according to Section 1 (1), second and third sentences, of the Trusteeship Act, to communes, towns and cities or rural districts, come under federal trusteeship upon the accession taking effect. . . . Financial assets shall be divided by federal law between the Federation and the Länder named in Article 1 of this Treaty in such a way that the Federation and the Länder named in Article 1 each receive one half of the total value of the assets. The communes (associations of communes) shall receive an appropriate share of the Länder portion. . . .

Article 23: Debt Arrangements

(1) Upon the accession taking effect, the total debts of the central budget of the GDR which have accumulated up to this date shall be taken over by a federal Special Fund without legal capacity, which shall meet the obligations

arising from debt servicing. The Special Fund shall be empowered to raise loans:

1. to pay off debts of the Special Fund,

2. to cover due interest and loan procurement costs,

3. to purchase debt titles of the Special Fund for the purposes of market cultivation. . . .

Article 24: Settlement of Claims and Liabilities vis-a-vis Foreign Countries and the FRG

(1) In so far as they arise from the monopoly on foreign trade and foreign currency or from the performance of other state tasks of the GDR vis-a-vis foreign countries and the FRG up to 1 July 1990, the settlement of the claims and liabilities remaining when the accession takes effect shall take place under instructions from, and under the supervision of, the Federal Minister of Finance. . . .

Article 25: Assets Held in Trust

The Privatization and Reorganization of Publicly Owned Assets Act . . . continues to be valid with the following stipulations, once accession goes into effect:

1) The Trusteeship Agency is also charged in the future with restructuring and privatizing the former publicly owned enterprises to bring them into line with the requirements of a competitive economy. It shall become a direct institution of the Federation vested with legal capacity and subject to public law. Technical and legal supervision shall be the responsibility of the Federal Minister of Finance, who shall exercise technical supervision in agreement with the Federal Minister of Economics and the respective federal minister. Stakes held by the Trust Agency shall be indirect stakes of the Federation. Amendments to the Charter shall require the agreement of the Federal Government. . . .

Article 26: Special Fund of the German Railroad

(1) Upon the accession taking effect, the property and all other property rights of the GDR and the Reich Property in Berlin (West) belonging to the special fund of the Deutsche Reichsbahn within the meaning of Article 26 (2) of the Treaty of 18 May 1990 shall become the property of the FRG as the special fund of the Deutsche Reichsbahn. . . .

Article 27: Special Fund of the German Postal Service

(1) The property and all other property rights belonging to the special fund of the Deutsche Post shall become the property of the FRG. . . .

Article 28: Economic Assistance

(1) Upon the accession taking effect, the territory specified in Article 3 of this Treaty shall be incorporated into the arrangements of the Federation existing in the territory of the Federal Republic for economic assistance, taking into consideration the competence of the European Communities. The specific requirements of structural adjustment shall be taken into account during a transitional period. This will make a major contribution to the speediest possible development of a balanced economic structure with particular regard for small and medium-sized businesses. . . .

Article 29: Foreign Trade Relations

(1) The established foreign trade relations of the GDR, in particular the existing contractual obligations vis-a-vis the countries of the Council for Mutual Economic Assistance, shall enjoy protection of confidence. They shall be developed further and expanded, taking into consideration the interests of all parties concerned and having regard for principles of a market economy as well as the competence of the European Communities. . . .

Chapter VII: Labour, Social Welfare, Family, Women, Public Health and Environmental Protection

Article 30: Labour and Social Welfare

(1) It shall be the task of the all-German legislator

1. to recodify in a uniform manner and as soon as possible the law on employment contracts and the provisions on working hours under public law, including the admissibility of work on Sundays and public holidays, and the specific industrial safety regulations for women . . . .

(2) Employed persons in the territory specified in Article 3 of this Treaty shall be entitled, upon reaching the age of 57, to receive early retirement payments for a period of three years, but not beyond the earliest possible date on which they become entitled to receive a retirement pension under the statutory pension scheme. The early retirement payment shall amount to 65 per cent of the last average net earnings; for employed persons whose entitlement arises on or before 1 April 1991 early retirement payments shall be raised by an increment of five percentage points for the first 312 days. The early retirement payments shall be made by the Federal Institute for Employment along similar lines to unemployment pay. . . .

(3) The social welfare supplement to pension, accident and unemployment payments introduced in the territory specified in Article 3 of this Treaty in conjunction with the Treaty of 18 May 1990 shall be limited to new cases up to 31 December 1991. The payments shall be made for a period not extending beyond 30 June 1995. . . .

(5) The details regarding the introduction of Part VI of the Social Code (pension insurance) and the provisions of Part III of the Reich Insurance Code (accident insurance) shall be settled in a federal Act.

For persons whose pension under the statutory pension scheme begins in the period from 1 January 1992 to 30 June 1995

1. a pension shall be payable which is in principle at least as high as the amount they would have received on 30 June 1990 in the territory specified in Article 3 of this Treaty according to the pension law valid until that time, without regard for payments from supplementary or special pension schemes. . . .

In all other respects, the introduction should have the goal of ensuring that as wages and salaries in the territory specified in Article 3 of this Treaty are brought into line with those in the other Länder, so are pensions. . . .

Article 31: Family and Women

(1) It shall be the task of the all-German legislator to develop further the legislation on equal rights for men and women.

(2) In view of different legal and institutional starting positions with regard to the employment of mothers and fathers, it shall be the task of the all-German legislator to shape the legal situation in such a way as to allow a reconciliation of family and occupational life.

(3) In order to ensure that day care centers for children continue to operate in the territory specified in Article 3 of this Treaty, the Federation shall contribute to the costs of these centers for a transitional period up to 30 June 1991.

(4) It shall be the task of the all-German legislator to introduce regulations no later than 31 December 1992 which ensure better protection of unborn life and provide a better solution in conformity with the Constitution of conflict situations faced by pregnant women – notably through legally guaranteed entitlements for women, first and foremost to advice and public support – than is the case in either part of Germany at present. In order to achieve these objectives, a network of advice centers run by various agencies and offering blanket coverage shall be set up without delay with financial assistance from the Federation in the territory specified in Article 3 of this Treaty. . . . In the event that no regulations are introduced within the period stated in the first sentence, the substantive law shall continue to apply in the territory specified in Article 3 of this Treaty. . . .

Article 33: Public Health

(1) It shall be the task of the legislators to create the conditions for effecting a rapid and lasting improvement in in-patient care in the territory specified in Article 3 of this Treaty and for bringing it into line with the situation in the remainder of the federal territory. . . .

Article 34: Protection of the Environment

(1) On the basis of the German environmental union . . . it shall be the task of the legislators to protect the natural basis of man's existence, with due regard for prevention, the polluter-pays principle, and cooperation, and to promote uniform ecological conditions of a high standard at least equivalent to that reached in the FRG.

(2) With a view to attaining the objective defined in paragraph 1 above, ecological rehabilitation and development programmes shall be drawn up for the territory specified in Article 3 of this Treaty, in line with the distribution of competence under the Basic Law. Measures to ward off dangers to public health shall be accorded priority.

Chapter VIII: Culture, Education and Science, Sport

Article 35: Culture

(1) In the years of division, culture and the arts – despite different paths of development taken by the two states in Germany – formed one of the foundations for the continuing unity of the German nation. They have an indispensable contribution to make in their own right as the Germans cement their unity in a single state on the road to European unification. . . .

(2) The cultural substance in the territory specified in Article 3 of this Treaty shall not suffer any damage.

(3) Measures shall be taken to provide for the performance of cultural tasks, including their financing, with the protection and promotion of culture and the arts being the responsibility of the new Länder and local authorities in line with the distribution of competence under the Basic Law. . . .

(5) The parts of the former Prussian state collections which were separated as a result of post-war events (including State Museums, State Libraries, Secret State Archives, Ibero-American Institute, State Musicology Institute) shall be joined together again in Berlin. . . .

(6) The Cultural Fund shall be continued up to 31 December 1994 on a transitional basis in the territory specified in Article 3 of this Treaty to promote culture, the arts and artists. . . .

(7) In order to offset the effects of the division of Germany the Federation may help to finance, on a transitional basis, individual cultural programmes and institutions in the territory specified in Article 3 of this Treaty to enhance the cultural infrastructure.

Article 36: Broadcasting

(1) GDR Radio and TV shall be continued as an autonomous joint institutions having legal capacity by the Länder named in Article 1 of this Treaty and

by Land Berlin in respect of that part where the Basic Law has not been valid to date for a period not extending beyond 31 December 1991 in so far as they perform tasks coming under the responsibility of the Länder. The institution shall have the task of providing the population in the territory specified in Article 3 of this Treaty with a radio and television service in accordance with the general principles governing broadcasting establishments coming under public law. . . .

(5) The institution shall be financed mainly by revenue raised through licence fees paid by radio and television users resident in the territory specified in Article 3 of this Treaty. To that extent it shall be the recipient of radio and television licence fees. For the rest, it shall cover its expenditure by advertising revenue and other revenue.

(6) Within the period laid down in paragraph 1 above the institution shall be dissolved in accordance with the federal structure of broadcasting through a joint treaty between the Länder named in Article 1 of this Treaty or converted to agencies under public law of one or more Länder. . . .

Article 37: Education

(1) School, vocational or higher education certificates or degrees obtained or officially recognized in the GDR shall continue to be valid in the territory specified in Article 3 of this Treaty. Examinations passed and certificates obtained in the territory specified in Article 3 or in the other Länder of the FRG, including Berlin (West), shall be considered equal and shall convey the same rights if they are of equal value. . . .

(4) The regulations necessary for the reorganization of the school system in the territory specified in Article 3 of this Treaty shall be adopted by the Länder named in Article 1. The necessary regulations for the recognition of examinations under educational law shall be agreed by the Conference of Ministers of Education and Cultural Affairs. . . .

Article 38: Science and Research

(1) In the united Germany science and research shall continue to constitute important foundations of the state and society. The need to renew science and research in the territory specified in Article 3 of this Treaty while preserving efficient institutions shall be taken into account by an expert report on publicly maintained institutions prepared by the Science Council and to be completed by 31 December 1991, with individual results to be implemented step by step before that date. . . .

(2) Upon the accession taking effect, the Academy of Sciences of the GDR shall be separated as a learned society from the research institutes and other institutions. The decision as to how the learned society of the Academy of Sciences of the GDR is to be continued shall be taken under Land law. For the time being the research institutes and other institutions shall continue to exist

up to 31 December 1991 as institutions of the Länder in the territory specified in Article 3 of this Treaty in so far as they have not been previously dissolved or transformed. . . .

(6) The Federal Government shall seek to ensure that the proven methods and programmes of research promotion in the FRG are applied as soon as possible to the entire federal territory and that the scientists and scientific institutions in the territory specified in Article 3 of this Treaty are given access to current research promotion schemes. . . .

Article 39: Sport

(1) The sporting structures which are in a process of transformation in the territory specified in Article 3 of this Treaty shall be placed on a self-governing basis. The public authorities shall give moral and material support to sport in line with the distribution of competence under the Basic Law.

(2) To the extent that it has proved successful, top-level sport and its development shall continue to receive support in the territory specified in Article 3 of this Treaty. . . .

Chapter IX: Transitional and Final Provisions

Article 40: Treaties and Agreements

(1) The obligations under the Treaty of 18 May 1990 between the FRG and the GDR on the Establishment of a Monetary, Economic and Social Union shall continue to be valid unless otherwise provided in this Treaty and unless they become irrelevant in the process of establishing German unity. . . .

Article 41: Settlement of Property Issues

(1) The Joint Declaration of 15 June 1990 on the Settlement of Open Property Issues (Annex III) issued by the Government of the FRG and the Government of the GDR shall form an integral part of this Treaty.

(2) In accordance with separate legislative arrangements there shall be no return of property rights to real estate or buildings if the real estate or building concerned is required for urgent investment purposes to be specified in detail, particularly if it is to be used for the establishment of an industrial enterprise and the implementation of this investment decision deserves support from a general economic viewpoint, above all if it creates or safeguards jobs. . . .

Article 42: Delegation of Parliamentary Representatives

(1) Before the accession of the GDR takes effect, the Volkskammer shall, on the basis of its composition, elect 144 Members of Parliament to be delegated to the 11th German Bundestag together with a sufficient number of reserve members. Relevant proposals shall be made by the parties and groups represented in the Volkskammer. . . .

Document 4:

Conservative historian Ernst Nolte replied to Niklas Luhmann's remarks (Document 1) by pointing out other areas of historical continuity and by reaffirming the legacy of West Germany.

Ernst Nolte on the Continuity of German History, 5 September 1990

(Source: "Untergang der Bundesrepublik: Zur Frage der Kontinuität in der Nachkriegsgeschichte," *Frankfurter Allgemeine Zeitung*, 5 September 1990)

Three main perspectives

There are nonetheless reasons which make it necessary to review these simple presentist statements [because they involve] historical perspectives which can be gained only by distancing oneself from the picture painted by the immediate present.

The first of these points seems to justify the claim that East Germany became a depressed area only because, at the Potsdam Conference, the Americans insisted on the condition that the region of the future GDR become the "province of reparations" for the Soviet Union, which had suffered particularly severely in the war. This was done for the protection of the western occupied zones, to counter what the United States considered the "provisional" separation of eastern Germany by the Soviet Union. . . . No matter how economically prosperous West Germany is, as one of the two successor states to the Third Reich, it differs from East Germany only on the surface. If the Soviet Union were to leave the GDR, the two states would be back on equal footing with each other. Unification would establish something new by reestablishing something old.

This perspective is not the only one, nor is it the most important. East Germany was also a "socialist state," and its economic system contributed essentially to its becoming a depressed area. Socialism was not simply imposed upon the country from outside, however. In 1945 and '46, all German parties, even the CDU in the western sectors, condemned the "capitalist economic system," and most of them sought salvation in socialism. But socialism was (and Niklas Luhmann correctly refers to this) "the experiment of the century, involving ethical control of the economy". . . .

Soviet (and later Chinese, North Korean and Cuban) socialism was thus not a "deformation," but the consistent realization of this idea under the existing conditions.

The fact that Germans in the future Federal Republic did not follow this course could only minimally be traced back to "social market economy" pioneers; it was primarily due to the will of the Americans, and even within their ranks there were quite a few anti-capitalists and pro-Soviets. The reason that

West Germany is now in such a better position than East Germany doesn't lie only in the fact that West Germans were spared suffering which East Germans had to endure; more importantly, West Germany had by far the more efficient economic system, even if it was more unjust – in the sense that justice means equality. From this perspective, the unification of the two states is nothing more than the annexation of the GDR by the FRG. But the residents of West Germany should not get credit for the strength which makes this annexation possible. This strength developed as part of a worldwide process which could be considered – not entirely correctly, as could be shown in a more extensive discussion – as a triumph of the United States.

The real difference and uniqueness of West Germany becomes apparent only through a third perspective. Separation from almost a fourth of the former territory of the German Reich and the expulsion of the population created a situation which could be referred to as a "westward shift of Germany" (or to be more exact: a westward shift within Germany). For the first time since the late Middle Ages, Germany's strength in terms of population and economic and political power is once again in the west and the south. This fact is fundamental, and could be changed only by a new "colonization of the east," which is in fact neither possible nor desirable. This merely means that West Germany would have represented the "core" German state even if the political and intellectual public had unanimously abandoned this concept, so that unification would have taken place solely on economic grounds. This was not the case, however; in terms of this exclusively German point of view, West Germany really is the "core state," whose history continues unbroken after retrieving the runaway, amputated fringe state which went astray.

Each of the three perspectives produces a different result. First, the demise of West as well as East Germany, in a new synthesis; second, the absolute victory of one of two antagonistic world economic systems in a Germany which, in the near future, would hardly be easier to distinguish from "capitalist" Eastern Europe than from the United States or Western Europe; and third, East Germany's joining of West Germany, a Germany fundamentally altered due to the "westward shift." Luhmann not sees the Federal Republic only in terms of its economic order, but also in terms of its characteristic "tradition of protest." More important than the protests, however, was the fact that forces always existed which tried to hold their ground against the protests, though in a very "flexible" way, as recently with the issue of the Euromissiles, a decision which presumably was one of the most significant reasons for the development of Soviet perestroika. GDR government authority collapsed after decades of totalitarian rule when it was no longer capable of preventing protest. In West Germany, on the other hand, protests and government authority – in the respective intellectual camps of the left and right wings – pursued a type of "double strategy," thereby supporting unification, though to some extent reluctantly. The former undermined the credibility of GDR propaganda against the "warmongering neo-fascist" state, while the latter prevented the instability which would have emerged from a total victory by demonstrators. This also articulated a characteristic of West German identity which was to spread to East Germany.

Three possible outcomes

The essential features and alternatives of the actual course can easily be predicted. The depressed area will blossom within several years by means of enormous subsidies, if the economy doesn't collapse. "Capitalism" will pass over East Germany like a whirlwind, stirring up the economy and sooner or later destroying the "earnestness" of the society, which represents the best part of the legacy inherited by GDR residents from four decades of separate history. Until recently, some political powers in West Germany have held to the idea of maintaining two states, in hopes of achieving a "better socialism." Even if they succeed in pushing through essential constitutional amendments, either in roundabout fashion or with a simple majority, the future Germany will resemble West Germany much more than East Germany. For this reason, the third perspective is the most likely and most significant alternative; the outcome will be that the FRG will not come to an end, but will continue in a combined Germany. . . .

In truth, Germans have three times played a leading role in the drama of world history triggered by the strongest and most motivating initiative of the twentieth century, the attempt to achieve socialism – the age-old dream of humanity – in Russia and areas under its rule or influence. This was a major experiment, the failure of which was only gradually recognized. In the Weimar Republic, Germans followed a promising and paradigmatic path. In the Third Reich, the majority, through their interpretation, took on the disastrous role of the main enemy. Not until the formation of the FRG did they succeed in finding a better and more successful track, in cooperation with Western powers. No matter which symbol it chooses, the Federal Republic should neither give itself up nor deny its history. This will enable it, in retrospect, to do justice to East German history as well.

Document 5:

Because Christa Wolf, a leading writer of the GDR, believed in democratizing socialism, conservative West German literary critics harshly attacked her for collaborating with the regime. Hanover political scientist Jürgen Seifert rejected these strictures by showing that her book *Kassandra* was a parable of Stasi repression.

Jürgen Seifert on the Christa Wolf Controversy, September 1990

(Source: "*Kassandra* und *Marmor-Klippen*. Christa Wolf's übersehene Stasi-Kritik," in: *DDR - Ein Staat vergeht*, T. Blank and R. Erd, eds., Frankfurt, 1990, 48ff.)

A double standard still prevails in Germany in its judgment of the left and right wings. Three years after the end of the war, Karl O. Paetel was able to write the following in his book on Ernst Jünger: "*Marmor-Klippen*[*] has correctly been called an anti-fascist book." No one questioned this statement, not even those who criticized Jünger for his earlier works. Everyone was forced to deal with *Marmor-Klippen*.

Christa Wolf's *Kassandra*[**] was published in 1983. It can only be interpreted as an anti-Stalinist book, severely criticizing the SED regime. But anyone not wanting to endanger Christa Wolf and her decision to stay in East Germany had to refrain from saying so at the time. It is, of course, no coincidence that *Kassandra* was first published in West Germany and [appeared] only in East Germany in 1984, with revisions. . . .

What's the matter with our literary criticism? How is it possible that the relationship between Christa Wolf and the GDR regime can be discussed today . . . without referring to *Kassandra* in the same way that *Marmor-Klippen* is mentioned in reference to Jünger? Why do critics fail to draw a connection between Christa Wolf's new text on the Stasi security apparatus, *Was bleibt,*[***] and corresponding passages in *Kassandra*? Is it merely forgetfulness? I believe it shows that our literary critics are not immune to manipulation by current political trends, leading them to overlook the specific political context of an encoded text.

Christa Wolf presented her entanglement in the SED regime and her renunciation of it in *Kassandra*. Just as Jünger did not deny his position in "Mauretanian" circles, Wolf deals with her "transition from the world of the palace."[****] Her "marble cliffs" are the heights of Mount Ida. She doesn't return, however – as Jünger does – to the "court in the old oak woods" and the "peace of my father's house;" instead, after deciding to speak up, she takes the path past the "grave of the heroes," via the common ground of women in rock caves, to a violent death which she neither can, nor wishes, to avoid. Jünger trusts in the "spirit" as a "magic sword whose glow pales the power of the tyrant." Christa Wolf, as Kassandra, declares that she has laid down her weapons, and "that was as much as I could change". . . .

When *Kassandra* was published, it was possible, both here and in East Germany, to recognize that the apparatus of the state security (Stasi) in East Germany was implied. Here is some evidence: "Eumelos's men" throw their

---

[*] Written during the Third Reich, Ernst Jünger's, *At the Marble Cliffs*, Penguin Publishers, was a veiled attack on the Nazi system from a neo-conservative point of view.

[**] Christa Wolf, *Kassandra*, Darmstadt, 1983.

[***] Christa Wolf, *What Remains and other Stories*, New York, 1991.

[****] All English quotes are from Christa Wolf, *Cassandra*, London 1984, translated by Jan van Heurch.

"security net" over the city. Service performed for Eumelos is considered "dishonorable;" there are "Eumelos's men in disguise." "Eumelos's men, who are at the bottom of everything," organize psychological defense. Eumelos decides on the "use of words," taking measures to "regulate speech" ("All of a sudden those of us who persisted in saying `welcome guest', including me, found themselves under suspicion.") Eumelos had "disciples among the palace scribes and the servants in the temple." He wants people "the way the war wants us." He stockpiles "mental armament" by "defamation of the enemy." Eumelos has power: "He tightened the screws." "Chains" and "security cordons," "strict controls" and "special authorizations for security personnel" are all part of the "height of his power." Eumelos "makes do without grounds." His people arrest Cassandra and take her to the "grave of the heroes." . . .

Anyone who wishes to judge Christa Wolf today has to deal with this position. Anyone – such as Ulrich Greiner. . . – who has the gall, as is widespread here, to accuse her of not having sought "refuge in the West" must face the following question: Why was something like "internal emigration" recognized as a legitimate response to national socialism, while the criticism expressed by Christa Wolf and her "distanced position" with regard to the SED regime are not? These judges need to reread *Kassandra* and ask themselves how much of the spirit of "Eumelos" and the "cold war" (which includes us as well) they have inside.

Document 6:

In place of a peace treaty, the Two-Plus-Four Talks produced an agreement that stipulated the international conditions of German unification, such as the extent of its territory and the return of its sovereignty.

Treaty on the Final Settlement with Respect to Germany, 12 September 1990

(Source: German Information Office, *Treaty on the Final Settlement with Respect to Germany*, September 1990)

The FRG, the GDR, the French Republic, the Union of Soviet Socialist Republics, the United Kingdom of Great Britain and Northern Ireland and the United States of America,

- Conscious of the fact that their peoples have been living together in peace since 1945;

- Mindful of the recent historic changes in Europe which make it possible to overcome the division of the continent;

- Having regard to the rights and responsibilities of the Four Powers relating to Berlin and to Germany as a whole, and the corresponding wartime and post-war agreements and decisions of the Four Powers;

- Resolved in accordance with their obligations under the Charter of the United Nations to develop friendly relations among nations based on respect for the principle of equal rights and self-determination of peoples, and to take other appropriate measures to strengthen universal peace;

- Recalling the principles of the Final Act of the Conference on Security and Cooperation in Europe, signed in Helsinki;

- Recognizing that those principles have laid firm foundations for the establishment of a just and lasting peaceful order in Europe;

- Determined to take account of everyone's security interests;

- Convinced of the need finally to overcome antagonism and to develop cooperation in Europe;

- Confirming their readiness to reinforce security, in particular by adopting effective arms control, disarmament and confidence-building measures; their willingness not to regard each other as adversaries but to work for a relationship of trust and cooperation; and accordingly their readiness to consider positively setting up appropriate institutional arrangements within the framework of the Conference on Security and Cooperation in Europe;

- Welcoming the fact that the German people, freely exercising their right of self-determination, have expressed their will to bring about the unity of Germany as a state so that they will be able to serve the peace of the world as an equal and sovereign partner in a united Europe;

- Convinced that the unification of Germany as a state with definitive borders is a significant contribution to peace and stability in Europe;

- Intending to conclude the final settlement with respect to Germany;

- Recognizing that thereby, and with the unification of Germany as a democratic and peaceful state, the rights and responsibilities of the Four Powers relating to Berlin and to Germany as a whole lose their function;

- Represented by their Ministers for Foreign Affairs who, in accordance with the Ottawa Declaration of February 13, 1990, met in Bonn on May 5, 1990, in Berlin on June 22, 1990, in Paris on July 17, 1990 with the participation of the Minister for Foreign Affairs of the Republic of Poland, and in Moscow on September 12, 1990;

Have agreed as follows:

Article 1:

(1) The united Germany shall comprise the territory of the FRG, the GDR and the whole of Berlin. Its external borders shall be the borders of the FRG

and the GDR and shall be definitive from the date on which the present Treaty comes into force. The confirmation of the definitive nature of the borders of the united Germany is an essential element of the peaceful order in Europe.

(2) The united Germany and the Republic of Poland shall confirm the existing border between them in a treaty that is binding under international law.

(3) The united Germany has no territorial claims whatsoever against other states and shall not assert any in the future.

(4) The Governments of the FRG and the GDR shall ensure that the constitution of the united Germany does not contain any provision incompatible with these principles. . . .

Article 2:

The governments of the FRG and the GDR reaffirm their declarations that only peace will emanate from German soil. According to the constitution of the united Germany, acts tending to and undertaken with the intent to disturb the peaceful relations between nations, especially to prepare for aggressive war, are unconstitutional and a punishable offense. The governments of the FRG and the GDR declare that the united Germany will never employ any of its weapons except in accordance with its constitution and the Charter of the United Nations.

Article 3:

(1) The Governments of the FRG and the GDR reaffirm their renunciation of the manufacture and possession of and control over nuclear, biological and chemical weapons. They declare that the united Germany, too, will abide by these commitments. In particular, rights and obligations arising from the Treaty on the Non-Proliferation of Nuclear Weapons of July 1, 1968 will continue to apply to the united Germany.

(2) The government of the FRG, acting in full agreement with the Government of the GDR, made the following statement on August 30, 1990 in Vienna at the Negotiations on Conventional Armed Forces in Europe:

"The Government of the FRG undertakes to reduce the personnel strength of the armed forces of the united Germany to 370,000 (ground, air and naval forces) within three to four years. This reduction will commence on the entry into force of the first CFE* agreement. . . ."

The government of the GDR has expressly associated itself with this statement. . . .

Article 4:

---

* Agreement on the reduction of conventional forces in Europe.

(1) The governments of the FRG, the GDR and the Union of Soviet Socialist Republics state that the united Germany and the Union of Soviet Socialist Republics will settle by treaty the conditions for the duration of the presence of Soviet armed forces on the territory of the present GDR and of Berlin, as well as the conduct of the withdrawal of these armed forces which will be completed by the end of 1994, in connection with the implementation of the undertaking of the FRG and the GDR referred to in paragraph 2 of Article 3 of the present treaty. . . .

Article 5:

(1) Until the completion of the withdrawal of the Soviet armed forces from the territory of the present GDR and of Berlin in accordance with Article 4 of the present treaty, only German territorial defense units which are not integrated into the alliance structures to which German armed forces in the rest of German territory are assigned will be stationed in that territory as armed forces of the united Germany. During that period and subject to the provisions of paragraph 2 of this Article, armed forces of other states will not be stationed in that territory or carry out any other military activity there.

(2) For the duration of the presence of Soviet armed forces in the territory of the present GDR and of Berlin, armed forces of the French Republic, the United Kingdom of Great Britain and Northern Ireland and the United States of America will, upon German request, remain stationed in Berlin by agreement to this effect between the government of the united Germany and the governments of the states concerned. . . .

(3) Following the completion of the withdrawal of the Soviet armed forces from the territory of the present GDR and of Berlin, units of German armed forces assigned to military alliance structures in the same way as those in the rest of German territory may also be stationed in that part of Germany, but without nuclear weapon carriers. This does not apply to conventional weapon systems which may have other capabilities in addition to conventional ones but which in that part of Germany are equipped for a conventional role and designated only for such. Foreign armed forces and nuclear weapons or their carriers will not be stationed in that part of Germany or deployed there.

Article 6:

The right of the united Germany to belong to alliances with all the rights and responsibilities arising therefrom, shall not be affected by the present treaty.

Article 7:

(1) The French Republic, the Union of Soviet Socialist Republics, the United Kingdom of Great Britain and Northern Ireland and the United States of America hereby terminate their rights and responsibilities relating to Berlin and to Germany as a whole. As a result, the corresponding, related quadripartite

agreements, decisions and practices are terminated and all related Four Power institutions are dissolved.

(2) The united Germany shall have accordingly full sovereignty over its internal and external affairs. . . .

Document 7:

In preparation for German Unity Day on 3 October 1990, the editor of the Warsaw journal *Polityka* reflected on the implications of German unification for Europe.

Adam Krzeminski on Germans and Poles, 2 October 1990

(Source: "Über die Geschichte der Polen mit den Deutschen: Polen ist zu der Hoffnung verdammt, daß alles anders wird," *taz*, 2 October 1990)

Does a foreigner have the right to intervene if a people is on the verge of adopting or granting or being granted a constitution? If I speak up now, then it is because we are not the only ones affected by our common German-Polish history. This tinderbox has sparked and inflamed all of Europe. . . .

In 1945, peace after Yalta and Potsdam was difficult. Germany lost the war of aggression and had to pay for the genocide. And Poland didn't win the war. It became smaller and was shifted to the West, since Stalin's "Devil's Pact" with Hitler in 1939 was still valid in the East. Millions of Germans and Poles were driven from the East to the West and resettled. The former eastern Germany became western Poland, and eastern Poland became the western Ukraine and western Belorussia. Germany was divided into the occupation zones, out of which two unequal states developed in 1949. One of them already recognized the border with Poland in 1950 in the Görlitz Treaty, though, of course, this did not receive any particular legitimacy from its population – as was the case regarding other issues as well. The other German state was more legitimate on account of free elections, but it took its time clarifying relations with its neighbors to the east.

Where does Germany end?

Why should it have clarified its neighborly relations anyway, when it believed that it existed "for a transitional period" only, as stated in the preamble of the constitution, until "the other parts of Germany" joined the Federal Republic. But Article 23, that has since become famous, doesn't say which parts are meant: Saxony, Brandenburg, Mecklenburg, etc., or maybe heading towards Memel: Silesia, Pomerania, East Prussia? And now the border is finally going to be officially recognized; the preamble and Article 23 are to become inapplicable. But who is "German" according to the constitution? The answer can be found in Article 116: it is "whoever holds German citizenship, or a spouse or descendant thereof, who resided within the territory of the German Reich as of 31 December 1937." So, someone of German heritage who lived in the part of Upper Silesia belonging to Poland before the war isn't German? But hundreds of thousands of people belonging to the Polish minority in the part of Upper Silesia which belonged to Germany at the time, including their spouses and descendants, they are all Germans. That has been one way in the last few years of miraculously increasing the number of qualified Germans. Article 116 makes it possible that not only Germans living in Germany and other ethnic Germans are considered "German," but also those who obtain this modern-day "Aryan Passport." The glaring affluence gap creates the suction; and Article 116 is the suction pump. . . .

The new Wall

Granted, it isn't as bad as we feared. But it's worse than we hoped. Many were afraid, we in Poland as well, that the massive strength of a united Germany would be used against its weaker neighbors. It's difficult to say how much we projected our own weakness onto what we considered Germany's strength. But in any case, we were angered by the national awakening which took the inferiority complex of the good East Germans – in comparison to their successful Western uncles – and dumped it on us in the East. . . . The Wall still exists in Europe – not in Berlin, but around the German embassy in Warsaw and at the Oder Neisse border. . . .

We never liked each other all that much, the Poles and the Germans. We Poles had more rights; we fought for them. You East Germans had more things; you worked for them to some degree, and you got some of them from those who wanted to achieve "humanitarian relief" by "filtering in" money. You think you're something better . . .

Did we really never like each other very much? Yes we did. We cheered you on, exactly a year ago, as you swam across the Oder-Neisse border in the middle of the night to get to Warsaw. And we also cheered you on in October when you finally overcame your fear of walking on the grass, taking on more than just billy clubs. And we were happy to see the people chipping down the Wall in November. And that was it. Then came the silent scream in Leipzig: We are one people, three times around the old city center and then into bed, with the operetta song on your lips: "Such a wonderful day as today". . . .

The dream of a beautiful Germany. . . .

And lately? One could imagine Germans will realize after 3 October that a considerable portion of their problems cannot be solved alone, but only together with their eastern neighbors. We need you, but you need us too, if we want to avoid friction in the neighborhood. Our mutual relations are morally grounded, not only because of a disastrous history but because of pragmatic interests for the future, so that the gap between us does not continue to deepen and have serious consequences. . . .

Many dream of a beautiful Germany – imbued with patriotism to the constitution and not controlled by patriotism to the German mark, federally bound. So that the weaker, pathetic part doesn't have to cower before the more popular and effective one; a Germany which is capable of insightful dialogue (so that something remains); a Germany that doesn't show its fists; one which knows its borders, even in the constitution, and its superior strength relative to its weaker neighbors; a Germany which does not greet these neighbors with a casual "This is nothing but junk; we'll take over the store," but rather helps them pull themselves together and become competitive. But that also demands a little "heroism of retreat" in the West, retreat from their own position of power, for example, in second and third world debt, in technology transfer and freedom of travel, which not too long ago was held out to us like candy, and which has since been taken away. . . .

Document 8:

In the early fall of 1990, surveys by Leipzig social researchers found the East German public skeptical about the immediate future but optimistic about long-term prospects.

Leipzig's Hopes for an Economic Miracle, October 1990

(Source: *Pressespiegel*, 1990, No. 17, 6f.)

They're back on the streets of Leipzig – the interviewers of the Central Institute for Youth Research. This time they're asking passers-by what name they would like to give to Karl Marx Square instead of the present one. In contrast to what used to happen, however, the findings of the survey, whether considered opportune or not, do not disappear into a safe somewhere, nor are the social scientists obliged to treat their work as confidential. . . .

For example, one of the questions went as follows: "What do you think your future will be like in the next two to three weeks with respect to . . .?" Several things were then mentioned. To "... with respect to your options and ability to cope with a totally changed living situation," 83 percent answered either "optimistic" or "more optimistic than pessimistic." With respect to their income, it was 63 percent; and with respect to job security, 61 percent. Only 43 percent of those asked were optimistic with respect to the future cost of living.

There were also questions about the economic outlook. "Definitely" or "probably" was the response given by 78 percent with regard to the chance of the unemployment level in eastern Germany reaching the millions. Seventy-three percent were convinced, however, that performance would still be rewarded.

Sixty-seven percent hoped for many new jobs, 61 percent for an "economic miracle in East Germany." Fifty-eight percent expected a high level of social security; only 21 percent, however, expected a considerable wage increase before too long.

Most responded with skepticism toward the relationship between East and West Germans in a united Germany. Not even half of those interviewed believed that West Germans would demonstrate any willingness to make sacrifices, or that former East Germans would be accepted as Germans having equal status to West Germans.

When asked about their general experiences with the market economy, 22 percent answered "mainly good" (at the end of July it was still 25 percent). This satisfaction (or dissatisfaction) varied among population groups: Unemployed – 18 percent; blue-collar workers – 18 percent; white-collar workers – 23 percent; farmers – 10 percent; self-employed – 33 percent; retired – 24 percent. The political views of those interviewed also played a significant role in their ratings. Thirty-four percent of CDU voters, 21 percent of SPD voters and only 14 percent of PDS voters had "mainly good" experiences so far. . . . The most obvious rejection of the new economic system (experience: "mainly bad") came from farmers – 20 percent, and the unemployed – 16 percent. Those people who were dissatisfied with their market economy experience estimated an average of 7.23 years until the present East Germany achieves the economic level of West Germany; those with positive experiences estimated 6.06 years

Another set of questions was dedicated to the national identity of GDR citizens on the eve of unification. Last November, 76 percent considered themselves "definitely Germans;" now the number decreased to 72 percent. Last November, 76 percent considered themselves to be "definitely GDR citizens;" in the meantime only 48 percent still gave this answer. . . .

Many questions dealt with citizens' trust in particular political parties and politicians. In answer to the question "Which party should govern united Germany?" 23 percent of those questioned in February wanted a CDU/CSU administration; this rose in August to 48 percent. An SPD government was favored by 77 percent in February and by only 52 percent in August. The strongholds of the parties and movements which had already become apparent in the previous elections were confirmed by the surveys by the Leipzig researchers and their large team of assistants. One question was as follows: "Which party or movement would you vote for in the upcoming Bundestag elections?" The CDU found the most support among the self-employed, farmers, and blue-collar workers, mostly under 25 years old and in smaller towns, primarily in Thuringia and Saxony-Anhalt.

The PDS, on the other hand, was preferred by white-collar workers as well as university and technical college graduates, by younger voters, and by those primarily in the large cities.

The grass roots citizens' movements were supported mostly by younger people in larger cities, particularly college graduates and the self-employed. . . .

Document 9:

At a ceremony in Berlin on German Unity Day, President Richard von Weizsäcker celebrated the achievement of external unification and called for efforts to achieve internal harmony.

Richard von Weizsäcker on the Consummation of Unity, 3 October 1990

(Source: *Frankfurter Allgemeine Zeitung*, 4 October 1990)

The preamble to our constitution, which from today on applies to all Germans, says the decisive words that move us today: In free self-determination, we complete the unity and freedom of Germany. We hope to serve world peace in a united Europe. In our tasks, we are aware of our responsibility before God and humanity.

From the bottom of our hearts, we feel gratitude and joy – and at the same time a great, serious duty. The history of Europe and Germany now offers us a chance never before available. We are experiencing one of the very rare historical periods in which things can truly be changed for the better. Let us not forget for a moment what this means to us.

There are pressing concerns here and abroad; we will not ignore this. We take our neighbors' reservations seriously. We also sense how difficult it will be to live up to the expectations, coming from every direction. But we do not want to, and will not, be steered by fear and doubt, but instead by confidence. Most important is our firm will to recognize our tasks with clarity and tackle them together. This will gives us the strength to bring our daily problems into the proper relationship to our past and future in Europe.

For the first time, we Germans do not form a point of contention on the European agenda. Our unity was not forced, but peacefully negotiated. It is part of an historical, pan-European process aimed at achieving the freedom of all peoples and a new, peaceful order on our continent. We Germans hope to serve this aim. Our unity is dedicated to it.

We now have a state that we no longer consider provisional and whose identity and integrity are no longer disputed by our neighbors. On this day, the united German nation takes its acknowledged place in Europe. . . .

The form of unity has been found. Now it must be filled with substance and life. Parliaments, governments, and parties must help. But unity can be carried out only by the sovereign people, in the hearts and minds of the people themselves. Each of us perceives how much remains to be done. It would be neither sincere nor helpful at this hour to conceal how much continues to separate us from each other.

The external coercion of division did not achieve its goal of alienating us. Anti-human as the Wall and the barbed wire were, they simply deepened the will to come together. We felt this most strongly in Berlin, this city of major significance for the past and the future. Seeing and feeling the Wall every day made us continue to believe in and hope for the other side. Now the Wall is gone; that is the most important thing. But now that we have freedom, we have to learn to live with it. We recognize more clearly than before the consequences of our different paths of development. The first to meet the eye is the material gap. Even though the people of the GDR were confronted daily with an economy of shortages, made the best of it, and worked hard, the full extent of the problem, and thus the distance from the West, has become completely clear only in recent months. If we are to succeed in overcoming this gap quickly, not only do we need mutual assistance, but above all mutual respect.

For Germans in the former GDR, unification is a daily existential process of adjustment that affects them directly and personally. It often makes superhuman demands on them. A woman wrote me that she was deeply grateful for freedom but didn't know the change would touch such a raw nerve by literally demanding that she bid herself farewell. She wanted nothing more than to be rid of her regime. But simultaneously replacing all elements of one's own life overnight with something new and unfamiliar exceeds human capabilities.

For the people of the West, joy at the fall of the Wall was infinitely great. But the fact that unification will have anything to do with their personal lives has not become clear, or is even highly unwelcome, to many.

It cannot remain this way. We must first of all come to understand each other better. Only when we truly realize that both sides have amassed valuable experiences and important qualities worth preserving in unity will we be on the right track. . . .

Today we have found our common state. No government treaty, constitution, or legislative decision can determine how well unity will succeed on a human level. It depends on the behavior of each one of us, on our own openness to one another. It is "the plebiscite of every single day" (Renan[*]) from which the character of our polity will emerge.

I am certain we will succeed in overcoming old and new divisions. We could combine the constitutional patriotism which evolved on one side with the human solidarity lived on the other to form a powerful whole. We have the common will to fulfill the great tasks our neighbors expect of us. We know how much more difficult it is for other peoples on this earth. The more convincingly

---

[*] French writer who defined the nation as a result of political approval by its citizens.

we manage to live up to our responsibilities for peace in Europe and in the world in a united Germany, the better it will be for our future at home. History has given us the chance. We must take advantage of it with confidence and trust.

Document 10:

The creation of states in the former GDR, prepared by designated officials, was completed with the legislative elections of 14 October 1990. The CDU, or a coalition of CDU and FDP, was able to achieve a majority in all of the new states except Brandenburg.

Results of the East German State Elections, 14 October 1990

(Source: *Pressespiegel*, 1990, No. 16, 1ff.)

Mecklenburg-West Pomerania

Voter Turnout: 65.22 Percent

(18 March: 92.97 Percent)

Party	14 Oct. (percent)	Seats	18 March (percent)
CDU	38.33	29	36.34
SPD	27.00	21	23.41
PDS	15.65	12	22.81
FDP	5.48	4	3.59
Bündnis 90	2.22	—	2.37
CSU	1.11	—	—
DSU	0.75	—	2.39
Greens	4.16	—	2.00
NPD	0.17	—	—
Neues Forum	2.92	—	—
Reps	0.89	—	—
Others	1.32	—	7.09

Saxony-Anhalt

Voter Turnout: 65.64 Percent

(18 March: 93.41 Percent)

Party	14 Oct. (percent)	Seats	18 March (percent)
CDU	38.99	48	44.54
SPD	26.00	27	23.70
FDP	13.51	14	7.71
PDS	11.98	12	14.01
Greens/ Neues Forum	5.29	5	3.97
DFD	1.11	—	—
DSU	1.71	—	2.40
Reps	0.64	—	—
NPD	0.15	—	—
Others	0.62	—	3.67

Thuringia

Voter Turnout: 72.13 Percent

(18 March: 94.46 Percent)

Party	14 Oct. (percent)	Seats	18 March (percent)
CDU	45.40	44	52.5
SPD	22.75	21	17.52
FDP	9.27	9	4.64
PDS/Left List	9.72	9	11.38
NF/Greens/DJ	5.47	6	3.80
DSU	3.28	—	5.76
NPD	0.23	—	—
Reps	0.83	—	—
Others	3.05	—	4.35

Brandenburg

Voter Turnout: 67.43 Percent

(18 March:93.54 Percent)

Party	14 Oct. (percent)	Seats	18 March(percent)
SPD	38.25	36	29.91
CDU	29.40	27	33.56
PDS	13.40	13	18.30
Bündnis 90	6.41	6	3.27
FDP	6.63	6	4.70
DSU	0.98	—	3.32
Greens	2.84	—	2.14
Rep.	1.15	—	—
NPD	0.13	—	—
Others	0.81	—	4.8

Saxony

Voter Turnout: 73.47 Percent

(18 March: 93.58 Percent)

Party	14 Oct. (percent)	Seats	18 March (percent)
CDU	53.82	92	43.31
SPD	19.09	32	15.05
LL/PDS	10.22	17	13.60
NF/Bündnis/ Greens	5.60	10	2.97
FDP	5.26	9	5.69
DA	0.57	—	—
DSU	3.58	—	13.09
NPD	0.68	—	—
Others	1.18	—	6.29

Document 11:

Though the unification treaty agreed on Berlin as the capital, it had left the location of government undecided. Mayor Hans Daniels argued that Bonn's performance as center of democracy spoke in favor of retaining the city as the seat of government.

Hans Daniels's Arguments for Bonn as the Seat of Government, 16 November 1990

(Source: *Die Zeit*, 16 November 1990)

It seems that all arguments pro and con in the debate over the capital have already been made. In taking stock of them, I reach the same conclusion as Countess Marion Dönhoff in her piece for the *Zeit* on 4 May. Neither Bonn nor Berlin; the decision should be Berlin and Bonn. Her words were, "Let us retain Bonn as an effective administrative capital and a pledge for Western integration, and make Berlin the intellectual and cultural center."

I have come to this conclusion not because it would be good for Berlin or Bonn, but because it would be good for Germany. In Germany's thousand-year history, until 1870, there was no dominant capital. In the past forty years, we have seen in the Federal Republic that the modest seat of parliament and government on the Rhine contributed greatly to the steady development of the cities and states. Is there a rational reason to transfer, at great expense, a seat of parliament and government that has functioned excellently for over forty years, and is recognized domestically and abroad? Especially at a time when it is necessary to concentrate all forces and prevent any unnecessary waste. . . ?

When Bonn was chosen as provisional capital in 1949, the *Neue Zürcher Zeitung* stated that no one in Germany or elsewhere in the world considered the decision reasonable, except for the members of the parliamentary council who voted for Bonn and a handful of students who cheered the decision. Over forty years have passed since then, and Bonn basks in the approval of numerous sympathizers in East and West. They attest that the capital of the Federal Republic of Germany has fulfilled its tasks superbly.

Against such a background, gentle ridicule of the city on the Rhine is replaced by thoughtfulness. Why shouldn't we share, as Lothar de Maizière requested for the sake of German unity? Would it really help Germany and Berlin if, in an unparalleled show of strength, the parliament, government, diplomatic corps, associations, and press offices were transferred to the already expanding metropolis? Would it be right to bring to an end a forty-year past that is widely approved in western Germany and considered by the people across the Elbe an object of their hopes and wishes?

I believe reason supports Bonn as the seat of parliament and government. Berlin and Bonn: that is the timely, visionary solution for a united Germany.

Document 12:

In countering Bonn's claims, Mayor Momper insisted on post-war promises that Berlin, as a symbol of German unity, had to be both capital and seat of the actual government.

Walter Momper's Plea for Berlin as the Capital, 16 November 1990

(Source: *Die Zeit*, 16 November 1990)

All of Berlin is the capital of all of Germany. History wrote this sentence; the unification treaty confirmed it.

For 45 years, limits on its sovereignty and the Cold War prevented Germany from installing democratically elected, all-German constitutional organs in Berlin. Now the limitations are gone. Those who turn their backs on history will be punished by the future. And those who casuistically deny their words of yesterday damage their political credibility.

Parliament and government belong in the capital. The word "capital" has never meant anything less than the center of political decision making. Serving as seat of the most important constitutional organs makes a city into a capital. The rarity of exceptions confirms the logic of the rule. The exceptions are based on historical features that cannot be applied elsewhere.

Parliament and government cannot reside in just any city. We are not looking for a location for the business headquarters of "Germany, Inc." We need a suitable central point for a great European people with significant traditions and a difficult history.

Today, Berlin is seen worldwide as a symbol of freedom, division, and unity. And even the link to the West, West Germany's raison d'être, is symbolized not in Bonn but in Berlin – from the airlift, to Kennedy's identification [with the city], to Checkpoint Charlie. The capital Berlin thus makes an essential contribution to German identity, to its process of growing together, to its self-image and its image abroad. In Berlin, parliament works face-to-face with sites of horror and shame. But where historical questions impose themselves, there is a better chance of finding answers for the future. . . .

Our hesitation, on the contrary, arouses doubt about the predictability and credibility of our current policies. We cannot avoid understandable concern at the weight of a united Germany by attempting to pass off a small capital as a pledge of modest policies.

A specter is haunting the discussion on the capital: an all-powerful, centralized Moloch[*] that could undermine federalism. Berlin can never be Paris,

---

[*] tyrannical ancient Semitic deity, to be propitiated by sacrifices.

because Germany has developed polycentrically and is federally constituted. A powerful Prussia, which once lent Berlin its predominance, no longer exists. Today, if we are worried about the federalist balance, we must establish the political center not in the largest state or the prosperous region along the Rhine but in the regions east of the Elbe in need of development and assistance.

The capital Berlin does not need to be built. From Bellevue Castle[**] to the Reichstag[***] to the many government buildings in the eastern part of the city that need to be renovated anyway, no less is available in Berlin than in Bonn. Building Bonn into an all-German seat of government would be no less expensive in the end. The least expensive and most socially acceptable solution would therefore be a distribution which would move the highly political core to Berlin, while leaving some ministries and administrative sections in Bonn.

Document 13:

During its Paris meeting the Conference for Security and Cooperation in Europe formulated a charter, affirming the goals of political and economic freedom. At the same time the CSCE also approved the unification of Germany.

CSCE Charter for a New Europe, 21 November 1990

(Source: Rotfeld and Stutzle, *Germany and Europe in Transition*, 219ff.)

A New Era of Democracy, Peace and Unity

We, the Heads of State or Government of the States participating in the Conference on Security and Co-operation in Europe, have assembled in Paris at a time of profound change and historic expectations. The era of confrontation and division of Europe has ended. We declare that henceforth our relations will be founded on respect and co-operation. . . .

Human rights, democracy and rule of law

We undertake to build, consolidate and strengthen democracy as the only system of government of our nations. In this endeavor, we will abide by the following:

Human rights and fundamental freedoms are the birthright of all human beings, are inalienable and are guaranteed by law. Their protection and promotion is the first responsibility of government. Respect for them is an essential safeguard against an over-mighty State. Their observance and full exercise are the foundation of freedom, justice and peace.

[**] former Hohenzollern castle, ceremonial seat of the Federal President.

[***] former German parliament building, burnt in 1933 and largely restored after the war.

Democratic government is based on the will of the people expressed regularly through free and fair elections. Democracy has as its foundations respect for the human person and the rule of law. Democracy is the best safeguard of freedom of expression, tolerance of all groups of society, and equality of opportunity for each person.

Democracy, with its representative and pluralist character, entails accountability to the electorate, the obligation of public authorities to comply with the law and justice administered impartially. No one will be above the law.

We affirm that, without discrimination, every individual has the right to:

- freedom of thought, conscience and religion or belief,
- freedom of expression,
- freedom of association and peaceful assembly,
- freedom of movement;

no one will be:

- subject to arbitrary arrest or detention,
- subject to torture or other cruel, inhuman or degrading treatment or punishment;

everyone also has the right:

- to know and act upon his rights,
- to participate in free and fair elections,
- to fair and public trial if charged with an offence,
- to own property alone or in association and to exercise individual enterprise,
- to enjoy his economic, social and cultural rights.

We affirm that the ethnic, cultural, linguistic and religious identity of national minorities will be protected and that persons belonging to national minorities have the right freely to express, preserve and develop that identity without any discrimination and in full equality before the law.

We will ensure that everyone will enjoy recourse to effective remedies, national or international, against any violation of his rights.

Full respect for these precepts is the bedrock on which we will seek to construct the new Europe.

Our States will co-operate and support each other with the aim of making democratic gains irreversible.

Economic liberty and responsibility

Economic liberty, social justice and environmental responsibility are indispensable for prosperity.

The free will of the individual, exercised in democracy and protected by the rule of law, forms the necessary basis for successful economic and social development. We will promote economic activity which respects and upholds human dignity.

Freedom and political pluralism are necessary elements in our common objective of developing market economies towards sustainable economic growth, prosperity, social justice, expanding employment and efficient use of economic resources. The success of the transition to market economy by countries making efforts to this effect is important and in the interest of us all. It will enable us to share a higher level of prosperity which is our common objective. We will co-operate to this end.

Preservation of the environment is a shared responsibility of all our nations. While supporting national and regional efforts in this field, we must also look to the pressing need for joint action on a wider scale. . . .

Unity

Europe whole and free is calling for a new beginning. We invite our peoples to join in this great endeavor.

We note with great satisfaction the Treaty on the Final Settlement with respect to Germany signed in Moscow on 12 September 1990 and sincerely welcome the fact that the German people have united to become one State in accordance with the Conference on Security and Co-operation in Europe and in full accord with their neighbors. The establishment of the national unity of Germany is an important contribution to a just and lasting order of peace for a united, democratic Europe aware of its responsibility for stability, peace and co-operation.

The participation of both North American and European States is a fundamental characteristic of the CSCE; it underlies its past achievements and is essential to the future of the CSCE process. An abiding adherence to shared values and our common heritage are the ties which bind us together. With all the rich diversity of our nations, we are united in our commitment to expand our co-operation in all fields. The challenges confronting us can only be met by common action, co-operation and solidarity.

Document 14:

In an interview, Minister of the Interior Schäuble, recovering from an assassination attempt, replied to the demands for constitutional change, raised primarily by the Greens and Social Democrats.

Wolfgang Schäuble on the Constitutional Debate, 28 November 1990

(Source: *Spiegel*, No. 48, 1990, 27)

Spiegel: How prepared is the CDU to oppose a referendum on a new constitution?

Schäuble: Consensus is necessary on constitutional issues. If we want to achieve this, there has to be some flexibility within the framework of our own position. I consider a referendum, under certain circumstances, to be perfectly conceivable, even in consensus with the Social Democrats. It must be clear that changes to the constitution are only possible through Article 79 of the Basic Law, that is, with the necessary amending and thus consensus-building majorities in the Bundestag and Bundesrat. As far as I can tell, this is no longer disputed by the Social Democrats, now that they have retreated from their demand for a constitutional council. Additionally, in a referendum for a new constitution, there can be only yes or no votes. In case of a no, we will have to have another constitution and the Basic Law will have to continue in force. Otherwise this would be a risk, at least theoretically, for which the minister of the interior, at any rate, could not take responsibility.

Document 15:

The SPD's candidate for Chancellor, Saarland premier Lafontaine, explained in a book published shortly before the federal elections why he felt social issues took priority over the national question.

Oskar Lafontaine on the Priority of Social Questions, Fall 1990

(Source: *Deutsche Wahrheiten: Die nationale und die soziale Frage*, Hamburg, 1990, 174ff. and 232ff.)

Those who seek German unity must ask themselves what is German and what is unity. It seems reasonable to take language as a criterion of "Germanness." However, this leads to a dead end as soon as one looks for the connection to unity under current conditions. Trying to make the German language the basis for German unity would mean including not only Silesia, Pomerania, and East Prussia, but also Austria, parts of Switzerland, and Lorraine, Alsace, and Luxemburg, as well as German-speaking enclaves in other countries. No one still seriously thinks in those terms today.

And what does unity mean? Merely living together in one single state? It is good that even those for whom this definition suffices can only imagine a modern, unified German state as a federal state. At least on this point, there is consensus that federalism is a good German tradition; one can assume it will continue in the future to help prevent misuse of centralized power and organize cultural variety regionally and democratically. But society is far from being united through state unity alone. As long as living conditions prevailing in the east of Germany are not even close to those in the western part of the country, German society will continue to be split under one common state umbrella. German state unity was established by state treaty. What is needed now is a sort of social treaty to introduce German social unity. I do not feel that state and social unity are opposites; one complements the other. But I make no secret of the fact that, of the two, social unity is more important to me. First comes the person, his or her freedom, his or her welfare; only then comes the state. Because social issues rank ahead of the national question in my value system, improvement of the living conditions of the people in the former GDR and integration of "foreigners" living in Germany are the most important and only visionary political goals. That is how I felt in the past, and that is how I feel today. Conservatives put the emphasis elsewhere. Preoccupation with the legal categories of German unity long kept the right wing from articulating practical policies on Germany. Not much could be done for the people in the GDR by political know-it-alls sulking in the corner. Belief in freedom and democracy, the call for a united Fatherland meant little when they were not followed by practical policies to bring these values home to the people in the GDR. It was more difficult and unpleasant, but made more sense, to deal with those in power in the GDR in order to achieve at least small, concrete steps to improve people's living conditions. . . .

Two corresponding, but in part also competing, solutions are characteristic for the epoch before us. They can be described as follows:

1. In the mid- and long-term, we must shape the market economy for all of Germany in such a way that it takes into account the lives of future generations: ecology equals long-term economy.

2. In the short and mid-term, we must do everything we can to rescue the states of the former GDR as production sites. We owe it to the citizens there not to replace more than forty years of top-down decision making by the Communist Party with top-down decision making by the West German economy. "Help towards self-help" – this as yet untested axiom should finally be taken seriously.

We are faced with an economic situation that does not appear in economics textbooks. Solutions according to a fixed plan are as useless as ideological concepts. Those who hope to create an Ecotopia in the GDR overnight will fail as badly as those who try to build up the GDR as a business-El Dorado. Instead, what is needed is intelligent pragmatism that preserves the chance for ongoing self-correction.

Document 16:

German Foreign Minister Hans-Dietrich Genscher dominated the FDP campaign. He presented himself as a determined promoter of domestic freedom who was at the same time working to secure unification internationally.

Frankfurter Allgemeine Zeitung on Genscher's Campaign, 28 November 1990

(Source: *Frankfurter Allgemeine Zeitung*, 28 November 1990)

The FDP is running a campaign of sure success. Party chairman Count [Otto] Lambsdorff seems almost relaxed, and top candidate Genscher appears calm and at ease when the FDP's two top men speak in small and medium-sized cities. This time they can enjoy their campaigning without worrying about the results. They like appearing in the East the best; there, the spontaneity of the audience and the responsibility of the politicians are directly related. . . .

Genscher West: In a hall in Oberhausen, not exactly an area favorable to the FDP, the audience crowds in even before the foreign minister arrives, many young people among them, even in the aisles and along the walls; every seat is filled. The faces show a willingness to be enthusiastic. Genscher immediately senses the agreement; applause greets him again and again. He speaks, as the foreign minister of all Germans, about the neighbors' assent to German unity, about the Paris Charter for Europe, and about Gorbachev. The 80 million Germans in one state don't want to be a great power, he says, but to live in freedom, democracy, harmony, and peace with all their neighbors. "Our need for power politics has been taken care of once and for all."

After twenty minutes of foreign policy, he goes on to the costs of unity; he compares them to the costs of division, a loss of freedom and opportunities for the people in the East. He says every bit of humanity had to be sold by the rulers of the GDR. The lower life expectancy was eloquent testimony to the supposedly human face of socialism. It is depressing that many people can still be found in the same positions. The fresh wind of privatization is necessary, says Genscher. He also speaks of higher taxes. The budget has to be tidied up, and West Berlin's positive experience with lower taxes should be applied to East Germany. "We must avoid dividing our people into two envious societies, where one says too little is happening, and the other says too much is happening." In speaking of responsibility for future generations, Genscher mentions not only retirement pensions but also, once again, foreign policy. It is impossible to hear the last few words over the applause: "If you are satisfied with me as foreign minister, and if you think I should carry on, you can make it possible by casting your second vote for the FDP." . . .

Genscher East: In the afternoon, on the Wood Market in Naumburg, interested spectators mix with shoppers by the stalls. Not everyone knows what the

FDP is. "They're the ones who always go with the CDU," a man explains to his neighbor, as Genscher arrives. Genscher makes more or less the same speech as in the West but emphasizes certain aspects more strongly. The German house, he says, must be built not with front and back yards, but with equal opportunity. In Naumburg, as people try to catch a glimpse of his face in the glare of the afternoon sun, Genscher seems more distant than in the hall in Oberhausen. His contact with the audience here does not seem as direct as the lively rapport achieved by Lambsdorff in Weimar. Genscher speaks more reflectively, and perhaps less personally, than Lambsdorff; the audience is diverse, and therefore not as attuned to him as the Oberhauseners and Lambsdorff's freezing Weimarers. However, many more people have gathered.

Carefully, and in contrast to Lambsdorff, Genscher avoids not only attacks during the campaign but also any reference to double-digit election returns, so as not to set a standard for the FDP that could be used as a measure of failure, even if the result, though good, is only single-digit. . . . The 1990 campaign is running more smoothly for the FDP than any since 1980. And the first FDP direct mandate since 1957 seems possible – in Halle[*].

Document 17:

The clear winners in the Bundestag elections were the CDU/CSU and, comparatively even more strongly, the FDP; the indisputable losers were the SPD and Greens. Bündnis 90 and the PDS made surprisingly good showings in the eastern states.

Results of the Federal Elections of 2 December 1990

(Source: *Die Zeit*, 7 December 1990)

---

[*] Genscher war born in this university city in Saxony-Anhalt.

Bundestag Election of 2 December 1990

Votes in Percent

	East	West	Germany	No. of Seats
Turnout	74.5	78.5	77.8	—
CDU/CSU	43.4	44.1	43.8	319
SPD	23.6	35.9	33.5	239
FDP	13.4	10.6	11.0	79
Greens[*]	—	4.7	3.9	—
Bündnis 90[**]	5.9	—	1.2	8
PDS[***]	9.9	0.3	2.4	17
Others[****]	3.8	4.4	4.2	—

Document 18:

Immediately after the elections, the distraught leftist journalist Klaus Hartung attempted an assessment. Instead of crediting Kohl, he saw the outcome as a plebiscite for Genscher, and sought reasons for the defeat of the SPD and Greens.

Klaus Hartung on the Defeat of the Left, 3 December 1990

(Source: *taz*, 3 December 1990)

The Bundestag elections proceeded as though there really were an ideal model voter who always opts for stability and limited change. The muse of history can hold a witches' Sabbath, and German unity can lead to an orgy of change, but Kohl received no historical bonus. The cloak of history has already been returned to costume storage. The spirit of history did not give a government greater chances. No great victory for the SPD, but no dramatic defeat for them either. The German voters did their best, almost like a collective subject,

---

[*] because of their refusal to combine with the eastern Greens, the western Greens fell short of the 5% in the West, needed to obtain parliamentary seats.

[**] by joining forces, the diverse groups of the civic movement managed to obtain more than 5% in the East and got into the Bundestag, since ballots were counted separately in East and West.

[***] the PDS had little success in the West, but obtained seats in the federal parliament on the strength of its votes in the East.

[****] the Reps, DVU or other right-wing groups failed to get enough votes for representation in the Bundestag.

to ensure equal political justice and balance. The implementation of unification was approved. The majority of voters has little criticism, but also little enthusiasm. Political management was rewarded, along with political activity and the true manager of unity; the manager of a new great power with international political consensus was in fact Genscher. If there was anything at all like a plebiscite in this election, it was a plebiscite for Genscher. Genscher is the distinctive all-German figure, Kissinger with a Saxon dialect, who can combine international political routine with attachment to his home. If you wanted to be subtle, you could interpret this as a mild rejection of Kohl.

The year of the executive is over. The SPD did relatively well, considering that, out of an overwhelming wealth of questions about the future, a great sociopolitical challenge, and the fascinating process of capitalist subversion of socialist security, the SPD election campaign produced breathtaking political poverty. Given all imaginable historical alternatives, the SPD decided to be opinionated in the area of deficit financing. Landslides are not popular in this country, and a fateful election doesn't even bother the voter. The question of change is dealt with in the struggle for third place. In the last decade, it was the third man, the third place, that held the actual political key. The fight for the center was exhausted, and it remains so after this election. The new classes of voters had decisive weight. The Greens lost this struggle for third place. Not merely lost; the election results were virtually a brutal punishment, a penalty card from their supporters. The alternative dentist [who voted previously for the Greens] is obviously seeking a new political home. And they lost even more: the prospects of a red-green coalition, the only chance for political modernization in the former Federal Republic, a change of generation, democracy beyond the party monopoly. The survival of the red-green option depended on the Greens. Lafontaine fought a campaign for the other Germany, a campaign against the German unification business. As the representative of this alternative, he can blame the defeat on his party and accept his increased esteem. However, he must consider whether the party he staged in the campaign will have any effect on the real-existing SPD any time soon. In any case, the Green disaster changes the party relationships of the eighties. That needs to be explained.

The Greens did almost everything wrong; more precisely, they preferred the sleepwalking security of the party milieu to reality. If we wanted to be malicious, we might suspect that it was mainly those nostalgic for the eighties, mourners for the lost Federal Republic, who continued to vote Green. It's possible that the resentment-ridden ability to accept responsibility among Green voters had as much force as that of the selfless friends of the PDS. But the PDS was more successful than the Western Greens. The Greens were not the party of the other Germany; they were the party of the former Federal Republic. Not only did they resist reunification; they rejected the newness, the change that unity brought. With pedantic distance, they bargained away the ideas of a new democracy, the strength of the citizens' movements in the East. Anyone who plays unification off against the climate catastrophe or thinks of the hole in the ozone layer in response to radical social change is not trying to make policy but to be in the right. And one shouldn't castigate the voters for not liking know-it-alls. What kind of a party is it that clutches at points of order during an earthquake and allows itself the luxury of doing without its best people? The seriousness of the defeat becomes even more apparent if we consider that ecology has by no means lost its importance during this year of unity. On the contrary, unity itself represents the greatest success of German environmental policies since the word ecology was coined. The nuclear power plants in the East have been shut down; environmental hells from Bitterfeld to Aue[*], where life expectancy averaged ten years less, are now being cleaned up. . . .

The rest of the election results simply confirm the depressing rationality of the all-German voter: the PDS is, to a certain extent, a protest party for those nostalgic for the GDR, although there were more privileged people in the former GDR than the PDS could gain as voters. The relationship between CDU and SPD in the so-called new states leveled off around the all-German average. Considering that mass unemployment and the collapse of social security have provided the first German lesson on the free market economy, one has to say that the voters in eastern Germany also have a great interest in political stability and abstain from expressing disappointment, hopes, and fears at the polls. The same is true of the ex-GDR opposition; it has seats in the new Bundestag. No more, but also no less. And the idea of a multivoiced opposition is far more pleasant than a large delegation of second-rate Greens. This new Bundestag guarantees that the ex-GDR will not disappear from politics without a sound. Ullmann and Gysi lend it a combative and mutually contentious voice. Those in the Green camp who think they sense an air of the fifties have their noses turned in the wrong direction. This election is a penalty. Should the Greens really disappear from the Bundestag, however, this penalty will have the nature of an historic injustice. Nevertheless, after election night, new policies begin. The election results do not define them; they simply inaugurate them.

Document 19:

In its initial analysis of the Bundestag elections, the Institute for Applied Social Sciences (INFAS) attempted to fathom voter shifts and structures.

INFAS Analysis of Voting Patterns, 4 December 1990

(Source: *Der Tagesspiegel*, 4 December 1990)

---

[*] environmentally damaged regions in the GDR, devastated by chemical industry and uranium mining.

In the first all-German Bundestag elections, the voters gave the "architects of German unity" a clear mandate. That is the conclusion of an analysis by the Institute for Applied Social Sciences (INFAS) in Bad Godesberg. The Social Democrats were unable to break through the opinion spiral that had mobilized against them. Given its historical significance, it seems remarkable that voter turnout was hardly higher than in the elections for state parliaments and that, at least in the West, there were no dramatic shifts. For such a momentous event, it has had few visible consequences so far. In the area of the Federal Republic, compared with the last Bundestag elections in January 1987, changes were between 0.1 (for the CDU/CSU) and 3.5 percentage points (for the Greens/AL[*]).

According to INFAS, however, shifting patterns in the western voting region show some movements not apparent in the net change. These patterns are characterized by a truly circular exchange between left and right. The pivot is formed by the liberals, who gained voters from all sides. Thus the Union [CDU/CSU] gained half a million votes, on balance, from the SPD and an additional 140,000 from the Greens but at the same time experienced a migration to the Republikaner (approximately 330,000 voters). The SPD won about 600,000 voters in an exchange with the Greens, but, in addition to losses to the Union, also lost to the FDP (approx. 420,000) and to the "Republikaner" (ca. 110,000). The Greens, on the other hand, once a growing party regardless of current trends, suffered losses in all directions.

Many SPD Voters Stayed Home

Particularly conspicuous is the varied effect of the decrease in voter turnout, which totaled over five percentage points in the West. A particularly large number of former SPD voters stayed home because of a widespread lack of motivation and morale; this caused a loss of about 550,000 votes. The Greens were unable to mobilize some 270,000 of their former supporters. Despite the widespread mood of victory, election fatigue caused the CDU/CSU and FDP far fewer problems. The Union lost 180,000 votes through abstentions, the FDP 75,000. . . .

The question of the extent to which the party landscapes in the two parts of Germany are beginning to resemble each other involves not only political issues and personal motives. Particularly significant is the fact that the social basis of the parties and the political orientation of individual population groups differ quite significantly. The link between industrial workers and "left-wing" parties, which existed in western industrial societies for over a hundred years and has only gradually begun to relax, dissolved completely in the eastern part of Germany. A majority of industrial workers, especially in Saxony and Thuringia, already gave their support to the conservative Alliance for

---

[*] AL are the initials of the alternative list, the name of Berlin Greens.

Germany in the Volkskammer elections, voting for rapid unity and free enter-prise. This time, too, as evidenced by broadbased election day surveys conduct-ed by INFAS, only 25 percent of blue-collar workers in the new Länder voted for the SPD; 48 percent voted CDU, and another 12 percent FDP. In the West, large segments of the working-class population (44 percent) remained loyal to the SPD; this time, the CDU garnered 40 percent of workers' votes (many from the Catholic working class), the FDP only six percent. These widely divergent loyalties represent a very new mentality.

Voting patterns according to age and sex, which were also recorded in sam-ple surveys of voting districts on election day, are also interesting. Men and women barely differed in their preferences. Young voters in East and West, on the other hand, were clearly less sympathetic to the CDU than a cross-section of the population. Among 18- to 24-year-olds in both voting regions, 35 percent voted for the CDU, nine or ten percent for the FDP. In the West, the SPD received 38 percent from young voters, that is, somewhat above the average; in the East they achieved 23 percent, somewhat below the average. The Greens attained 12 percent of young peoples' votes in the West; Bündnis 90 garnered 16 percent in the East.

Document 20:

SPD politician Egon Bahr compared the implications of German unifi-cation with the problems of a late marriage. He mused that the dif-ferent backgrounds of the partners would require a lengthy process of growing together to create internal unity.

Egon Bahr on Prospects for Unity, 14 December 1990

(Source: *Die Zeit*, 14 December 1990)

Truth demands that, in retrospect, we record that unity did not start in the Federal Republic. Almost no one here was impatient, nor did he bring pressure to bear to make a problem out of this illusion or utopia. There was as little in-terest in GDR reality among the West German public as in the SED Politburo. The whole thing began with a man, Mikhail Gorbachev, who, with enormous courage, linked the necessity of basing Europe's future on national self-deter-mination with the consequence that this principle must also apply to the German people. This led to the decision that Russian troops – unlike on 17 June 1953 – would remain in their barracks, creating space for the people of the GDR – a space that is still not without risk.

The smaller, distressed segment of the German people was the decisive fac-tor. It forced peaceful unification by rebelling and streaming through walls that could no longer be held up. It thereby compelled Bonn to introduce the D-mark and also forced agreement in the four capitals, where they did not really want it so quickly in any case. The West Germans were never strong enough to achieve this. The people have Gorbachev and the East Germans to thank for unity. West Germans are in the fortunate position of being able to provide the money, although it has become more expensive than necessary due to the unfortunate accident that unity had to be organized not in the middle, but at the end, of the legislative period.

The heralds of German unity can continue to blow the same fanfare that ear- lier had less to do with the subject itself than with soothing consciences and appeasing our brothers' and sisters' justified suspicion that we had forgotten or turned our backs on them. The call for change through greater contact was already an annoying disturbance almost thirty years ago. Those who preferred to attack hypocrisy, who sought Germany's chance in division and, if necessary, replacing the unkept promises of the victors with German self-determination through two peace treaties, were suspected of having resigned themselves to partition. And yet every day the heralds document how completely unpre- pared unity caught them. There were no plans. There was nothing on the draw- ing board. The budget did not provide for unity. The costs are still incalculable.

Now we have the problems we always hoped for. It's wonderful. So let us look ahead.

I do not want to deal with the economic issues that rightly take center stage today. Even though we have not yet reached rock-bottom and the West German economy is profiting more than it is investing, we can hope for recovery and upswing. The people can wait and expect that things will start looking up in the second half of next year.

As little as national and international unity should and can be diminished, it is still obvious that psychological unity among the people is only just begin- ning. Choosing unity and living with unity are two different things. To use a metaphor, we, the Germans in the East and the Germans in the West, have come together, not without affection, in an indissoluble marriage, with the possibility of belated love. The wedding ceremony was really beautiful, but now we have to get acquainted.

The problems aren't surprising in such a late-wedded couple, of the same age, who do not deny having had other serious relationships in their previous lives. This can be all the more difficult when one party brings a truly impres- sive dowry, while the other can only point to his inner worth – which does not prevent him from expecting a decent new car as a wedding present. And as far as equal rights, one expects difficulties when the economically stronger party not only points to the proven adaptability of the other, but also, and with rea- son, to the fact that, in the final analysis, it was the other who made the first move, who carried out the union, or the accession to the union, or whatever this Article 23 calls the wedding. If the prognosis is to be positive given all these conditions, then in all sobriety only because this German union is indissoluble.

It is important in such cases to recommend that the past not burden the future. This is easier said than done, because it also means that the past must not be suppressed. The Germans in East and West have had forty years of separate experiences, from which we are now taking our leave; but we dare not take leave of our own past lives. . . .

7

Post-Unity Problems and Perspectives

After the achievement of political unity, unexpected problems emerged. The official optimism about an economic "upswing East" (Document 1) gave way to skepticism about unification as a large-scale social experiment (Document 2). The Trusteeship Agency faced severe difficulties in privatizing and salvaging the moribund East German economy (Document 4). In contrast to the speed of the political merger, economic and social integration turned out to be more of a long-term challenge than expected (Document 9). As a result of start-up problems, observers perceived widespread disappointment in the five new states (Document 22).

Issues left open by the unification treaties also had to be resolved. One of the most contentious was the symbolic question of the capital. The Bundestag decided in June 1991 that Berlin and not Bonn should be the seat of most important offices of government (Document 3). Another controversial question was abortion, heatedly debated between "pro life" and "pro choice" advocates. Though a moderate compromise for choice seemed to settle the matter, it was partly repudiated by the Supreme Court (Document 12).

The legacy of the GDR created many unforeseen problems. The material damage caused by pollution (Document 6) was appalling. The shocking revelations of collaboration by the Stasi files spread psychological poison (Document 7). The dismantling of the East German "National People's Army" (Document 8), and the reconstruction of education and research created much resentment (Document 13). The attempts of the courts to wrestle with the legal consequences of GDR repression proved unsatisfactory. Though Erich Honecker was accused of authorizing the killings at the Wall, he was eventually allowed to leave for health reasons (Document 16). The acrimonious debate about collaboration in the example of prominent East German writers left a trail of suspicion (Document 18).

No wonder that the public was irritated and dismayed. In several West German elections the voters blamed the politicians for post-unification difficulties (Document 10). The strains of this rapid transformation caused much psychological suffering in East Germany (Document 14). Especially youths engaged in ugly attacks upon foreigners during the second half of 1992 (Document 15) which raised old fears of German racism abroad (Document 17). But eventually the moderate majority denounced such xenophobia in spontaneous mass demonstrations for tolerance (Document 19). Ultimately the tension was somewhat reduced by a compromise that tightened the asylum provisions of the Basic Law (Document 21).

United Germany also had to find a new international role. The Persian Gulf War and the Yugoslav civil war raised the question of German participation in worldwide military action (Document 5). In European questions, the Bonn government advocated further integration and supported monetary union, planned by the Maastricht Treaty (Document 11). The internal and external questions came together in a renewed search for German identity (Document 20). With the problem of division resolved, the new German question became whether the reunited country could find a national purpose and a sense of multicultural responsibility (Document 23).

Document 1:

The liberal Bavarian paper described the Bonn government's belated measures to bring about an economic recovery in the former GDR.

Süddeutsche Zeitung on the "Upswing East," 13 February 1991

(Source: *Süddeutsche Zeitung*, 13 February 1991, translation based on *German Tribune*)

Chancellor Helmut Kohl says help for the former East Germany is the top domestic policy goal. Economics Minister Jürgen Möllemann wants to give the eastern German states DM 10 billion more than planned each year.

The Länder and municipalities there will receive an immediate advance payment of DM 5 billion from the German Unity Fund in order to overcome current payment problems. The SPD is saying that the government's economic policy for eastern Germany has failed.

Kohl feels that a united effort must be made during the coming months to create new jobs in the new Länder. This should show the people of the former GDR that German government, industry, and society are acting together. . . .

With the help of a concept entitled "Strategy Upswing East," Economics Minister Möllemann hopes to strengthen industry in eastern Germany and cushion the impact of structural change. The FDP politician said in Bonn that the realization of economic and social unity was "much more difficult" than expected and could not be achieved in one year. . . .

In a ten-point plan, Möllemann recommends the increased promotion of private investments and the establishment of new businesses, through, for example, special depreciation allowances and a 12 percent increase in the capital investment bonus. Furthermore, three-year special programs would be needed for regions with very high unemployment. This would require DM 2 billion in federal funds. It is hoped that an "Initiative Program" for the new Länder will speed up public investments designed to improve the infrastructure. Möllemann estimated that DM 8 billion would be needed here over a two-year period. The parliamentary state secretaries in the German Interior and Finance Ministries, Horst Waffenschmidt and Manfred Carstens, announced that the new Länder and municipalities would immediately receive a further partial payment of DM 5 billion from the German Unity Fund to avert payment difficulties. This means that DM 14.6 billion will be transferred from the Fund's planned volume of DM 35 billion in 1991.

The economic policy spokesman of the SPD's parliamentary group in the Bundestag, Wolfgang Roth, accused the government of covering up the failure of its economic policy with respect to the new Länder through "hectic and belated improvements." What was needed was a new concept. Roth called for immediate 100 percent write-off provisions of the 25 per cent investment bonuses. New roads should be built only in the east or as east-west links.

The Trusteeship Agency should take on responsibility in the industrial and regional policy fields and have a stake in companies at a later stage.

Document 2:

This well-known West German sociologist suggested that transformation of the former GDR from 1989 on offered a unique opportunity for observing a large-scale social experiment.

Claus Offe on Unification as Experiment, Summer 1991
(Source: *German Politics*, 1, 1992, 1ff.)

The collapse of state and society in the GDR did not just overthrow the former regime but turned on its head the agenda for research and reflection in the social sciences. . . .

The overwhelming attraction of this theme is not merely a result of the political, moral, historical and emotional associations it evokes. It is also a consequence of the pragmatic recognition that researchers have had the good fortune to see a natural experiment, of such dimensions as could not even approximately be reproduced under "laboratory conditions," get under way before our very eyes. Just as the massive accelerators of modern physicists make it possible to observe the collisions of subatomic particles and their patterns of decay, so too the events of German reunification – only but begun as a constitutional fact of life, and by no means worked out in all its social consequences, let alone completed – place us in the unique position of being able to study the impact of the characteristic West German variety of democratic-capitalist institutions on a society which has not been democratic for nearly 60 years, and for 40 years has certainly not been capitalist. . . .

The potential for explosive social and political conflict results above all from the high rate of unemployment in the old GDR which seems likely to continue for the foreseeable future. In spite of all the efforts, and promises, of the government in Bonn, the number of unemployed in the new Länder amounts to nearly four million, which represents a rate of around 40 per cent. This rate is far in excess of that which obtained during the world economic crisis of the early thirties.

Quite apart from its startling extent, there are three qualitative characteristics which distinguish the current unemployment in the GDR, and may tend to render its effects more acute.

(1) The inhabitants of the GDR have had no experience of the phenomenon of unemployment. . . .

(2) The citizens of the old GDR well know that effective relief can only come from "outside" (that is to say, from political forces in the old Federal Republic) and from "above" (in other words from the Federal Republic government in Bonn, from its budget and from the Trusteeship Agency which it has set up). . . .

(3) Where there do exist spontaneous and energetic efforts for economic betterment, they tend to follow the logic of "lifeboat economics": everybody is looking for an individual way to escape, whether by migration, long-distance commuting, retraining or whatever. The result is an acute and, compared with the previous conditions in the GDR, quite extreme inequality of opportunity depending on age, region, sex, marital status, number of children and professional qualifications. The society of the old GDR has developed an internal cleft between those who get by and those who, at any rate for the time being, have turned out to be the losers. . . .

The coincidence of these three political/cultural dispositions in the population of the GDR (lack of experience of collective action in practice; high-quality expectations as to social advancement; absence of a background of prosperity or of protest) together with the quantitative and qualitative features of GDR unemployment, prevents any favorable prognosis of the course or the end result of economic and political conflicts in the new Länder. Four different forms of such conflicts may be distinguished according to the mode of acting of the participants: *individual* or *collective* action; and *institutional* action, within the framework of legality, which must be contrasted with the *non-institutional* kind. These types of action may be represented by the following matrix:

	Institutional	**Noninstitutional**
Individual	Individual migration and adaptation	Anomie, violence, suicide, etc.
	1	2
	3	4
Collective	Action through political parties, groupings, trade unions	Protest movements, wildcat strikes

Cell 4: the phenomena summarized here have unmistakably and rapidly diminished in frequency, and since mid-1990 have lost all significance and fallen from prominence. Only for a few months in the autumn of 1989 and winter 1989-90 was GDR society a "society in flames;" nowadays one might characterize it as rather an apathetic society, frustrated in its hopes and thoroughly resigned.

Cell 3: the system of political parties, trade unions, professional associations, funded health schemes, manufacturers' groups and chambers of commerce, which plays such an important role in the former West German "corporatist" system, has certainly been swiftly transferred into a GDR context; but, as was demonstrated above, it there lacks the favorable circumstances which only come with long-standing routine and experience. As a consequence these bodies are inappropriate instruments for dealing with the transitional conflicts of GDR society, since they are all controlled by their West German masters. . . .

Cell 2: it is among conflict phenomena of this individual and non-institutional type, which often include illegal or pathological acts, that the highest rates of increase are recorded. Acts of violence at sporting events, or against foreigners, or when driving, or against private property, or within the family, or in self-destructive form are on the increase however you measure them, and delineate the contours of a distinctly *non-civil* society.

Cell 1: individual strategies of going in search of work and adapting to new economic circumstances are certainly the most commonly practised form of coping with conflicts, difficult situations and frustrations, even if they are less automatic than the administrators in Bonn hoped when they set about the process of reunification! The consequences are not only a division of GDR society into a weakened majority, who manage to make ends meet by these methods, and a substantial minority of losers; but also a further hardening of the obstacles on the way to the *solidarity* of this society.

Document 3:

A bare nonpartisan majority in the Federal Parliament voted to make Berlin the seat of parliament, residence of the president, and nucleus of government. As a concession, Bonn would, however, remain the "administrative center" of the Federal Republic.

Bundestag Decision to Make Berlin the Capital, 20 June 1991

(Source: *Blätter für deutsche und internationale Politik*, 1991, 1013f.)

To implement the many resolutions in which the German Bundestag has declared its political desire to return parliament and government to the German capital, Berlin, following German unification, the German Bundestag resolves:

1. The seat of the German Bundestag is Berlin.

2. The federal government, in cooperation with the administrations of the German Bundestag and the Berlin Senate, is instructed to draw up a plan to implement this decision by 31 December 1991. They should rapidly begin to create the necessary facilities in Berlin for sessions of the German Bundestag, its parliamentary groups, and committees. Working conditions should exist within four years. Until then, plenary sessions of the German Bundestag will take place in the federal capital only in special cases, upon decision of the parliamentary advisory committee. Berlin should be completely functional as the seat of parliament and government in ten to twelve years at the latest.

3. The German Bundestag expects the federal government to take suitable measures in Berlin to fulfill its responsibilities to the parliament, and to ensure a political presence in Berlin by moving the main government functions to Berlin.

4. A fair division of labor will be established between Berlin and Bonn, so that Bonn will remain the administrative center of the FRG even after the parliament is moved to Berlin. In particular, ministerial departments and parts of government of primarily administrative character will remain in Bonn; thus the majority of jobs in Bonn will be retained. In addition, proposals will be drafted

for the Bonn region by the federal government or an independent commission, with the assistance of the states of North Rhine-Westfalia and Rhineland Palatinate, with the aim of compensating for the loss of parliamentary and governmental functions through new functions and institutions with national and international significance in politics, science, and culture.

5. The Capital Agreement between the federal government and the city of Bonn will be developed into a Bonn Agreement to compensate for the financial burden placed upon Bonn and the region by the change in function.

6. The President of the Bundestag is requested to create a commission of representatives of all constitutional organs, top federal authorities, and additional independent persons. This independent Federalism Commission will draw up proposals for the distribution of national and international institutions. It will strengthen German federalism by devoting special attention to the new states; its goal will be to locate federal institutions in each of the new states. Existing federal institutions in Berlin may also be used for this purpose. . . .

Document 4:

This East Berlin economist analyzed the Trusteeship Agency and warned of reducing an economic reform to mere privatization. Instead, he pleaded for an industrial policy in order to integrate Eastern Germany into the Western market economy.

Hans Luft on the Trusteeship Agency, December 1991

(Source: *Deutschland Archiv*, 25, 1991, 1270ff.)

Although trusteeship management of property is nothing unusual in civil law, the Berlin *Treuhand* is working under conditions unprecedented for such an authority.

First of all, unlike post-war developments in the former West Germany, the transition to a market economy in the former GDR also involves changing the social system, that is, the desocialization of society.

Secondly, in contrast to other Eastern European countries, this transition to a market economy is tied to the end of the GDR state, including a preliminary phase in which the West German D-mark is introduced into the GDR, signaling the abandonment of East Germany's own currency. This means that each and every business must calculate an opening D-mark balance, which brings up complicated questions of determining the value of existing assets and having this certified by an independent audit, usually by someone from West Germany.

Third, the size of the Treuhand makes it unique in the world. It is responsible for over 8,000 former state-owned companies [VEB], ranging from branches of raw material industries to the various fields of mechanical engineering, light industries, and the food industry. Approximately 15,000 vacation apartments belonging to state-owned companies need to be assigned a new use. And finally, the Trusteeship Agency is responsible for around 25,000 buildings in the trade and hotel sector. In addition, formerly state-owned construction and transportation agencies and newspaper publishers are to be privatized. . . .

Privatization of such great magnitude is without historical precedent. If eastern Germany were to be privatized at the pace with which privatization was carried out in Great Britain during the Thatcher Administration, it would take about 600 years. . . .

Giving privatization a higher priority than rehabilitation of the economy has preordained future problems in eastern Germany, since it inevitably pushed the maintenance of jobs and social services into the background. The primacy of privatization as stated in the Treuhand Law of 17 June was somewhat relativized by the Unification Treaty of 31 August 1990. However, the Trusteeship Agency was still expected to rapidly provide the federal budget with income from the sale of former state-owned companies, to serve as liquidity aid for companies not yet sold. . . .

There is a perpetual battle as to whether businesses should be returned to their former owners or whether the owners should instead receive some sort of financial compensation. It has already been demonstrated that returning the companies nationalized in 1972 is relatively simple. As far as property expropriated after 1945 is concerned, the situation is more complicated, as this involved large companies, often with very complex distributions of ownership that will take years to clarify. Regardless of the theoretical position with respect to the property basis in a market economy – whether exclusively or primarily private property or multiple forms of ownership exist – favoring the return of property over compensation results in discouraging interested investors, since they are left in the dark regarding the future of the company. The resulting production shutdowns can be justified neither in terms of employment policy, nor economically or legally, assuming the property is not and cannot be used or expanded by the former owners in the meantime, so that in any case, compensation will be made only for the originally existing capital. . . .

Making companies profitable without assuring their liquidity is impossible. This represents a major challenge for the Treuhand. In the second half of 1990, it was granted power to take over companies at amounts up to 4.7 billion D-marks without assuming any debts. The German Ministry of Finance also agreed to the Treuhand taking over sureties, guarantees, and other securities. In connection with the opening D-mark balance, starting on 1 July 1990, a former VEB could declare a deficit not covered by its assets as a separate interest-yielding claim (compensatory claim) to the Treuhand.

I believe the entire issue of guaranteeing liquidity needs to take into account that the former VEBs, under the fiscal regulations in the former GDR, were obligated to pay a major portion of their profits, including part of amortization, to the state to finance social policy and the military. On the other hand, investments were financed mostly with loans on basic assets, and 60-70 percent of circulating capital was also financed through loans. . . .

The problem of assuring liquidity for all companies in the former GDR is complicated by the collapse of COMECON and the conversion of trade in Eastern Europe from transfer rubles[*] to hard currencies. The conditions for both new and old supply contracts must be renegotiated. Falling dollar exchange rates have always posed problems for Western European exporters. Imagine how much greater the problems are for Eastern European companies that had exported almost their entire production to former COMECON countries, and all of a sudden have to pay in convertible currency. . . .

Regardless of one's standpoint concerning concrete Treuhand decisions, the theoretical fact remains that economic reform cannot be boiled down merely to privatization, liberalization, and new fiscal policy. It requires at the same time a reallocation of resources and structural changes with respect to social security for the people. This cannot be left up to the market alone; instead, a regulatory state influence is necessary. This does not mean a planned economy, but instead creation of conditions that make it possible for economic decisions to be based on the public interest, and not to erode the foundation for future generations.

Document 5:

This British scholar commented on Germany's post-unification international role, calling it "Gulliver unbound."

William E. Paterson on the Changing Context of Foreign Policy, Winter 1991/92

(Source: *Developments in German Politics*, G. Smith, et al., eds., London, 1992, 137ff.)

German unity removed nearly all the dependent features which defined the role of the Federal Republic in the international arena. By the time unity was achieved on 3 October 1990, Germany had regained its full sovereignty though it accepted a continued constraint on the possession of biological, chemical and nuclear weapons. The resolution of the Berlin issue was particularly important since it had been a major source of leverage on successive governments of the Federal Republic by the Soviet adversary and the Western allies. Indeed the transformation of Berlin's status from Four Power occupation to future German capital is perhaps the most potent symbol of the changes wrought by unity. . . .

---

[*] COMECON unit of account, non-controvertible into hard currency.

The erosion of Soviet power was quickly reflected in the downfall of communist regimes throughout Eastern Europe. This transition was entirely welcome to the Federal Republic and it presented it with a number of new opportunities.

The opening up of Eastern Europe created a huge potential market of 118 million people, excluding the Soviet Union, 118 million people with a hunger for an individualistic Western consumer lifestyle. The geographical position of Germany, its contacts in the area and the strength of its export oriented economy guarantee that Germany will be the major beneficiary of a growth in East European demand. East Europe is also a promising alternative to southern Europe for the siting of the more labour intensive sections of German industrial production. Unlike southern Europe, which is at some distance from the golden triangle, Poland, Czechoslovakia and Hungary are neighbors of Germany. German investments in Eastern Europe have accordingly dwarfed those of its European neighbors. The successful transformation of the economies of Eastern Europe will of course also dramatically improve the prospects of the five new Länder. . . .

Undoubtedly the most difficult problem for Germany is the situation in Yugoslavia. German inhibitions in the security area rule out active support for military intervention. It is also much more difficult than in the Polish or Czech cases to jump over the shadow of Germany's history. In these two cases, the federal government was able to take a generous attitude and to discount the voice or votes of the refugee element. In an intra-ethnic struggle, it is a question of choosing sides, and the Federal Republic has decisively sided with the former German allies of Slovenia and Croatia. This policy has been justified in terms of support for the principle of self-determination that was played down in the morally much more clear cut case of the Baltics. Perhaps even more crucially, it has led to extreme strain on a common European position with the German government announcing its intention to recognize Slovenia and Croatia some time before its European partners. The reasons that have been adduced for this step include the presence of 700,000 Yugoslav workers, mainly Croats and Slovenes, in Germany and heavy lobbying by the Catholic Church. Whatever the grounds, Germany's contribution to a common European foreign policy in Yugoslavia has been regarded as less than helpful by all its Community partners. Its insistence on persisting with its recognition policy also indicates a departure from Germany's normally automatic support for EC foreign policy positions. . . .

The political horizon of the Federal Republic was largely restricted to the European area. Its views on areas outside Europe have rarely been advanced or sought, and when they have been articulated, as on South Africa and the Middle East, it has been from within the protective lager of the European Political Cooperation mechanism. The ending of the Cold War, the virtual demise of the Soviet Union and the weakening economic readiness of the United States to underwrite international public goods like security has coincided with a greatly increased expectation of what Germany can contribute to the maintenance of international order. The United States in particular was keen to offer Germany a "partners in leadership" role. Unfortunately for the United States this is a role, as the Gulf Crisis demonstrated, which neither German public opinion nor German elite opinion is equipped to respond to. The German response to the Gulf Crisis was hesitant, unsure and put some considerable strain on the German-American relationship.

In a damage limitation exercise the German government made very considerable financial contributions to the allies, but this brought it no increase in influence. The government intends to remove the constitutional inhibition to participating in out of area conflict (Article 87A), but this will not take the issue much further. For real change to occur what Germany needs is a sustained public discourse on the specific geopolitical strategic interests of Germany, and under what circumstances force might be employed. There is little sign of such a debate as yet.

The hesitations Germany displays about essaying a more ambitious security role are largely absent in terms of contributing to global economic stability. Germany is bearing the lion's share of the burden in Eastern Europe and the Soviet Union without much help from either the United States or Japan. It has also played a key role in the GATT negotiations though it has not yet unequivocally decided to throw its weight in the direction of concluding the Uruguay Round at the expense of domestic interests, especially agriculture. . . .

The traumatic political history of twentieth-century Germany will ensure that Germany remains a "civilian power;" it will continue to resist efforts by the United States to tie it into some more ambitious security role. Germany will also persist in giving priority to multilateral frameworks. A gradual reduction of the American presence in Europe is assumed, and the Federal Republic will continue to push for the development of a strengthened European defence identity, but it will go to great lengths to avoid a breach with the United States. It will, of course, also bring the incoherence of its own security discussion and its reluctance to make choices into the debates taking place within multilateral frameworks.

Document 6:

The leading Protestant weekly printed a report on water pollution in the East with the bleak prediction that the population would have to continue to drink polluted water in the foreseeable future.

Wolfgang Heinemann on Water Pollution in the East, 28 February 1992

(Source: *Deutsches Allgemeines Sonntagsblatt*, 28 February 1992, translation based on *German Tribune*)

Almost half of all East Germany's 17 million people did not have clean drinking water under the communist regime, according to the last environment report compiled in the GDR. Fertilizer, liquid manure, pesticides, and the inadequately purified industrial effluent and waste water of the municipalities polluted the lakes and rivers. These surface waters are extremely important for the new Länder in eastern Germany.

As the geological requirements for extracting groundwater are often missing, the water-supply enterprises have to take 36 percent of the water required from polluted lakes and rivers. The corresponding figure in western Germany is 27 percent. It was hoped that things would improve following unification – including drinking water. Politicians in Bonn promised to raise the environmental standards in eastern Germany to the western level within just a few years.

The pollution of the most vital of foodstuffs with heavy metals, nitrate, and pesticides would be brought down to the ceiling levels by the end of 1995, they said. Until then, the European Community has suspended its Drinking Water Directive but placed the German government under an obligation to present a sanitation plan for the eastern German sources of drinking water by the end of February. Can people in the new Länder hope, at long last, for clean water?

Up to now, the German government has claimed that the ceiling levels for [the] Drinking Water Directive would soon be reached. Within the framework of the "Upswing East" project, DM 116 million was invested to this end in the new Länder in 1991. Another DM 800 million is earmarked this year.

SPD environment expert Klaus Lennartz and the nature conservation organizations, however, fear that this is just a drop in the ocean. Greenpeace and the Environment and Nature Conservation Association (Bund) speak of a permanent drinking water crisis in the former GDR. Lennartz takes the view that what comes out of the taps in some areas is dangerous to life. This was panic-mongering, the German Health Ministry declared. Studies had shown that such a health hazard did not exist.

However, one Ministry expert admitted that only 50 percent of the 7,600 wells of the eastern German waterworks had been checked. An extensive analysis was not to be expected until the end of 1992. The critics feel that this is not good enough. As long as the drinking water plants were not improved, 1.4 million people would have to drink mainly nitrate-polluted water.

Nitrate primarily finds its way to the fields through the liquid manure from mass livestock farming in agricultural factories and then flows via ground and surface water into the waterworks. According to a Greenpeace study, as much as two-thirds of the water channeled into the network does not always meet the stipulations of the Drinking Water Directive. . . .

Toxic heavy metals, such as arsenic and mercury, solvents, and other chemicals make drinking water in eastern Germany a dangerous cocktail. In the 839 supply enterprises reviewed, the German Environment Ministry confirmed that ceiling levels were exceeded in 169 cases. The situation was so drastic in 31 cases that the authorities immediately closed down the wells and mixed the water with clean water until pollution fell below the ceiling levels. . . .

And this is probably just the tip of the poisonous iceberg. Due to the lack of means of analysis, water in the new Länder has by no means been examined to check all dangerous substances, such as, for example, the highly nondegradable pesticide cocktails. Even the most modern waterworks in western Germany do not have standard methods of detecting the pesticides commonly used in farming. Each of the roughly 280 authorized active substances and their known number of highly toxic breakdown products would have to be examined in a special, and extremely expensive, procedure. What is more, there is no suitable analytical method for a third of these substances. . . .

Professor Wolfgang Levi, a Research Ministry adviser, believes that cleaning up the open-cast mines is [a] most difficult environmental problem. Greenpeace, Bund and the German Gas and Water Industry Association (Bgw) are sceptical, therefore, that the German government will be able to keep its promise of providing clean drinking water by the end of 1995. . . .

Document 7:

In December of 1992, West Germany's leading expert reflected upon the poisonous legacy left by the Eastern secret service and assessed the effect of the Stasi Files Law of 20 December 1991.

Karl-Wilhelm Fricke on the Stasi Legacy, Spring 1992

(Source: *Aussenpolitik* [English edition], 43, 1992, 153ff.)

A good two-and-a-half years after the decision by the Modrow government to dissolve the Ministry for State Security (MfS) and its successor institution, the Office for National Security (AfNS), the overall picture of the enormous apparatus of surveillance and repression created by the SED has become clearer. The structures of the MfS have been exposed, the names of the former leading cadres are no longer anonymous, and more and more revelations have been appearing in newspapers, radio and television since the Stasi dossiers and documents in the archives were made accessible.

The most fatal legacy of the Stasi is the absolutely unimaginable quantity of written material of all kinds, files, dossiers and documents, which have by no means been completely sorted out, let alone examined, registered and evaluated. Realistic assessments of the stocks of files in the central archives of the former MfS and in the archives of its formerly fifteen district administrations claim that [placed back to back] they would extend over a distance of over two hundred kilometers! "In the Berlin central archives there are at least 18 kilometers of personal dossiers; 7 kilometers of these are court files, 11 kilometers relate to the so-called operational activities, in other words files which directly document the surveillance of one person. The F 16 card file alone, which contains the names of all citizens registered, is one-and-a-half kilometers long." The man who said this knows what he is talking about: Joachim Gauck, who is the Federal Commissioner for the Documents of the State Security Service of the former GDR and has been setting up his authority since the day of German unification. The last Volkskammer of the GDR, which was freely elected for the first time on 18 March 1990, tried to find a solution for the problem. On 24 August 1990 it adopted a law relating to the protection and use of the personal data of the former MfS/AfNS. The attempt, however, was unsuccessful. One of the law's main shortcomings was that the persons concerned were not guaranteed the right to see their personal files. Contrary to the recommendation of the Volkskammer, the law was not adopted in the Unification Treaty drawn up between the two German states on 31 August 1990. This treaty stipulated that the corresponding data files and documents should be taken into custody and protected against unauthorized access by the so-called Gauck authority. First of all, neither the persons concerned nor research and journalism had access to the files. Only parliaments and courts were allowed to investigate the dossiers if they had to examine suspects.

The regulation triggered protests, which included the nonviolent occupation of the archives in the MfS building complex in the Normannenstrasse in Berlin-Lichtenberg by civil rights campaigners. Finally, an additional agreement was drawn up between Bonn and East Berlin on 18 September 1990 that the principles of the law from 24 August 1990 would be "comprehensively taken into account" when the all-German legislature adopts a Stasi Documents Act. As already emphasized earlier on, this took place in the form of the Law on the Documents of the State Security Service of the Former GDR on 20 December 1991. It was the will of the legislature to regulate the registration, administration and use of the documents of the former MfS in such a way that each individual would have access to the personal information stored by the MfS in order to help that person clarify the influence the Stasi took on his personal fate. Furthermore, each individual should be protected against an infringement of personal rights in the form of access by others to his Stasi file. The law also seeks to guarantee and encourage the historical, political and legal reappraisal of Stasi activities. Finally, it is laid down in detail which public and non-public institutions are to have access to the documents.

The examination of the files by the individuals affected began on 2 January 1992. Prominent civil rights campaigners and authors, all of them persecuted by the Stasi, were among the first to take a look inside their files. At present, the number of applicants exceeds 300,000. The first experience was depressing. The quantity and quality of the information gathered extend beyond anything previously assumed. For many people, the files were full of bitter surprises. "Alongside banal observation protocols we can flick through the measures planned by the Stasi," said civil rights campaigner Bärbel Bohley after being confronted with her files. "The planned target was the subversion and destruction of human beings. We read assessments about us made by unofficial Stasi employees. These IMs are generally anonymous. They hid behind names such as Tilly, Rudi or Maximilian. . . . These names stand for a friend, who had become a traitor, the crawler, at work, who wants to speed up his career, the comrade who has gone astray and who wants to kowtow to the state, the student who wants the post of research assistant at all costs, or quite simply people who were envious, resentful, avaricious, whom life had treated badly, or people who just couldn't say no." The banality of evil becomes tangible in these files.

Apart from the problems of the victims of this system, the political problems regarding its perpetrators must also be considered. What can be done with the, at the last count, 85,600 full-time employees of the MfS? The slogan: "Stasi into production" – a motto from the period of revolutionary upheaval in the GDR – still fails because prospective colleagues refuse to work together with former Stasi members. Nevertheless, social integration is necessary. Of course, former members of the Stasi should never again be allowed to wield power over other people. And, of course, those who are guilty must, in terms of criminal law, be taken to court. Yet this does not rule out that the majority of former MfS employees must be occupationally and socially integrated. Their ostracisation would create a dangerous political conflict potential.

Document 8:

The commander of the Eastern Corps, Lieutenant General von Scheven, presented a rather favorable account of the integration of the East German National People's Army into the Federal Army.

Werner von Scheven on the Merger of the Two Armies, Spring 1992

(Source: *Aussenpolitik* [English edition], 43, 1992, 164ff.)

On 3 October 1990, the Federal flag was hoisted in all garrisons and barracks of the former National People's Army (NVA). On the same day the supreme power of command over the 1,500 units and agencies of the NVA passed over to the Federal Minister of Defense, who established the Bundeswehr Eastern Command and the Military District Administration VII at Strausberg near

Berlin. Approximately 90,000 service personnel and about 47,000 civilian employees joined the Bundeswehr on the basis of special preliminary terms of service. The 6,000 remaining regular members of the border troops and the civil emergency preparedness organization of the GDR were taken over by the Bundeswehr on special terms. Nearly 2,000 servicemen and several hundred civilian officials from the western Bundeswehr took over commanding and other leading functions in the newly established commands, units and agencies. The material and the facilities or installations of the NVA (war strength: 350,000) and of the border troops (40,000) as well as weapons and other military equipment of the workers' militia (400,000), the civil emergency preparedness organization (500,000), the Society for Sports and Technology (600,000), the Ministry of State Security and the police forces (120,000) were taken into safekeeping and identified in proper stock records. . . .

On 31 December 1991 the first conscripts called up by the Bundeswehr in the new Länder were discharged from service after completion of a basic term of 12 months. Approximately 25,000 young men are serving as conscripts in the Eastern Corps and Territorial Command at present. These young men have [already] undergone some preinduction training at school; they are disciplined and able to endure great strain, and they have been accorded a social status equal to that of their western counterparts. About 50 per cent of the conscripts have undergone a basic training period of three months in western units. This is probably the only major group of young ex-GDR citizens who officially shared the living conditions of young West German men of the same age for three months. The number of applicants for long-term service in the Bundeswehr is satisfactory. Within 3 or 4 years it will thus be possible to form the junior NCO corps from East German recruits called up by the Bundeswehr. In the NVA there was no NCO* corps of the kind the Bundeswehr has. NCOs generally were specialists without any command authority. For this reason it is necessary to transfer a major number of NCOs of the western Bundeswehr component to eastern garrisons. This programme started in December 1991, when about 850 NCOs were transferred to the east.

Some 4,000 former NVA regular officers have now enlisted for a preliminary service period of two years. Their applications for enlistment as long-term volunteers or regulars in the Bundeswehr will be decided on in 1992. A central decision will not be taken until an independent commission in Bonn has been heard. At the same time the usual personnel security investigation will be carried out with inquiries as to former membership in the GDR State Security Service (Stasi) being made to the Gauck agency. Social security for all those who are going to remain in the Bundeswehr will not be established before 1993. Until then the individual former NVA regular will be faced with the possibility of having to leave the armed forces upon expiry of his two-year term of enlistment. Nearly all former NVA regulars have undergone training

---

* non-commissioned officers, i.e. sergeants, the backbone of any military force.

or practical service in the West and, in doing so, have gained some decisive learning experience. Only those former NVA staff will be designated Bundeswehr reservists who served in the Bundeswehr after 3 October 1990. . . .

People often ask about the former NVA regular officers' self-image in the new Bundeswehr. On 3 October 1990 Germans came together with Germans and German servicemen with German servicemen in order to set about a common national task. This is how the situation can be described in simple terms. After the turn of events in the former GDR the NVA's regular cadres were given new opportunities to inform themselves, thus opening up new perspectives. Many of them, for instance, bitterly speak of their "stolen life" in isolation when comparing the different alert statuses of the two German armies. Many of them are convinced [they] made a contribution to peace according to European standards, because they helped to keep the system of stability intact which NATO and the Warsaw Pact had created. In addition, many former NVA regulars are convinced [they] rendered essential services to an internationally acknowledged antifascist state. Internal discussions on this misunderstanding have already begun. The officers who have enlisted for an interim service period of two years are highly motivated and loyal soldiers. Many of them are truly shocked about what the media and public prosecutors have found out about the communist leadership. It was hard for them to cope with the loss of their status, the loss of identity and the invalidation of private and professional [orientation and] knowledge. But the inherent requirement to roll up the sleeves and cooperate will help them.

The service personnel's self-image and self-confidence will increase with the vocational qualifications. The Bundeswehr can, however, only accept service personnel who correspond to the dual concept of a soldier and a citizen in uniform. The reappraisal of existing deficiencies in this area will require longstanding and [consistent] efforts. The acquisition of a democratic concept of man as well as general historical and political knowledge will take many years. A lot of guidance, education and supervision will be required to make former NVA regular cadres assume the same attitude towards conscripts that Bundeswehr members are supposed to have and most of them actually have. Many former NVA members lack the courage of having their own convictions and to express them vis-à-vis others as well as the courage to take the initiative. Discriminating thinking and discriminating use of the German language were not desired in the SED state which used to view things in black and white. Those who come from a world of ideological certainties will find it difficult to [face new] situations in a free world. . . .

Document 9:

In the spring of 1992 the SPD Finance Minister of the East German state of Brandenburg voiced short-term concern about integration, tempered by long-term optimism.

Klaus-Dieter Kühbacher on Economic and Social Unification, Spring 1992
(Source: *Aussenpolitik* [English edition], 43, 1992, 153ff.)

From the end of 1989 until well into the year 1990, the prevailing mood, especially in eastern Germany, could be most aptly described as one of "euphoria." Particularly high hopes were pinned on the speedy introduction of the D-mark within the framework of the economic and monetary union on 1 July 1990. The people in the East believed that this would give them immediate access to all the blessings of the market economy: the unrestricted availability of all commodities and services, complete freedom to travel, and increased and guaranteed purchasing power. . . .

Today, the drawbacks are all too obvious. In many places, they are responsible for a mood marked by disappointment, resignation and embitterment. Politics, at least in the eyes of many of the people affected, has failed. Perhaps none of the politicians – or only a handful – were able or willing to imagine the actual scale of the structural crisis which in the meantime affects the entire economy and the entire territory of the former GDR. The dramatic extent of mass unemployment may not have been predictable in its current form. . . .

Time is running out in the new Länder. If politics fails to take determined action, the people will have no option but to migrate. In Brandenburg, the number of jobless persons in January 1992 passed the 200,000 mark; in addition, there are roughly 80,000 short-time workers – with a potential workforce of just under 1.4 million people. As I said earlier on, one in five. A further 60,000 people are involved in job creation measures. This basically means that every family in Brandenburg is more or less directly affected by structural change and unemployment.

What should these people do? Move to the West? Wait for better times? Bearing in mind the labor market and housing situation in western Germany, it is obvious that a new migration movement in Germany is the worst of all conceivable solutions in the short, medium and long term. On the whole, it would lead Germany into new social friction in many policy fields.

This is why the subject of social, economic and societal unity must be given top priority in political activities. We will only be able to play our part in the solution of European and global problems if we successfully come to terms with the economic, social and political upheaval in Germany and if we prove our ability and credibility.

Finally, I would like to comment on the situation in Brandenburg in order to demonstrate with reference to a specific case how we are tackling problems in the new Länder. . . .

We began government in Brandenburg last November under adventurous circumstances: no offices, no furniture, no working telephones, no personnel apparatus. A great deal had to be organized from phone booths, for example, the one on the Glienicker Bridge on the outskirts of West Berlin. Despite all the stress, it was an exciting period with its own kind of romanticism.

The active support from the West, in our case mainly from our partner state North Rhine-Westfalia, soon pulled us through the worst. Within just a few months we built up new administrations from scratch.

Today, well over 1,000 helpers from our West German partner region are working in Brandenburg, and we shall need them for some time to come. Most of them work in finance offices, land registry offices or for the police. Without them, the systemic change from the centralist dictatorship of the various apparatuses to democracy and the market economy as well as the introduction of a new legal system, a new economic system and a new finance system would not have been possible. . . .

Apart from establishing a functioning administrative apparatus, the Land government is concentrating on the rapid reconstruction of the economy. We need fresh capital and new ideas to provide new and guaranteed jobs for people who have been made redundant. In many cases, people will need to acquire new qualifications. We estimate that one in two Brandenburgers will have to learn a new job.

Our aim is to take as many people as possible out of their former jobs, give them retraining and advanced training, and then immediately place them in new fields of activity. So far, we have provided qualification and labor promotion measures for roughly 160,000 people from Brandenburg. A further 100,000 will follow during the next few months. We continue to count on the full support of the Federal Government and the Federal Labor Office. This approach costs a great deal of money, but it is a good investment.

We can also show promising results with respect to contacts with investors. Up to now, we have acquired almost DM 16 billion in large-scale investments, guaranteeing well over 40,000 jobs. One of the key aspects is the timetable: people must be given the corresponding qualifications in the one to two years it takes for investments to be completed.

I feel extremely optimistic about Brandenburg's future. Our finance offices have been able for some months now to extensively list the number of registered employers and their employees. There has been an increase in new business creations, especially in the crafts and medium-sized industries.

A further signal of hope is the fact that people are rethinking their consumptive behavior. After the Wall fell, eastern products were completely "out" and everything from the West completely "in" – from the shiny car to the shiny European Community apple. This caused particular problems for the agricultural sector. In the meantime, the people have discovered that not all that glitters is good. They are returning to their own products, the quality of which is often not just not inferior but in fact superior. . . . This guarantees jobs, provides tax revenue for the Finance Minister, and saves social welfare payments.

Document 10:

As a result of post-unification disenchantment, state elections showed a decline in ballots for the moderate governing parties and an increase in votes for the right-wing Republicans and the German People's Union.

Results of State Elections in Western Germany, 5 April 1992

(Source: *German Politics* 1, 1992, 123, 284, and 287.)

Results of Bremen Bürgerschaft[*] Elections on 29 September 1991

	1987 (percent)	1991 (percent)
SPD	50.5	38.8
CDU	23.4	30.7
Greens	10.2	11.4
FDP	10.0	9.5
DVU	3.4	6.2
Reps	1.2	1.5
Others	1.3	1.9

Results of Schleswig-Holstein Landtag[**] Elections on 5 April 1992

	1988 (percent)	1992 (percent)
SPD	54.8	46.2
CDU	33.3	33.8
FDP	4.4	5.6
Greens	2.9	4.9
Danes (SSW)[***]	1.7	1.9
DVU	—	6.3
Reps	0.6	1.2
Other	2.3	0.1

[*] Bremen city state legislature.

[**] state legislature.

[***] Danish minority in the state of Schleswig-Holstein.

Results of the Baden-Württemberg Landtag Elections on 5 April 1992

	1988 (percent)	1992 (percent)
CDU	49.0	39.6
SPD	32.0	29.4
Reps	1.0	10.9
Greens	7.9	9.5
FDP	5.9	5.9
Others	4.2	4.7

Document 11:

The Federal President sought to allay German worries about the creation of a common European currency as a part of the political union foreseen by the Maastricht treaty.

Von Weizsäcker on Maastricht and the Future of Europe, 13 April 1992

(Source: *Frankfurter Allgemeine Zeitung*, 13 April 1992, translation based on *German Tribune*)

The Maastricht summit, regardless of the criticism that has been leveled at it, was a milestone. It pointed the way toward Europe, a way on which we depend. . . .

In eight months we will have a single European market, a Europe without frontiers for goods and services, for manpower and capital. What is now lacking are the crucial stages leading up to European unity: Economic and Monetary Union and Political Union.

This is where criticism begins. Too many of the decisions that affect Europe as a whole, on issues such as asylum, immigration and aliens policy, the environment, research and development, and, finally, foreign and security policy, will arguably continue, after Maastricht, to be made in different ways in EC capitals.

They will merely be harmonized in Brussels rather than referred to the Community for a uniform decision to be reached. And inasmuch as national governments' powers have been transferred, they have accrued to a body that isn't satisfactorily subject to parliamentary control.

This critical view is accompanied by an almost traumatic worry. It is that the European Economic and Monetary Union, as agreed at Maastricht, will deprive us of the D-mark.

Its place will be taken, or so it is feared, by a European currency the value of which will be seriously at risk, robbing us in the long run of our savings and jeopardizing our future. Is that true?

The first point to make concerns our own currency. At present it is living on its good repute. It isn't the [most] stable or the one with the steadiest value in Europe. And that is mainly a result of German unification. . . .

The national debt is on the increase, with all the attendant effects on the capital market and interest rates of which we are now feeling the pinch. . . .

It goes without saying that all European Community member states will need to do their utmost in budget discipline and currency stability. But that is precisely where the strong points of the Maastricht treaties lie.

At Maastricht strict criteria were agreed upon that must be met before a member-state qualifies for the final stage of Economic and Monetary Union. At the moment these criteria are not met even by the Germans.

The Economic and Monetary Union will be run on principles that must, in any case, apply to us: an independent central bank, a stable currency, budget discipline.

It is no exaggeration to say that our monetary concept has been adopted by Europe and that our social free-market economy has now been accepted as the economic constitution for Europe.

That is the unique significance of Maastricht in the economic and monetary context. It is particularly important for us Germans. Ours is the strongest economy in the Community; one third of our national product is earned in exports and nearly 60 percent of it in Europe.

But are the political safeguards that have been agreed on in the Economic and Monetary Union sufficient? critics ask. The terms agreed on in the Political Union certainly leave much to be desired, especially where parliamentary powers in Europe are concerned.

We must continue to aim at reducing the democracy deficit in European institutions, but that is no reason for voting against Europe itself.

The process of European integration has grown virtually irreversible, with the history of European unification being one of institutional competition.

No matter how skeptical people may be, what proves its worth will, in the final analysis, prevail. The principle of an independent central bank is a case in point. . . .

For nearly a half-century after World War II, the Federal Republic of old was safe and secure as a part of the Western alliance. Inhuman though the division of Germany may have been, our peripheral position preserved us from the serious tension that accompanies a mid-continental geographical location.

The first two post-Wall years have been enough to drastically demonstrate what problems this geographical location can entail – a location that Germany has been exposed to since the end of the Holy Roman Empire and that has led it into two world wars this century.

The challenges we now face extend further still. Our neighbors to the east are keen to forge closer links with the EC. A new and permanent wall of poverty bordering on Germany would pose a threat to us as well as others.

Nuclear burdens bequeathed to us by the erstwhile East Bloc are more threatening than the balance of terror that has been superseded. There can be neither an intercontinental deterrent nor German security in the face of rogue nuclear warheads.

Dangers and problems of this kind cannot be dealt with by Germany alone. Alongside the new tasks set for the Atlantic alliance, the prospect of enlargement of the EC is inevitable.

That will call for an intensification of [the EC's] ability to act, which is one of the targets of the Maastricht treaties.

A further task is set by the growing technological lead enjoyed by America and Japan. We definitely don't want an interventionist industrial policy, but we will lag behind unless Europe mobilizes its forces.

If anyone in Europe needs Political Union and, as its present gateway, Economic and Monetary Union, it is us. We may still be too close to the event to appreciate it, but on the threshold to the twenty-first century Maastricht offers us an opportunity.

Document 12:

According to the Unity Treaty, the Bundestag, on 26 June 1992, voted 355 to 283, with 16 abstentions, for a compromise between Eastern and Western abortion practices. But the Constitutional Court wanted stronger protection of unborn life and declared the combination of choice with mandatory consultation unconstitutional.

The Bundestag Decision to Allow Choice in Abortion, 26 June 1992

(Source: *Deutschland Archiv*, 25, 1992, 675)

Law to Protect Unborn and Developing Life, Promote a Child-Friendly Society, Assist in Pregnancy Conflicts, and Regulate Abortions (Pregnancy and Family Assistance Law)

Paragraph 218 a: Abortion Non-Punishable

Abortion is not illegal if

1. it is requested by the pregnant woman, and it has been confirmed by a doctor in accordance with Paragraph 219 (Pregnancy Counseling in a Situation

of Need and Conflict), section 3 that she has undergone counseling at least three days prior to the operation

2. it is performed by a doctor, and

3. no more than twelve weeks have passed since conception. . . .

Paragraph 219: Pregnancy Counseling in a Situation of Need and Conflict

(1) Counseling serves to protect life by offering advice to the pregnant woman, in acknowledgement of the great value of unborn life and of the woman's responsibility. Counseling is intended to help overcome the need and conflict situation arising due to pregnancy. It should enable the pregnant woman to make a responsible choice, based on her own conscience. The task of counseling is to provide the pregnant woman with extensive medical, social, and legal information. Counseling includes an explanation of the legal rights of mothers and children and available practical assistance, particularly that which eases continuation of the pregnancy and the situation of mother and child. Counseling also aims to avoid future unwanted pregnancies.

(2) Counseling is to occur at a legally authorized counseling office. The doctor performing the abortion may not be the counselor.

(3) No records will be kept of the counseling session, and it may occur anonymously at the request of the pregnant woman. The counseling office is to immediately supply a dated confirmation of the fact that counseling has taken place according to section 1 and that the woman has thus been provided information for her decision.

Document 13:

A year and a half after unification, this West German commentator tried to draw up a balance sheet on the dismantling of the GDR Academy of Sciences and the reconstruction of eastern scholarship.

Dieter Zimmer on the Restructuring of Eastern Research, 31 July 1992

(Source: *Die Zeit*, 31 July 1992)

No, contrary to all fears a neutron bomb did not explode here on New Year's Eve, said Jens Reich, not only one of the most sensitive interpreters of inter-German chaos, but a bio-mathematician at the former Central Institute for Molecular Biology in the Buch district of eastern Berlin. The institute used to play a leading role in the entire Eastern Bloc; today it continues to exist as one of three major new East German research facilities belonging to the Max Delbrück Center for Molecular Medicine (MDC). The three MDC institutes in Buch used to have a combined staff of 1,600; now it has shriveled to 360. Nevertheless, almost 80 percent of the former staff initially found work on the

Buch campus. Most of them are still here and doing what they used to do, said Reich. But then he mentioned the other side of the coin: The insecurity that paralyzed the work there for two years still exists. As does bitterness of some older employees and the brain-drain luring some of the younger ones to the West. And once again, an emergency program for German scientific research is long overdue.

One view of the research scene in the former East Germany reveals countless people who have not only lived through a break in their careers, but often lost their positions or even their occupations altogether, and who considered themselves lucky if they were old enough to retire early or be pensioned off – at an offensively low pension at that. The other view, one concentrating on the structures, observes that new research institutes are being established everywhere; many scientists continue to work there, and some of them might soon be working even under better conditions than before. It is not an easy matter trying to get the two views to jibe. Nevertheless, both are true.

Scientific statistician Werner Meske, currently at the Berlin Center for Social Science Research, converted East German statistics to West German standards. He determined that, relative to the population, East Germany had the same proportion of researchers as West Germany. In both countries, the large majority of everything falling within the scope of research and development was sponsored by industry – 65 percent in the East and 74 percent in the West. The share of university research with respect to total volume of research was also almost the same in both countries: 11 percent in the East and 14 percent in the West.

The greatest difference was in non-university state-funded research. In East Germany this category represented 24 percent, or twice that of the West. It was concentrated in the East in the centrally organized research facilities of the three academies: the Construction Academy, the Agriculture Academy, and the Academy of Sciences. These consisted of approximately 60 institutes and, at final count, 24,000 employees. The Unification Treaty declared that all three of these would be closed. The end of 1991 marked the dissolution of the last of the institutes, and the last of the employees were let go. But where did they go? . . .

The balance is as follows: Of the 32,000 people employed by the three academies at the end of 1989, approximately 13,000 can continue working for the time being. That represents a 60 percent reduction. Cuts in the size of university staffs have just begun. If the situation everywhere turns out as it did in Saxony, where 7500 of 18,500 positions were eliminated, then at the most 60,000 will remain of the 104,000 positions at East German universities, a decrease of [about] 42 percent. The greatest dismantling has taken place in industry. Of approximately 74,000 R&D positions, at most 18,000, or a mere 24 percent, still exist. . . .

Altogether, 210,000 positions used to exist. Soon, only 91,000 will remain, many of which are temporary. In addition, 10 percent of the positions will be filled by Westerners; in the final analysis, therefore, German-German unification means the professional end for considerably more than half of the scientific personnel of East Germany.

And that is more than just a personal catastrophe for a large number of people. It is a structural catastrophe for the entire country. Relative to population size, there are now only half as many R&D positions in eastern as in western Germany. With respect to the number of employees in industry, this amount shrinks to about one-tenth. The best and most flexible people leave for the West, and the extremely depressed economy, desperately in need of new products and procedures, is even further handicapped by a thinning of innovative potential.

Document 14:

One of the biggest difficulties of unification was the loss of familiar routines and the onslaught of new demands. Counselling professionals therefore discussed how to deal with the widespread adjustment problems of disoriented individuals.

Rosemarie Stein on Psychological Distress, 3 August 1992

(Source: *Der Tagesspiegel*, 2 August 1992)

"We slipped into a marriage without having been engaged, but we weren't young enough to do that. A divorce is out of the question, so the only thing left is to try to get to know each other better after the fact." That is how East Berlin physician Monika Haas, who works as a psychotherapist, characterized the overhasty German-German unification. The Humboldt University conference "Origins, Crisis, and Changes in Modern Medicine" had set up a committee on problems resulting from the fall of the GDR that doctors in eastern Germany have to deal with daily.

The former East Germany has become a major field for psycho-social study, commented Dr. Dieter Seefeldt of Potsdam. There is a lot of resignation and depression, he says. Based on the southwestern suburbs of Berlin, Dr. G. J. Fischer, a neurologist who has worked in Teltow for the last 14 years, has described the observations made in the course of this natural "field study." The part of this major experimental field with which he is most familiar includes the village of Stahnsdorf, the relatively rural area of Teltow, and the exclusive Berlin suburb of Kleinmachnow, where a disproportionate number of artists and intellectuals, as well as officials and border guards, lived during the period when East Germany still existed. Starting in the 1950s, this area was developed into East Germany's second-largest electronics center. Three major companies employed 35,000 to 40,000 people.

"And all of this was dismantled before my very eyes. For example, a huge factory was torn down within three days by a big steel ball swinging back and forth. And the people who had worked there are my patients," reported Dr. Fischer, who also chairs the Brandenburg Medical Association. Unemployment started out harmlessly as a reduction of working time to zero hours. In fact, everyone really liked it, since they got their money, but could still relax in their gardens or go on trips in the summer. And they all hoped for a economic recovery.

But now unemployment is no longer disguised as something else, and it has grown to a most frightening extent. Entire families are hit; some of them have worked for one company for three generations, enjoying the "same social nest." And now? Not only the 40- to 50-year-olds are at a loss; even the young people realize that there are few, if any, options open to them in their fields. Everyone is desperately looking for new jobs, but there aren't any available. Some people are venturing to western Germany in their search, which is also breaking up many families.

On top of all this, 5,000 of 5,800 lots of land have been "claimed," according to Fischer. That means former owners have registered claims for the property. (Most of the residents of Kleinmachnow, for instance, gradually moved to the West when their suburb was cut off from West Berlin.) The Teltow doctor mentioned that political circles in Bonn referred to the "Kleinmachnow Syndrome." Loss of work, threatened loss of one's home, destruction of the family structure – existential security has been shaken and the future is uncertain. Neurologists have observed that epileptics who had shown no symptoms for years are losing control and having relapses, thus requiring much more medication. This also applies to patients with other chronic neurological diseases, such as neuralgia or Parkinson's Disease. There has also been an increase in eye diseases that are psychosomatic to some degree, such as tunnel vision. The situation of patients with so-called "classical" psychiatric disorders (e.g., schizophrenia), on the other hand, does not appear to have changed as much. Fischer admitted, however, that he did not have complete information in this area, since he opened his own practice a year ago and no longer has the services of a nurse who used to make regular house calls.

He referred to new problem areas of substance addiction, depression (which is often hidden behind physical symptoms), violence, and rootless people deceived into joining dubious sects in their search for a sense of security. The Teltow neurologist is surprised by the fact that colleagues only a third of a mile down the road lead a sheltered existence, continuing to practice as though nothing had changed. . . .

Document 15:

Eastern resentment against unemployment and Western tutelage exploded in a week of riots at a refugee hostel in the coastal city of

Rostock. Especially in the former GDR, feelings of inferiority focused on the only people even more helpless, namely foreigners.

John Eisenhammer on the Explosion of Racism, 30 August 1992.

(Source: *The Toronto Star*, 30 August 1992)

For five nights, hundreds of police and special riot units battled to contain the worst explosion of violence against foreigners since reunification.

The local police chief, Siegfried Cordus, said he has never seen such viciousness and brutality. "People clapped at every stone which hit a policeman," said a bystander.

Chancellor Helmut Kohl condemned the attacks, calling them "a disgrace to the nation," and urged Germans to "make it clear to the world that hatred of foreigners is totally unacceptable."

But many authorities predicted this was only a beginning.

Lothar Kupfer, interior minister of the state of Mecklenburg, in which Rostock lies, warned of a "civil war." Sporadic attacks on foreigners continued throughout the week in several other east German cities as well.

But the crucial moment came late on Monday night when the police in Rostock were forced to withdraw, apparently to re-group or change shifts.

In doing so, they left the hostel at the mercy of the hooligans. Some were just kids, most from the [surrounding area] and Rostock, reinforced by neo-Nazis from far and wide, hardened by street battle. They were well-organized with petrol containers in nearby bushes from which they filled their beer cans, once drunk to make fire-bombs.

The crowd of onlookers, some 3,000 strong, bigger than on either of the previous two nights of rioting, egged them on. Once inside the building the youths smashed everything on two floors. A few jagged bits of porcelain are all that is left of the toilet. Water drips everywhere from broken pipes.

The hostel was destroyed despite the fact that, in desperation, the authorities had evacuated all the 200 residents, mainly Romanian Gypsies, earlier in the day, busing them to temporary hostels in other towns.

But there were about 100 Vietnamese families with children in the adjoining block – not refugees, but still living and working in Rostock since their guest-worker days under the communists.

Terrified, they barricaded themselves in their flats as flames leapt from the windows nearby. For well over an hour the fire service looked on from afar, terrified by the rioters. The police were still re-grouping. Finally, the Vietnamese were slipped to safety over the roof.

The fires still burnt.

"And the fires will continue burning wherever they take these so-called asylum-seekers. People here are fed up," says Dietmar, gesticulating wildly. He is [in] one of the small groups that continually form in front of the scarred building.

"It was disgusting, the way they sat around here, rubbish everywhere," says 15-year-old Alex. "The city dump is paradise compared to this shit-heap. They had to be got rid of."

On the fifth night of rioting, the police finally got on top of the extreme-right thugs. Stung by nationwide accusations of incompetence, and having promised a "hard-as-nails approach," they moved in quickly, with massive reinforcements of special riot police, encircled the Molotov cocktail throwing hordes, and restored a semblance of order.

In the minds of many, it was precisely what should have been done at the outset.

By Thursday, moderation was gaining the upper hand as some 2,000 people marched in silence through the center of Rostock to protest the rioting against foreigners and police.

"If we capitulate to violence, we have lost democracy," Christoph Kleermann, president of the city council, told demonstrators on Rostock's historic University Square.

"I am ashamed of what has happened here the last five nights," Kleermann said. "I want to live in Rostock but not in a city which shuts out foreigners."

The crowd, carrying banners reading, "Don't give xenophobic hatred a chance" and "Light candles, not houses," marched to a church where a peace service was to be held later.

But the damage had been done.

Document 16:

In 1992 the Russian government deported the former East German party leader to face charges in Berlin for authorizing shootings at the Wall. Shortly after Honecker defiantly defended his policy, the trial was called off because he was suffering from cancer.

Honecker's Legal Defense, 7 December 1992

(Source: *Blätter für deutsche und internationale Politik*, 1993, 118ff.)

I will not grant the charges and this trial any semblance of justice by defending myself against the obviously baseless accusation of manslaughter. It is also unnecessary to prepare a defense, since I will not be here to hear your verdict. I will not serve the sentence you obviously have in store for me. That is already clear to everyone. For that reason alone, a trial against me is a farce. It is political theater. . . .

Only one argument is used at this trial, and other trials in criminal, labor, social welfare and administrative courts in which other GDR citizens are being persecuted for their close involvement with the system. Politicians and lawyers say, "We have to convict the communists, since we did not convict the Nazis. This time, we have to come to terms with our past." That is convincing to many, but it is merely a spurious argument. The truth is that West German justice was not able to punish the Nazis because judges and prosecutors could not convict themselves. The truth is that the justice of the Federal Republic has the Nazis who continued in office to thank for its current standards, no matter how one wishes to judge them. The truth is that the communists, GDR citizens, are persecuted for the same reasons today as they were in the past in Germany. This was only reversed during the forty years of the existence of the GDR. This omission now has to be "rectified." Of course it is all done according to law. It has nothing at all to do with politics. . . .

We – as I already said – obviously did not personally kill anyone, nor directly order the killing of any individuals. Therefore, the building of the Berlin Wall, its maintenance and the enforcement of the prohibition to leave the GDR without state authorization, are seen as an act of killing. And it supposedly has nothing at all to do with politics. German jurisprudence makes it all possible. It will not stand the test of time, nor the logic of common sense. It merely demonstrates its origins once again, revealing its true self and where it has come from, and where Germany is on the verge of going. . . .

I dedicated my life to the GDR. Particularly since May 1971, I have carried a major part of the responsibility for its history. I am therefore partial, and beyond that, I am weak on account of my age and failing health. Yet at the end of my life I am still certain that the GDR was not founded without reason. It made its mark, showing that socialism is possible and can be better than capitalism. It was an experiment that has failed. But never has failure caused humanity to give up the search for new insights and new methods. The present task is to investigate why the experiment failed. Certainly one reason is that we, and here I mean those responsible in all of the European socialist countries, made mistakes which could have been avoided. Certainly it failed in Germany, among other reasons because GDR citizens made the wrong decision, as other Germans have also done in the past, and because our opponents were still more powerful. The experience gained through the history of the GDR and through the histories of other former socialist countries will all be useful for the millions of people living in socialist countries which still exist, and for the world of tomorrow. All those who dedicated their work and their lives to the GDR did not do it in vain. More and more *Ossis* will begin to realize that living conditions in the GDR deformed them less than the *Wessis* have been deformed by the so-called "social" market economy. And they will realize that children in the GDR grew up happier, with fewer problems, freer, and better educated in day-care centers, preschools, and schools than children growing up in the violence-ridden schools, streets, and squares of the FRG. . . .

Many will also come to understand that the freedom to choose between CDU/CSU, SPD, and FDP is only the freedom to participate in a sham vote. They will realize that in the GDR, they enjoyed an incomparable amount of freedom in their daily lives, particularly at their workplaces, compared to the freedom they now have. And finally, the care and security that the GDR – though small and, compared to the FRG, relatively poor – guaranteed its citizens will no longer be taken for granted, since daily life in capitalism will make it perfectly clear to everyone what such security is really worth. The balance of the forty-year history of the GDR looks different than it is presented by politicians and the media in the FRG. In the course of time, that will become more and more clear. . . .

Document 17:

The former editor of the Italian communist journal *Rinascita* and professor of political philosophy called on other countries for a more balanced response to the problems of the new Germany.

Angelo Bolaffi on Foreign Reactions to Xenophobia, 14 December 1992

(Source: *Der Spiegel*, 1992, No. 51, 28f.)

An anti-German syndrome is spreading throughout Europe – a genuine allergy to the new reality of a united Germany. Journalists, intellectuals, and of course those nostalgic for the "good old days" (when there was still a Wall, tanks at the Brandenburg Gate, SS-20 nuclear missiles, and a constantly-growing mountain of Stasi files) seem to have nothing better to do than repeat a single dramatic question: Will the new, larger Germany try for the third time in this century to storm the heavens in order to rule the old continent?

Everything that happens between the Oder and the Rhine is observed by the majority of the public in other countries with a distrust that can only be attributed to a high degree of provocative disinformation and resentful prejudice. It seems post-Communist Europe is seeking a new enemy with all its might, as though the vacuum created by the disintegration of communism simply had to be filled. . . .

The European left – not excluding the Germans, and with the Italians at the forefront – has taken on a special role in this orgy of unfriendly suspicion and even falsification. The left suffers from the same intolerance with regard to Germany that it exhibits with regard to Israel. This attitude bears a dangerous resemblance to racism. . . .

There is great danger that the increasing mistrust of Germany could be fatal for Europe. Although it is not easy, we cannot avoid acknowledging that the days when Europe could punish an unloved Germany by pointing to its historical guilt are over. No country can proceed forever like Paul Klee's Angelus Novus[*], which so impressed Walter Benjamin[**]: with its back to the future, its eyes on the ruins of the past.

Germany took advantage of the historical opportunity to regain the right to normalcy. It should be treated like any other nation. No European balance is imaginable without Germany, and certainly not against it. It doesn't make much sense to counter the desired goal of a European Germany with warnings against a German Europe. Any form of European unity, should it ever become reality, must have a German motor.

But how can we avoid the concern that Germany could be seized anew by the illusion of a special path, the attractions of a dangerous tightrope walk between East and West, and once again become an uneasy Reich? Only in such a case would our fear of Germany be justified. Only such a mistaken political path would be capable of turning into a mass phenomenon something that, at present, is little more than the behavior of lost groups of young people, and not, as at the beginning of this century, the myth behind an entire leadership.

Several basic factors distinguish the present situation in Europe and Germany from that prior to 1945.

The presence of the Americans on the old continent and Germany's integration into NATO obligate Germany to pro-Western decisions. Following World War II, the USA became the protectors of the European balance of power. Will we reach a point someday when the European left will have to revise its hostility toward "Yankee imperialism" out of fear of Germany?

Demographically, the former Federal Republic makes up four-fifths of the new Germany. Economically, however, it is almost the entire country. Culturally and demographically, it has undergone a radical Westernization. This change makes Germany a completely different country from the one created by Bismarck, which vanished completely following the unconditional surrender of 8 May 1945.

Germany's roots in the West are the most effective antidote to the shades of its history. Surprisingly, the same left that today particularly stresses the German danger flirted in the past with the irresponsible hypothesis of a "united, neutral" Germany.

---

[*] famous painting by Ernst Klee of an angel, facing the past rather than the future.

[**] leftist writer and literary theorist of the Weimar Republic.

Another anchor preventing any attempt by Germany to go it alone are its material interests. The days are gone when Germany was capable of reaching the tragic conclusion that it had to conquer living space; today the country is a cornerstone of the international economic system. For this reason, it needs others to survive – especially the Western industrial nations, which buy over 85 percent of its exports. . . .

Is it right to always ask whether, behind their insufferable efficiency, the Germans are still hiding those secret demons that brought forth the banality of evil? Maybe. But what use are such concerns if not to spur on old hatreds and dangerous resentments? Certainly they do not help build up a united Europe. Europe's states would do better to stick to empirical facts than to myths. The key to German success can be found in the special kind of cooperation among its social subjects – in a type of capitalism, regulated by a welfare state based in the rule of law, that an expert once aptly termed "Rhenish capitalism."

So there is the "other" Germany; today, it is once again possible to link up the torn threads of another German history. Germany is not only the Germany of the Kaiser and the Führer, the Reich and the concentration camps, the Wall and the Stasi. It is not, as people would have us believe, old and new anti-Semitism, old or new intolerance. Germany was the first country to implement the welfare state. It is a country of education and culture, tolerance and cosmopolitanism. Over Bismarck's winged Goddess of Victory stretches Wim Wenders' "Sky Over Berlin."[***]

"They laugh to hear the words that come from your house. But those who see you reach for their knives." This, as Brecht put it, is the Europeans' eternal dilemma regarding Germany. What to do? Laugh, or reach for the knife? When the cemetery at Dachau is desecrated, there is certainly cause for sadness and concern. Nevertheless, the old disinformation campaigns against Germany do no good – and hate helps even less.

Document 18:

This American journalist tried to find out why a nation of readers had dumped its writers. Shortly after the publication of her article, new charges forced authors Heiner Müller and Christa Wolf to admit their active collaboration with the Stasi.

Katie Hefner on Attacks against East German Writers, 10 January 1993

(Source: *New York Times Magazine*, 10 January 1992)

In the summer of 1990, barely six months after the Berlin wall fell, residents of Kömmlitz, a small village near Leipzig in southeastern Germany, made a

---

[***] German title of the postmodern pre-unification film "Wings of Desire."

bizarre discovery. Their local garbage dump had been turned into a mountain of books. It looked as if a city library had been turned upside down and had its contents shaken out. It was a curiously arbitrary collection. Communist tracts were discarded along with German classics; Lenin's "State and Revolution" lay next to the works of Tolstoy. But most of the books were by East Germany's most celebrated fiction writers: Christa Wolf, Stefan Heym, Hermann Kant and Anna Seghers. . . .

The rejection of their own authors' books was the rejection of a collective soul. The collapse of communist East Germany has taken its writers with it. Once among that nation's most elite and privileged citizens, they have suffered a summary fall from grace. Once heroes, they are now being accused of timidity and are falling into discredit. Once looked to for the truth, they are now mistrusted and, still worse, ignored.

East Germany was called the Nation of Readers. Its citizens adored their authors. Writers were the Oprah Winfreys and Phil Donahues of the nation, the ones to whom people turned for what the Germans call *Lebenshilfe*, or life help, the ones designated to answer the question: How do you get by in an authoritarian regime? It was in the pages of East German novels that such topics as alcoholism, homosexuality and abortion were first broached. Public readings were always standing room only, and often they turned into mass public confessionals. It was at readings, says Therese Hörnigk, a literary historian in Eastern Berlin, that people realized they weren't alone. "People went to readings to experience solidarity and build up self-confidence," she says.

Christa Wolf, in particular, East Germany's most famous writer, was a kind of Mother Confessor. Wolf's cathartic, intensely personal and multilayered prose inspired thousands of people to write to her about their own lives. She employed a secretary just to help her answer the dozens of letters she received every day. . . .

After an initial flurry of essays once the wall came down, and a handful of memoirs, writers from the former East Germany stopped producing. The fall of Communism should have liberated writers – instead it crippled them and exposed them to the world of harsh criticism. It pointed up the difference between writers in the West, who write because they believe they have something to say, and writers in the East, who wrote because their readers needed them to say something.

Schirrmacher started the onslaught in 1990, with an unprecedented attack on Christa Wolf. For years rumored to be on the short list for the Nobel Prize, Wolf had gained a worldwide reputation. Her subtly critical fiction and her readiness to take on contemporary German history made her a hero both to East German readers and West German critics. Through the years, the 63-year-old novelist's writing, translated into 27 languages, has engendered a voluminous body of secondary literature. She has a particularly large following among American feminists.

Shortly after the Berlin wall fell, Wolf published a 100-page book titled "What Remains," a novella she had written a decade earlier and kept in a desk drawer. The book is based on a period she spent under Stasi surveillance in the late 1970's after she protested the expulsion of Wolf Biermann.

As soon as Christa Wolf's book appeared in the spring of 1990, Schirrmacher did the unthinkable. With brazen disrespect, Schirrmacher, then 33, attacked older critics for having perpetuated the myth of an East German literature of dissent, and he attacked Wolf herself for having lacked the courage to publish the book 10 years earlier. If she had done so, Schirrmacher argued, she could have forced into public a discussion of the Stasi – a topic conspicuously absent from East German literature - much earlier. She claimed to be complaining about the Stasi, but she waited until it was safe to do it. She claimed to be a victim but was in fact a tacit collaborator.

Sensitive and unaccustomed to such harsh treatment, Wolf largely withdrew from public view. . . .

Document 19:

Troubled by xenophobic violence, decent German citizens started a series of candlelight demonstrations that gradually changed the public climate toward greater tolerance of foreigners.

Stephen Kinzer on Demonstrations for Tolerance, 13 January 1993

(Source: *The New York Times*, 13 January 1993)

The anti-racism movement that has brought huge numbers of Germans into the street in recent weeks to protest rightist violence had its start over steak and Chianti in a Munich living room.

The occasion was a quiet mid-November dinner for four at the home of a young Munich businesswoman. Even before the main course was served, conversation turned to the wave of neo-Nazi attacks that had broken out across Germany. All four diners agreed that it was time for the country's "silent majority" to break its silence and show its repudiation of these attacks.

One of the guests, Giovanni di Lorenzo, a newspaper reporter and television host who holds an Italian passport but has lived in Germany for most of his life, suggested the idea of organizing a protest demonstration in Munich. By the time the party broke up, the four had agreed to call a meeting and propose the idea to some friends and colleagues.

From that dinner has sprung, in the space of a few weeks, one of the largest mass movements in Germany since the end of World War II. About two million people, or one of every 40 people in the country, have poured into the street in every section of the country to show their repudiation of rising racial violence.

"The reaction has been amazingly positive, far beyond anything we had imagined," Mr. Di Lorenzo said in a recent interview. "It shows that the majority of Germany are not secretly hostile to foreigners or sympathetic to fascism. I really think this movement has changed the climate in Germany."

Many Germans agree that the protests, most of them silent vigils held at dusk and illuminated by candlelight, have had a profound effect on the national consciousness. The sight of seemingly endless chains of flickering light is deeply impressive to participants and bystanders alike, and has moved more than a few to tears.

The vigils began as Government officials were stepping up pressure on neo-Nazis by banning their organizations and increasing police surveillance. There are indications that the number of attacks on foreigners has dropped since the police crackdown and the peace vigils began. Fire-bombs are still being thrown at hostels for asylum-seekers, but officials in Saxony and other regions have said there are fewer such incidents now than there were a few months ago.

"There has definitely been a change," said Ignatz Bubis, the head of Germany's principal Jewish organization. "More still needs to be done, but I think these demonstrations have been great. They show that most Germans reject all forms of violence."

The four Munich residents who organized the first candlelight vigil, all in their early 30's, began their work by inviting about 100 people to a meeting at a popular downtown bar called Babalou. Nearly every guest agreed to support the idea and enlist 10 other supporters.

Within days, the idea was spreading across the city, and spontaneous support began pouring in from businesses, schools, churches and civic groups.

Encouraged by the response, organizers predicted that 100,000 people would join the Dec. 6 vigil, which would have made it the largest demonstration in Munich's recent history. They and the country were amazed when 400,000 turned out.

Inspired by the Munich success, citizens in other cities quickly set about organizing similar vigils. Nearly 500,000 marchers turned out in Hamburg, and 200,000 others took to the streets in Berlin. In the four weeks after the Munich vigil, similar ones attracted 100,000 people or more in Frankfurt, Nuremberg, Stuttgart, Karlsruhe, Hanover, Wuppertal and Essen. . . .

On the eve of a candlelight vigil in Dresden at the end of December, the city's principal newspaper, *Sächsische Zeitung*, asked in an editorial whether such protests were truly effective or whether they were "only theater."

"The great value of the candlelight vigils is moral and psychological," the newspaper said. "They tell violent rightwing extremists and those who support them that they are on the wrong side, and that society will not silently accept their acts". . . .

Document 20:

From 2 November to 18 December 1992, the polling organization EM-NID asked a representative sample of the German population for its current opinion about eastern and western Germany.

Opinion Polls on Inner Division, 18 January 1993

(Source: *Der Spiegel*, 1993, No. 3, 52ff.)

	WEST	EAST
Many working people in the East are not up to Western efficiency.		
Agree:	73 percent	23 percent
Many East Germans want to live like the West and to work like in the former East.		
Agree:	70 percent	30 percent
Former GDR citizens will remain second-class citizens for some time.		
Agree:	33 percent	77 percent
East Germans tend towards self-pity.		
Agree:	62 percent	25 percent

How is the general situation in East Germany now in comparison to the time before 1989?

	WEST	EAST
Better :	76 percent	41 percent
The Same:	13 percent	11 percent
Worse:	20 percent	48 percent

Document 21:

In response to popular fears of a flood of "so-called asylum seekers," the governing coalition and the opposition compromised on a revision of the Basic Law that would retain the right to asylum, while restricting its application in practice.

Party Compromise on Tightening the Asylum Law, 22 January 1993

(Source: *This Week in Germany*, 22 January 1993)

In a debate in the Bundestag on Thursday (January 21) during the first reading of draft legislation that would amend the constitution to restrict the right to asylum in Germany, it appeared that sufficient support would be found among the major parties to ensure passage of the proposed law. The legislation contains provisions on other categories of emigrants to Germany, but is primarily aimed at asylum-seekers. Three readings in the Bundestag are required; the government hopes to pass the legislation before Easter.

If the new legislation passes, which it seems sure to do, a list of countries will be drawn up which will be deemed safe; these will include the countries of the European Community and others that adhere to the Geneva convention on refugees. A person entering Germany from one of these "safe" countries will automatically be rejected. Because it is generally assumed that the countries surrounding the Federal Republic will be considered safe, the great majority of asylum-seekers will be sent back.

The governing coalition, in particular the Christian Democratic Union and the Christian Social Union, have long sought to make the asylum provision, now the most liberal in Europe, more restrictive, arguing that the law is being abused. After many months of discussion and negotiation, a majority within the Social Democratic Party agreed to an amendment of the constitution. The agreement of at least some of the Social Democrats is necessary, because a change in the constitution requires a two-thirds majority vote in the Bundestag, which the governing coalition parties cannot muster alone; at least 44 Social Democrats must vote for the measure. Critics of the legislation, who come from within the SPD as well as from the Alliance '90 and the Party for Democratic Socialism, charge that Bonn is caving in to "the pressure of the street," that is, to those who inflame sentiment against foreigners. In a broader sense, opponents argue that Germany needs to recognize that it is a nation of immigrants, i.e., those who come there seeking a better life should be allowed to stay in reasonable numbers, which could be established through a quota system.

When Germany's constitution, the Basic Law, was drawn up in 1949, its authors were concerned with including a passage that would reflect recognition of the fact that many Germans were forced to seek refuge in other countries during the National Socialist regime. Thus Article 16 came about, which in its second part states that "persons shall enjoy the right to asylum." A person claiming political persecution can apply for asylum and has the right to an individual hearing of her case; because of a large backlog of cases, she may wait several years before the claim is disproved or granted. During the waiting period, applicants are housed and given a small cash allowance. The great majority are rejected, on the grounds that they are economic refugees, not political ones.

Despite the 90-95 percent rejection rate, the number of asylum-seekers has increased steadily over the years. It remained under 100,000 for most of the

1980s, but jumped above that mark in 1988 (103,076) and has increased in large increments since then. 1992 saw a total of 430,191 applicants, a 71 percent increase over the preceding year. The asylum-seekers do not take away jobs from Germans, because they may work only under certain strict conditions, nor do they deprive Germans of housing, although their presence in steadily increasing numbers has exacerbated what was already a severe housing shortage. Nonetheless, the asylum-seekers are a source of continued, and increasing, resentment for some sectors of the population, especially since unification in 1990; they were the target of many of the more than 2,000 attacks on foreigners in 1992.

Document 22:

In Mecklenburg, one of the poorest areas in eastern Germany, the transition difficulties were particularly intense. With collectivized agriculture collapsing and industrial unemployment rising, the future looked bleak.

Neue Zürcher Zeitung on Eastern Resignation, 28 January 1993

(Source: *Neue Zürcher Zeitung*, 28 January 1993)

Next to the official notices on the bulletin board of the district administrative office in Teterow hangs an invitation from the People's Solidarity[*] to a concert and dance. Admission: 60 cents. Coffee and cake "at affordable prices". . . . The figures are one more sign of the consequences of the unemployment that looms over this part of Mecklenburg-Western Pomerania like a threatening shadow. Yet the inhabitants of this small city of 11,000 don't look any different from their counterparts elsewhere. In this still primarily agricultural state between Brandenburg and the Baltic Sea, the residents have the same skeptical looks, and wear the same heavy parkas – more colorful since the fall of the Wall – to keep out the winter cold. Here, too, the stores have modeled their presentation and stock on Western examples. Scaffolding has been erected on many streets; car traffic occasionally causes traffic jams; and many other details indicate that a minority, the size of which is difficult to estimate, has profited from reunification.

But the 757-year-old city, which succeeded in preserving its seven churches and the old roads near the center from the century's turmoils, is only the hub of a district with the same name. Thirty-one thousand people live here in two cities, twenty-nine communities, and 110 villages. The latest statistics show 22.4 percent unemployment – and that's an improvement. When the rate was 30 percent at the beginning of 1992, Teterow was the unhappy leader among the Federal Republic's four hundred districts. The reason is the decline

---

[*] Name of the social service agency of the former GDR.

of agriculture, the consequences of which have been especially harsh in Mecklenburg, where only 17 percent of all workers are employed in industry. Branches of industry here – shipyards and producers of consumer goods – have lost their regular Eastern European customers, and are thus unable to pick up the slack; in fact, they have themselves become a constant source of concern for the state government in Schwerin, which continually preaches optimism and even has – on paper – a cure for the troubled farmers.

Minister President Seite gives his government high marks for beginning the restructuring; he believes the 375 to 450 acre farms, large in comparison with [farms in] western Germany, will in the long run boast the most modern agricultural techniques in the EC. His experts would like to see small villages and thinly settled parcels tilled with the most up-to-date technology and interspersed with middle-class centers in the right proportions. All this would be a positive reversal of the GDR's failed agricultural policies, which created huge agrarian factories – areas of 12,300 acres tilled with squadrons of combines, and stalls with 5,000 cows or 100,000 pigs run by brigades of shift-workers. The utopia became a rigid ideology, from which the environment will suffer for a long time to come.

For Agriculture Minister Brick, the past and the future are useful settings for speeches; but what really concerns him is the present. Of 190,000 agricultural workers, a third, at most, still has full-time or seasonal work. Brick favors any solutions that save jobs; he is proud of the fact that Trusteeship agency sales of land are generally limited to two-year leases, though long-term leases are also possible. Nevertheless, there are 22,000 unemployed in the villages, of whom only one in three receives more than DM 800 per month.

Even such figures do not reveal the extent of the crisis. This is apparent only when one examines the decay of village structures. Many Konsum grocery stores have closed, forcing people to pay higher prices to travelling vendors or take long bus rides to the next city. When funds ran out, communities shut down their cultural centers, so few theaters and discos remain. The post office closed unprofitable branches, and bus routes were reduced. New small businesses appeared only slowly. And young people looking for work went either to the cities or straight to western Germany. An economic upturn that could keep them at home is not expected until 1995, and opinion polls predict that an additional 400,000 Mecklenburgers will move by the year 2015, leaving only 1.5 million. In the villages, the old people remain – those who, in the pointed words of an eastern German colleague, wait only for the food cart and death. "Restructuring" means closing day-care centers; consequent loss of purchasing power has also closed the restaurants, which used to serve as meeting places. . . .

Document 23:

One of the founders of the East German Social Democratic Party, this Berlin theologian pondered the problems of creating a common German identity after unification.

Richard Schröder on German Identity, 29 January 1993

(Source: *Die Zeit*, 29 January 1993)

Whether we want to be Germans or not, we are not the only ones who determine who we are; we are also told. If any of us, in Italy or elsewhere, were to say we are Europeans and prefer not to be called Germans because we feel European and not German, we would be received with laughter or a shake of the head: "We recognize your accent, my dear," and perhaps also the remark, "He's crazy, typically German!"

In fact, such behavior would be the old arrogance in new clothing: exalted over the rest of the world of ordinary nationalities, with all their rough edges and embarrassments; flight from the fact of having a homeland.

Those who declare that they do not feel German and those who, in contrast, declare that they feel German, agree that it is a feeling which determines whether one is German or not – typically German?

What do we mean when we – Germans in the East and Germans in the West – say, "We are Germans?"

I would answer: *Nothing special, but something specific.* When someone says, "I am a carpenter," he or she is not saying that this vocation is far superior to all others but, instead, that among many honorable vocations, this happens to be my vocation. It is the one I know; others I do not know, or do not know as well

Although we Germans lived forty years in *separate* states, the similarities between us are much greater than those between Serbs and Croats, who lived (with a four-and-a-half year intermission) in *one* state for seventy-three years. This natural belonging together was claimed concretely by the four million refugees who left the GDR over the past forty years. Few of them went to Austria or Switzerland or America. One reason for this was certainly their easy admission to West Germany; but another was most likely the fact that the Federal Republic was not a foreign country, not alien.

It was the millions of GDR refugees who, despite the eastern policy of separation, kept creating new links between East and West. Each refugee, each prisoner bought out by the West, each case of "family reunification" led to separation from friends and relatives who remained, thus constantly creating new contacts across the borders – though these were admittedly perceived more strongly in the East than in the West, where people were more likely to emigrate to Australia than to East Germany.

Viewed in this way, the sentence "I am German" is more modest than the sentence "I am an East German citizen," which included, at least officially, a claim that one was part of the best state in German history and represented historical progress – "the world shall be saved by socialism," as it were. It was not good that some flattered themselves with this. We Germans are nothing special, but something specific, not above, but on a par with other nations. We have a particularly large number of neighbors. This gives us a particular obligation to be good neighbors.

What is the specific thing that links us Germans? It is a substance that we should completely show and preserve as "Germandom." It is a *common responsibility*. We are responsible for our entire history with its highs and lows, and we are responsible to one another for our common future.

By the highs, I mean our culture. We, the Germans, have a duty to preserve it as part of European culture and human culture, not only for ourselves, but for others. We can expect from one another that we preserve ours, for ourselves and for them, and that they preserve theirs, for themselves and for us. Culture comes from *colere*, and that means cultivate.

By lows, I mean Germany's historical responsibility. Some would deny that anything like historical responsibility even exists. What do I have to do with what my ancestors did? The answer is that the descendants of the victims see in us the descendants of the perpetrators. Jews and Poles can expect us not to rely upon the good fortune of having been born later, as though nothing terrible ever happened in our country. In return, we can ask Jews and Poles not to make us personally liable for what happened. Our responsibility for the historical culpability of our ancestors is to acknowledge and consider what happened in our dealings with other peoples. Understanding among nations doesn't happen according to Schiller's[*] recipe – Embrace one another, millions – which would erase history, but only if we accept what has happened among peoples and together seek a reasonable relationship to what has been. . . .

But who, exactly, is part of this community; *who is German*? The precise answer must be: *Whoever has German citizenship*. It is granted either by birth or, under certain conditions, by application. It has nothing to do with hair color, skin color, or race and must never again have anything to do with them, or, as in the GDR, with a prescribed world view; it involves only *rights and duties*, as well as, it must be said, a declared desire to be part of this community. Those to whom citizenship is granted thus become part of our community, with their various backgrounds, cultures and religions.

For those of us in eastern Germany, this is nothing new. In the past, Dutch, French, and Bohemian immigrants came to Brandenburg. Brandenburg profited from this. The Sorbs[**], who have preserved their Slavic culture and

---

[*] famous liberal German poet of the late 18th century.

[**] Slavic minority in Brandenburg.

language, are German citizens without reservation and do not wish to be anything else. And I recall the German Jews who made such important contributions to German culture and science.

Then there are those with whom we share language and culture but not a fatherland; I am speaking of the *ethnic Germans*, for example in Romania and the former Soviet Union. They are not German citizens and not fellow citizens, but they are closer to us than other foreigners.

Finally, there are the *foreigners who live among us* and are thus fellow citizens but not German citizens. With them, too, we are linked by clear rights and duties.

We will make quite a mess if we approach this complicated area with an axe, setting up incorrect alternatives. Both have their place: Germany as a homeland characterized by its history and culture, and Germany as a state that, regardless of standing, guarantees all its citizens equal rights and requires equal duties; that is, Germany as a *cultural nation* (*Kulturnation*), and Germany as a *legal nation* (*Staatsnation*.) In our dealings with one another, the legal entity must take precedence.

Germany as a cultural concept will be opposed by those who desire a multicultural society. Like all catchwords, this one is ambiguous. It can mean a cosmopolitan society, hospitable and open to immigrants. Because of its new central location, because the East has merged with the West and the West with the East, Germany is predestined to be cosmopolitan.

GLOSSARY

ABM (Arbeitsbeschaffungsmassnahmen). Public works and retraining measures for unemployed.

Abwicklung. Dissolution (sometimes replacement) of East German cultural institutions in 1990.

Accession. The joining of five new East German to eleven West German states on October 3, 1990.

Alliance for Germany (Allianz für Deutschland). Alliance of >CDU, >DA, and >DSU for East German elections in March 1990.

Alliance 90 (Bündnis 90). Alliance of East German civic movements >Demokratie Jetzt, >Initiative für Frieden und Menschenrechte, >Neues Forum. Joined >Greens in 1993.

Amt für Nationale Sicherheit (AfNS). East German Office for National Security, founded as successor organization to >MfS in December 1989. Dissolved in 1990.

Article 23. Article of >Basic Law that gave right of accession to other parts of Germany. Deleted after >Unification Treaty.

Asylum Problem. Controversy about influx of several hundred thousand foreigners per year during 1990s. Resolved by constitutional change in 1993.

Basic Law (Grundgesetz). De facto constitution of >FRG, adopted in 1949.

Basic Treaty (Grundlagenvertrag). Treaty establishing relations between the two Germanys, adopted 1972.

Bloc Party. Non-Communist party within East German "Democratic Bloc" under the leadership of >SED.

Bund Freier Demokraten (BFD). Alliance of East German >LDPD and other liberal groups for elections of 1990. Merged with West German >FDP in 1990.

Bundestag. Freely elected West German parliament.

Bundeswehr. West German army, established during 1950s.

Bundesrat. Federal Council, representative body of eleven, later sixteen states. Upper house of West German parliament.

Bündnis 90. >Alliance 90.

Bürgerbewegung. East German >Civic Movement.

Central Committee (ZK). Highest formal body of East German >SED between party congresses. Dissolved in December 1989.

Christian Democratic Union (CDU). In East Germany, Bloc Party from 1946 to 1989. In West Germany, a long-time governing party with centrist and moderately conservative leanings.

Christian Social Union (CSU). Fiercely independent Bavarian sister party of West German >CDU.

Civic Movement. East German opposition movement of fall 1983. >Alliance 90, DA and SDP.

Confederation. Plan for merger of two German states while retaining sovereignty of both partners.

Conference on Security and Cooperation in Europe (CSCE). Helsinki conference of thirty-three states in 1975 that recognized post-World War II frontiers and established standards for human rights.

Democracy Now (DJ). Citizens' initiative of autumn 1989. Joined >Alliance 90 in 1990.

Democratic Awakening (DA). East German civic initiative. Founded in autumn 1989 and joined >CDU in 1990.

Demokratische Bauernpartei Deutschlands (DBD). Democratic Farmers Party of Germany, East German Bloc Party, founded 1948. Merged with >CDU in 1990.

Demokratischer Frauenbund Deutschlands (DFD). Democratic Women's League of Germany, official East German women's association.

Deutsche Soziale Union (DSU). German Social Union, East German sister party of Bavarian Christian Social Union.

Deutsche Volks-Union (DVU). German People's Union, minor right wing party that made a splash in 1992 regional elections.

East Germany. Former Soviet zone, later >GDR.

Federal Republic of Germany (FRG). West German state, also known as Bundesrepublik Deutschland (BRD). Founded in Western zones of Germany in 1949. Was joined by >GDR in 1990.

Four Powers. France, Great Britain, Soviet Union and United States, victors of World War II, responsible for Germany and Berlin.

Free Democratic Party (FDP). West German liberal party.

Freie Deutsche Jugend (FDJ). Official East German youth organization. Dissolved 1990.

Freier Deutscher Gewerkschaftsbund (FDGB). Free German Trade Union Association, umbrella organization of East German trade unions. Dissolved 1990.

German Democratic Republic (GDR). East German state, also known as Deutsche Demokratische Republik (DDR). Founded in Soviet zone of Germany in 1949. Joined >FRG after free elections in 1990.

Greens. West German environmental party also known as Die Grünen, founded in 1978. Was joined by Eastern sister party (founded 1989) in 1990. Merged with >Alliance 90 in 1993.

Initiative für Frieden- und Menschenrechte (IFM). Initiative for Peace and Human Rights, East German citizens' initiative, founded in mid-80s.

Länder. German federal states, eleven before 1989 and sixteen after unification in 1990.

Liberaldemokratische Partei Deutschlands (LDPD). Liberal Democratic Party of Germany, >Bloc Party, founded 1946. Joined all-German >FDP in 1990.

Maastricht Treaty. Agreement of EC member states on European Political Union and creation of single currency, December 1991.

Ministerium für Staatssicherheit (MfS). Ministry for State Security, East German agency for domestic surveillance and foreign espionage. Dissolved 1989. Popularly known as >Stasi, transformed into >AfNS.

Monetary Union. Extension of West German D-mark and of its economic and social system to the >GDR in July 1990.

Nationaldemokratische Partei Deutschlands (NDPD). Nationalist Bloc Party in East Germany, merged with western FDP.

Nationale Front. East German umbrella organization for >Bloc Parties and mass organizations such as >FDGB and >FDJ.

Nationale Volksarmee (NVA). National People's Army, East German army established during late 1950s.

New Forum (NF). Also known as Neues Forum, most popular East German civic group during autumn 1989. Joined >Alliance 90 in 1990.

Oder-Neisse Line. Post-World War II eastern border of >GDR, running along Oder and Neisse rivers. Recognizes the transfer of Silesia, Pomerania, and East Prussia to Poland and Russia. After 1990, frontier between united Germany and Poland.

Ossi. Colloquial term for "Easterner," marking lingering identity of former citizens of GDR.

Ostpolitik. Policy of reconciliation with East European countries, pursued by social-liberal coalition during the early 1970s.

Paragraph 218. Section of >Basic Law dealing with abortion. Termination of pregnancy permitted in >GDR during the first trimester, but restricted to medical or social reasons in >FRG.

Partei des Demokratischen Sozialismus (PDS). Party of Democratic Socialism, succeeded >SED after December 1989.

Politburo. Political Bureau of >Central Committee of >SED. Highest authority of ruling party, dissolved in December 1989.

Republikaner (Reps). Republicans, West German right-wing party founded in 1982.

Reunification. Concept calling for restoration of single German state. Often replaced by "unification" or "unity" in 1990 to ease fears of a resurgence of old Germany.

Round Table. Also known as Runder Tisch, institution of power-sharing in East Germany 1989 and 1990. Representatives of >civic movement and >SED-dominated government attempted to reform the >GDR. Dissolved after the elections of March 1990.

Skinheads. Right-wing youth subculture, influenced by "oi" rock music. Predominantly chauvinistic and xenophobic.

Sozialdemokratische Partei (SDP). East German Social Democratic Party. Founded as civic initiative in October 1989. Joined West German >SPD in 1990.

Sozialdemokratische Partei Deutschlands (SPD). Social Democratic Party of Germany. Oldest German party, existed only in West Germany, because Eastern branch was compelled to join Communists in >SED.

Sozialistische Einheitspartei Deutschlands (SED). Socialist Unity Party of Germany founded in 1946 by forced merger of Communists and SPD in Soviet zone of Germany. Governing party of >GDR until 1989. Since December 1989 called >PDS.

Stasi (Staatssicherheitsdienst). State Security Service of >GDR, run by >MfS.

Treuhandanstalt. Trusteeship Agency in charge of privatization and restitution of state property in former >GDR.

Two-plus-Four. Negotiations between two German states and >Four Powers, i.e. France, Great Britain, USA and USSR, on settlement of questions concerning unification of Germany.

Unabhängiger Frauenverband (UFV). Independent Women's Association of East Germany, founded in the fall of 1989 to replace the Communist >DFD.

Unification Treaty. Treaty between >GDR and >FRG on the >accession of the five new states, creating German unity, 31 August 1990.

United Left. Leftist challenge to >SED, founded in September 1989 and dedicated to worker's democracy.

Volkseigener Betrieb (VEB). People-Owned Company, nationalized industry in East Germany.

Volkskammer. East German legislature, consisting of representatives of the >SED, the >Bloc Parties and the mass organizations. Became freely elected in March 1990.

West Germany. Former Western zones of Germany, later >FRG.

Wessi. Colloquial term for "Westerner," marking presumed arrogance of West German citizens.

SELECTED BIBLIOGRAPY

ANZ, Thomas, ed. *"Es geht nicht um Christa Wolf": Der Literaturstreit im vereinten Deutschland* (Munich, 1991).

ASH, Timothy Garton. *In Europes Name: Germany and the Divided Continent* (New York, 1993)

ASH, Timothy Garton. *The Magic Lantern: The Revolution of '89 Witnessed in Warsaw, Budapest, Berlin, and Prague* (New York, 1990).

ASMUS, Ronald D. *German Unification and its Ramifications* (Santa Monica, 1991).

BARK, Dennis, and GRESS, David. *A History of West Germany* (Oxford, 1989), 2 vols.

BESCHLOSS, Michael R., and TALBOTT, Strobe. *At the Highest Levels: The Inside Story of the End of the Cold War* (Boston, 1993).

BEYME, Klaus von. *Das politische System der Bundesrepublik Deutschland nach der Vereinigung* (Munich, 1991).

BEYME, Klaus von. *Hauptstadtsuche* (Frankfurt, 1991).

BORNEMAN, John. *After the Wall: East Meets West in the New Berlin* (New York, 1991).

BRYSON, Philip, and MELZER, Manfred. *The End of the East German Economy* (London, 1991).

CONRADT, David P. *The German Polity*, fifth edition (New York, 1993).

DAHRENDORF, Ralf. *Reflections on the Revolution in Europe* (New York, 1990).

DALTON, Russel J., ed. *The New Germany Votes: Unification and the Creation of a New German Party System* (Oxford, 1994)

DARNTON, Robert. *Berlin Journal, 1989-1990* (New York, 1991).

FRITSCH-BOURNAZEL, Renata. *Europe and German Unification* (Oxford, 1992).

FULBROOK, Mary. *The Divided Nation: A History of Germany 1918-1990* (London, 1991).

Germany in Transition, DAEDALUS, 124 (1994), No. 1

GLAESSNER, Gert Joachim, and WALLACE, Ian, eds. *The German Revolution of 1989* (Oxford, 1992).

GOECKEL, Robert F. *The Lutheran Church and the East German State* (Ithaca, 1990).

GRANSOW, Volker. *Problems and Perspectives of German Unification.* (Toronto, Center for International Studies, 1993)

GRANSOW, Volker, and JARAUSCH, Konrad H., eds. *Die deutsche Vereinigung: Dokumente zu Bürgergewegung, Annäherung und Beitritt* (Cologne, 1991).

GREENWALD, G. Jonathan. *Berlin Witness: An American Diplomat's Chronicle of East Germany's Revolution* (University Park, PA, 1993).

GROSSER, Dieter, ed. *German Unification: The Unexpected Challenge* (Oxford, 1992).

HANCOCK, M. Donald, and WELSH, Helga, eds. *German Unification: Processes and Outcomes* (Boulder, 1994)

JAMES, Harold, and STONE, Marla, eds. *When the Wall Came Down: Reactions to German Unification* (London, 1992).

JARAUSCH, Konrad H. *The Rush to German Unity* (New York, 1994).

JARAUSCH, Konrad H., ed. *Zwischen Parteilichkeit und Professionalität: Bilanz der Geschichtswissenschaft der DDR* (Berlin, 1992).

JARAUSCH, Konrad H. and MIDDELL, Matthias, eds. *Nach dem Erbeben. (re-) Konstruktionen ostdeutscher Geschichte und Geschichtswissenchaft* (Leipsig, 1994).

JOAS, Hans, and KOHLI, Martin, eds. *Der Zusammenbruch der DDR* (Frankfurt, 1993).

KENNEDY, Ellen. *The Bundesbank: Germany's Central Bank in the International Monetary System* (London, 1991).

KOLINSKY, Eva, ed. *The Federal Republic of Germany: The End of an Era* (Oxford, 1991).

KRISCH, Henry. *The Political Dissolution of a Communist State: The German Democratic Republic 1987-1990* (Boulder, 1992).

LEMKE, Christiane. *Die Ursachen des Umbruchs* (Opladen, 1990).

LIEBERT, Ulrike, and MERKEL, Wolfgang, eds. *Die Politik zur deutschen Einheit* (Opladen, 1991).

MAIER, Charles S. *After the Wall* (Princeton, 1994).

MARCUSE, Peter. *A German Way of Revolution: DDR Tagebuch eines Amerikaners* (Berlin, 1990).

MCADAMS, A. James. *Germany Divided: From the Wall to Reunification* (Princeton, 1993)

MERKL, Peter. *German Unification in the European Context* (Boulder, 1992).

MEUSCHEL, Sigrid. *Legitimation und Parteiherrschaft: Zum Paradox von Stabilität und Revolution in der DDR 1945-1989* (Frankfurt, 1992).

NAWROCKI, Joachim. *Relations Between the Two States in Germany* (Bonn, 1985).

PHILIPSEN, Dirk, ed. *We Were the People: Voices from East Germany's Revolutionary Autumn of 1989* (Durham 1993).

POND, Elisabeth. *After the Wall: American Policy Toward Germany* (New York, 1990).

POND, Elisabeth. *Beyond the Wall: Germany's Road to Unification* (New York, 1993).

RAMMSTEDT, Otthein, and SCHMIDT, Gert, eds. *BRD ade! Vierzig Jahre in Rück-Ansichten* (Frankfurt, 1993).

ROTFELD, Adam B., and STÜTZLE, Walther, eds. *Germany and Europe in Transition* (Oxford, 1991).

SCHNEIDER, Peter. *The German Comedy: Scenes of Life After the Wall* (New York, 1991).

SPENCE, David. *Enlargement without Accession: The EC's Response to German Unification* (London, 1991).

STERN, Frank. *The Whitewashing of the Yellow Badge: Antisemitism and Philosemitism in Postwar Germany* (Oxford, 1992).

STOESS, Richard. *Politics against Democracy: Right-wing Extremism in West Germany* (Oxford, 1991).

STOKES, Gale. *The Walls Came Tumbling Down: The Collapse of Communism in Eastern Europe* (New York, 1993)

SZABO, Stephen F. *The Diplomacy of German Unification* (New York, 1992).

WALLACH, H. G. Peter and FRANCISCO, Ronald A. *United Germany. The Past, Politics, Prospects* (Westport, CT, 1992).

WEIDENFELD, Werner, and Korte, Karl-Rudolf, eds. *Handwörterbuch zur deutschen Einheit* (Frankfurt, 1992)

WELFENS, Paul J. J., ed. *Economic Aspects of German Unification: National and International Perspectives* (Berlin, 1992)

IMPERIAL GERMANY, 1871-1914
Economy, Society, Culture, and Politics

Volker R. Berghahn, John P. Birkelund Professor of European
History at Brown University, Rhode Island

Twenty years after the appearance of Hans-Ulrich Wehler's classic
work, this comprehensive history of the German Empire offers
fresh perspectives, incorporating as it does the results of further
research carried out since then. While providing a broad survey of its development, the volume is organized thematically and designed to give easy access to
the major topics and issues of the Bismarckian and Wilhelmine eras. The sta-
tistical appendix contains a wide range of social, economic and political data.
Written with the English-speaking student in mind, this book will become a
widely used text for this period.

380 pages, 86 tables, bibliog., index,
hardback, ISBN 1-57181-013-7   paperback, ISBN 1-57181-014-5

POLITICS AND GOVERNMENT IN GERMANY, 1944 - 1994
Basic Documents

2nd, revised edition
Edited by C.C. Schweitzer, Detlev Karsten, Robert Spencer, R. Taylor Cole†,
Donald P. Kommers and Anthony J. Nicholls

This revised and enlarged edition brings the successful original volume of
1984, published as *Politics and Government in the Federal Republic of Germany:
Basic Documents,* commmpletely up to date by taking into account the most
recent developments. It contains key documents on the political development
of postwar Germany, selected by an international team of specialists from the
United States, Canada, Britain and Germany. Each section begins with an
introduction which provides the context for the following documents. There is
no comparable volume of its kind available in English, and most of the documents have not been translated before. Students of German politics and history,
of comparative politics and government, journalists and other professionals will
find this volume an indispensable work of reference.

ca. 500 pages, 20 tables, 6 fig., gloss., bibliog., index,
hardback, ISBN 1-57181-854-5   paperback, ISBN 1-57181-855-3

THE AMERICAN IMPACT ON POSTWAR GERMANY

Edited by **Reiner Pommerin**

It is only with the benefit of hindsight that the Germans have become acutely aware of how profound and comprehensive was the impact of the United States on their society after 1945. This volume reflects the ubiquitousness of this impact and examines German responses to it. Contributions by well known scholars cover politics, industry, social life and mass culture.

hardback, ca. 200 pages, ISBN 1-57181-004-8

VOLUME 1: **TOWARD A GLOBAL CIVIL SOCIETY**

Edited by **Michael Walzer**, School of Social Science, Institute for Advanced Study in Princeton

The demise of Communism has not only affected Eastern Europe but also the countries of the West where a far-reaching examination of political and economic systems has begun. This collection of essays by internationally renowned scholars of political theory from Europe and the United States explores both the concept and the reality of civil society and its institutions.

hardback, 288 pages, ISBN 1-57181-054-4

EUROPE AFTER MAASTRICHT
American and European Perspectives

Edited by **Paul Michael Lützeler**, Rosa May Distinguished University Professor in the Humanities at Washington University, St. Louis and Director of its European Studies Program

During the era following the Second World War world peace was largely assured through American-European cooperation on the political, military, and economic level. This status quo was upset by the ratification of the Treaty on the European Union (Maastricht Treaty) which will, whatever obstacles still remain, inevitably lead to closer a cooperation among (West) European countries and to a shift in Europe's position within world politics. This raises a number of questions such as to what extent and in what way Europe's relationship with America will be affected? Will Europe become a fortress? Will NATO continue to function as an alliance dominated by the US? How will the changes in Eastern Europe affect European and American policies? What do these changes mean on a cultural level? These and other issues are discussed by an international team of experts from Europe (East and West), Russia and the United States.

hardback, ca. 224 pages 10 tables., bibliog., index, ISBN 1-57181-020-X